T0265665

THE ENLIGHTENMENT'S MOST DANGEROUS WOMAN

THE ENLIGHTENMENT'S MOST DANGEROUS WOMAN

Émilie Du Châtelet and the Making of Modern Philosophy

Andrew Janiak

OXFORD
UNIVERSITY PRESS

Oxford University Press is a department of the University of Oxford. It furthers
the University's objective of excellence in research, scholarship, and education
by publishing worldwide. Oxford is a registered trade mark of Oxford University
Press in the UK and certain other countries.

Published in the United States of America by Oxford University Press
198 Madison Avenue, New York, NY 10016, United States of America.

Library of Congress Cataloging-in-Publication Data
Names: Janiak, Andrew, author.
Title: The Enlightenment's most dangerous woman : Émilie du Châtelet and
the making of modern philosophy / [Andrew Janiak].
Other titles: Émilie du Châtelet and the making of modern philosophy
Description: 1. | New York, NY, United States of America :
Oxford University Press, [2024] | Includes bibliographical references. |
Identifiers: LCCN 2024012792 (print) | LCCN 2024012793 (ebook) |
ISBN 9780197757987 (hardback) | ISBN 9780197758014 |
ISBN 9780197758007 (epub)
Subjects: LCSH: Du Châtelet, Gabrielle Emilie Le
Tonnelier de Breteuil, marquise, 1706–1749.
Classification: LCC PQ1981.D55 J36 2024 (print) |
LCC PQ1981.D55 (ebook) | DDC 848/.509 [B]—dc23/eng/20240620
LC record available at https://lccn.loc.gov/2024012792
LC ebook record available at https://lccn.loc.gov/2024012793

DOI: 10.1093/oso/9780197757987.001.0001

Printed by Sheridan Books, Inc., United States of America

No account of the authentic history of philosophy can remain purely historical and be oriented toward history alone. For the consideration of the philosophical past is and must always be an act of genuine philosophical self-examination and self-criticism.

—ERNST CASSIRER,
Philosophy of the Enlightenment, 1932

Each philosopher has seen something, and none has seen everything; there is no book so bad that nothing can be learned from it, and none so good that one may not improve it.

—ÉMILIE DU CHÂTELET,
preface to *Foundations of Physics*, 1742

CONTENTS

Acknowledgments | ix

1. The Rise and Fall of Émilie Du Châtelet | 1

2. What Was the Scientific Revolution? | 24

3. Du Châtelet's Vision of Science and Philosophy | 70

4. The Enlightenment's Most Famous Woman | 115

5. The Enlightenment's Most Dangerous Woman: or the Making of Modern Philosophy | 157

6. Du Châtelet's Enlightenment: Philosophy for Freethinkers | 186

NOTES | 197
BIBLIOGRAPHY | 249
INDEX | 277

ACKNOWLEDGMENTS

When I was a little boy, my mother, Joan Saperstan, came out of the closet. That was just a few years after Stonewall—it was a courageous act. Ever since those early days, Mom has been a constant source of love and of wisdom. Maybe that's why I wanted to be a philosopher.

A little more than twenty-five years ago, right after our father's life was tragically cut short, my sisters and I struggled to put our lives back together. It wasn't easy. As fate would have it, each of us was embarking on a new journey back then: Liz was beginning high school, Melissa college, and I grad school. I know I couldn't have made it through those first few years without their love and support. So I dedicate this book to my wonderful feminist sisters, Elizabeth Janiak and Melissa Oliver-Janiak. And Dad, we still miss your gentle presence and sparkling intelligence.

Back in those days, I was struggling to find a place for myself in philosophy. I loved its promise of clarity and rigor, but often bemoaned its approved topics of study. I thought of switching to political science, where the topics seemed more pressing, but the methods less promising. I took courses in feminist theory, as I had in college. Progress can happen in fits and starts. In my very first semester in grad school, I took Sally Haslanger's fabulous metaphysics seminar: things were beginning to connect. I am grateful to Sally for her sage advice over the years. But I still needed to make more progress on my own.

A little more than twenty years ago, I was finishing grad school as a visiting student at Berkeley. One afternoon, I spent a few hours at the Bancroft library, studying their copy of Émilie Du Châtelet's magnum opus. It amazed me. I resolved then and there to research her philosophy for a planned postdoctoral fellowship. After submitting my proposal, I had the good luck of working as a postdoctoral fellow at MIT's Dibner Institute for the History of Science. The Dibner was paradise: an entire building overlooking the Charles River and downtown Boston, filled with brilliant colleagues and a world-class library in the basement. (Alas, paradise never lasts: The Dibner building was eventually demolished to make way for the business school.) Even more luckily, one of the world's leading Newton scholars, George Smith, was running the Dibner in those days, and Sally had by then moved to MIT, where she led the famous Workshop on Gender and Philosophy. The Workshop was a haven for someone like me, who still felt like a fish out of water. I spent countless hours talking with George about Newton, a growing interest of mine, and learned feminist philosophy from the wonderful people visiting Sally's group. But for all that, the two parts of my life remained stubbornly separate and I couldn't figure out how to connect them. In the end, I abandoned my Du Châtelet research, choosing a "sensible" career path involving Newton. Fits and starts.

But I did not abandon the project of connection. A little more than ten years ago, with tenure behind us, Karen Detlefsen and I began collaborating on a new project concerning Du Châtelet's philosophy. Our early work received a huge boost from an American Council of Learned Societies collaborative research grant, which enabled us to take time off and study the archives in St. Petersburg and Paris; many thanks to Rebecca Manley for her expert guidance in Russia. We scoped out the project, giving ourselves plenty of time to get lost in the thicket of Du Châtelet's milieu in the early

Enlightenment. We're still wandering around in that thicket; the book in your hands is merely an offshoot.

Modern philosophy's vaunted obsession with becoming "scientific," exemplified by Kant's notion that he had set it on the "secure path of a science," reinvigorated more recently by Quine, remains a fixation for many. Yet even as science has grown larger and more collaborative, philosophy remains stubbornly individualistic. I find that aspect of our discipline misguided. Over the past decade, Liz Milewicz, Will Shaw, Cheryl Thomas, and I have tried to promote a more collaborative approach through our work with Project Vox. So let me give what our student team members would call a "shout out" to all of them for their wonderful work on every aspect of our digital humanities project. I hope we have bequeathed to the next generation a collaborative model of philosophy.

The book in your hands would not exist without the support of my editor at Oxford, Lucy Randall. Indeed, I first conceived of a popular book during a memorable lunch in New York with Lucy. Four years later, when the book was finished, we had another memorable lunch. Throughout that whole period, Lucy provided encouragement, criticism, and guidance in equal measure.

Many friends, colleagues, and students have contributed their suggestions to this work. First and foremost, I would like to thank Karen Detlefsen, a wonderful and thoughtful collaborator, and Katherine Brading, the Platonic ideal of a colleague, for their helpful suggestions over many years. Katherine read the entire manuscript and sent me many useful criticisms and comments. Christia Mercer has been a constant guide and interlocutor for years, and the late Eileen O'Neill gave me great encouragement in the early days of this project.

My home for more than twenty years now, Duke University, has been a wonderful place to teach and learn. I would like to thank the members of a Du Châtelet seminar that Katherine and I recently co-taught—especially Qiu Lin, Tayfun Gur, Michael Veldman, and Aurora Yu—for their numerous excellent suggestions. During my years at Duke, I've had many conversations about history, philosophy, and literature with colleagues and friends: I would especially like to thank Ásta, the late Srinivas Aravamudan, Rey Chow, Erdag Göknar, Luciana Feillin, Toril Moi, Charmaine Royal, and Barbara Herrnstein Smith. When I left the departmental nest, several university leaders took me under their wings: for their guidance and mentorship, I thank Valerie Ashby, Dick Brodhead, Peter Lange, and Susan Roth. To Susan, and especially to Kevin Moore, I am also grateful for friendship and good humor over the years.

In the wider world, many students and colleagues listened to my talks on the Marquise and provided me with extremely valuable feedback, including at venues in Bergamo, Bucharest, Copenhagen, Ghent, Groningen, Halifax, Hannover, Paderborn, and Paris, and at Boston University, Columbia, Denison, Harvard, Indiana, Oxford, Notre Dame, Wayne State and Washington University in St. Louis. Special thanks to Mihnea Dobre and Dana Jalobeanu in Bucharest, Niccolò Guicciardini in Bergamo, Sabrina Ebbersmeyer in Copenhagen, Anne-Lise Rey in Paris, and Fritz Nagel in Basel, for their hospitality during memorable visits. For discussions over the years, I would also like to thank Wilda Anderson, Sandrine Bergès, Nico Bertoloni Meli, Jacqui Broad, Jonathan Cottrell, Nicholas Cronk, Adela Deanova, Marguerite Deslauriers, Mary Domski, Moti Feingold, Barbara Fultner, Bryce Gessell, Banu Görkariksel, Kristin Gjesdal, Ruth Hagengruber, Sarah Hutton, Andrew Jainchill, Chike Jeffers, Marcy Lascano, Antonia LoLordo, Scott Mandelbrote, Jonathan Maskit, Dalia Nassar, Bill Newman, Calvin Normore, Alison Peterman, Tinca Prunea, Andrea Reichenberger, Vincenzo De Risi, Eric Schliesser, J. B. Shank, Lisa Shapiro, Alison Simmons, Marius Stan, Sarah Abrevaya Stein, Richard Stein, Mary Terrall, Tom Vinci, Aaron Wells, and finally Judith Zinsser, who has always been encouraging.

Last and the opposite of least, I thank my family, Rebecca, Isaac, and Saul. Although the research and thought underlying this book occupied the last decade, much of the actual writing occurred during the first pandemic year of 2020–21. Without the love, support, and good cheer of my family, expressed most sublimely in our nightly boisterous dinners, I would never have made it. Rebecca is a thoughtful interlocutor, a courageous public intellectual, a lifelong friend. Isaac and Saul are smart and considerate young feminists who mean more to me than any words could hope to convey. So, I will not try. Instead, I'll quote the teenage Saul, from a recent dinner: "Dad, now we know more about Du Châtelet's history than our own!" As the comic books of my youth had it, 'nuff said.

1

The Rise and Fall of Émilie Du Châtelet

In the eighteenth century, the Café Gradot was found near the Louvre in the heart of Paris. It was one of many such establishments in the capital. But the Gradot was no ordinary café. In those days, it served as the home for famous philosophers, authors, and mathematicians to discuss the intellectual controversies of the time. Meetings at midday would be followed in the evenings by long conversations over drinks. The Gradot served as a kind of intellectual and literary home, much as the Café de Flore was the meeting place for Simone de Beauvoir and Jean-Paul Sartre. Yet there was one key difference between the Parisian institutions from these two eras. Unlike the Flore, where Beauvoir founded modern French feminism, the Café Gradot was a male-dominated enclave. The only women allowed inside were those serving the famous men lounging in its chairs. That exclusion was typical in the Enlightenment: none of the major French institutions admitted women. Unlike the author of the *Second Sex*, who helped to shape intellectual history from her perch in a Parisian café, a woman in eighteenth-century France had no public place to think.

Pierre-Louis Maupertuis was one of the fixtures at the Café Gradot. During the 1730s, he conducted significant research, published important papers, and built a considerable scientific reputation across Europe. As was common in that era, he also made time to tutor students in science and mathematics. His pupils knew better than to interrupt him while he was holding court among the writers sipping drinks in the Gradot. So they would wait outside until they could catch his attention, perhaps to ask a pressing question about a tricky math problem or to share a new insight. On an unusual evening, one of his pupils finally decided that the wait had been long enough and simply barged into the Gradot to grab Maupertuis. But this was no ordinary pupil, a young scholar who had broken the rules of politesse. This was Émilie Du Châtelet (see Figure 1). As a member of one of France's oldest aristocratic families, Du Châtelet had the privilege of attending court at Versailles. She could gossip with the Queen of France. Few in Paris had a higher social standing. But as a woman, she was not even allowed inside the Gradot. The crowd in the café that evening would have been aghast.

Like the famous story of a young Isaac Newton sitting in the English countryside watching an apple fall, a supposed inspiration for his theory of gravity, the story of the day when Madame Du Châtelet broke protocol and stormed into the Café Gradot is probably just a fairy tale. One biographer proudly relates the episode, but modern accounts find little evidence for it.[1] The question of historical accuracy in this case misses a larger point, for fairy tales are often no less instructive than histories; perhaps they are even more so. Just as the tale of Newton's apple encapsulates our conception of the lone genius solving a great scientific problem, the story of Du Châtelet and the café captures our desire to see social injustice vanquished by a brave woman. Learning that Newton took years to perform the calculations necessary to derive his theory of gravity does little to undermine our recognition of his scientific genius. The fall of the apple, that fateful fruit in western civilization, makes for better bedtime reading, but Newton's genius is secure. The same is true of the tale of a young woman who changed from a dress into a pair of pants, rushed through the streets of Paris, and broke into an all-male enclave to join a heated intellectual discussion. Even if it's apocryphal, the narrative of Du Châtelet's courageous breaking of social barriers endures. Indeed, as with Newton's apple, the story of Du Châtelet and the café contains a kernel of truth. For if one wants to find a woman who broke the gender norms of Enlightenment Europe and changed the course of intellectual life, there is no better person to study than Émilie Du Châtelet.

An Academy of Her Own

Born in Paris in late 1706 to a powerful aristocratic family, Gabriele Émilie le Tonnelier-de-Bretueil was the luckiest of young women. She lived in the center of Paris in the Place Royale—now known as the Place des Vosges—in the early days of the Enlightenment (Figure 2).[2] Her family's lovely stone and brick apartments still stand today, surrounding the great equestrian statue of Louis XIII. Émilie's youth was filled with intellectual excitement. Her father ran a well-known *salon*, which meant that famous visitors came for regular discussions at her home. He also quickly recognized her talents: she was tutored along with her brother, and had access to the family's extensive library. France was the center of the Enlightenment at that time, so her perch in Paris and her youthful studies prepared her to participate in the main discussions of European intellectual life.

When she turned eighteen, Émilie married into an even more prominent aristocratic family, one with an ancient lineage. The wedding ceremony, important enough to be presided over by a bishop, was held at Notre Dame Cathedral on a warm June day in 1725 (Figure 3). The marriage gave her the title "Marquise Du Châtelet," and she was to be addressed as "Madame." After getting married, she quickly had several children. Her husband Florent-Claude was a colonel in the army, so while he was off fighting King Louis XV's various battles, Émilie devoted herself to intellectual pursuits. She began to build on the lessons of her youth: she learned from tutors like Maupertuis, as aristocratic men would also do; she studied Latin, Greek, and the classics; she read numerous treatises and began to shape an intellectual life for herself.

There was only one problem: where could she go next? Women were systematically excluded from learned institutions at this time. Although the famous Bernard Fontenelle, secretary of the Academy of Sciences, had been a frequent dinner guest at her father's salon since Émilie's youth—starting when she was ten, he would explain astronomy to her—the Académié Française and the Royal Academy of Sciences excluded women.[3] These academies were the twin pillars of French intellectual life and the burgeoning centers of the Enlightenment. Formal education in a college like Louis-le-Grand (Voltaire's alma mater) or La Flèche (Descartes's) was similarly out of the question for women.

Du Châtelet was keenly aware of the barriers she faced to participating in public life. She later described them movingly in the preface to her planned translation of Bernard Mandeville's controversial moral work, the *Fable of the Bees*:[4]

> I feel the full weight of prejudice that excludes us universally from the sciences, and it is one of the contradictions of this world, which has always astonished me, that there are great countries where the law permits us to decide our destiny, but none where we are brought up to think.

In another famous passage in the preface, she bemoaned the fact that no woman had yet written "a good book of physics." Before long, she set out to rectify that particular situation. But how could she do so?

The institutional barriers to intellectual life facing women in Europe at this time would turn out to be little match for Du Châtelet, one reason that the tale of the Gradot resonates. If she could not go to college, she would bring the best tutors to her, which she did in her early years in Paris. More profoundly, if she could not officially join academic life, she would create her own academy. Having seen to the care of her children, and with her husband the marquis busy in the service of the king, she made a courageous choice. She left Paris, moving to a newly renovated family chateau in Cirey-sur-Blaise, deep in the countryside of Champagne, near the ancestral home of the Du Châtelet family in Lorraine (Figure 4). It was roughly a three-day-ride from Paris to Cirey. The stone chateau, which still stands today, had lovely gardens, ample room for guests, an accompanying farm, and eventually a small theater.[5] Before long, she aptly called it "mon académie." A famous Prussian intellectual told a correspondent in 1739 that "Cirey looks like an Academy of Sciences."[6]

In the chateau, Du Châtelet hosted a wide range of major intellectuals from throughout Europe. The guests included the great Swiss mathematician Bernoulli, the Italian philosopher Algarotti, and France's leading poet and writer Voltaire. Together they read the latest scholarly journals, discussed ideas, shared sumptuous meals, and drank local wine—they were, after all, in Champagne. An academy of her own, but one with more wit and better cheer than the stodgy Parisian institutions. One is tempted to think that an evening at the Gradot back in Paris would pale in comparison to one in her chateau.

Throughout those heady days, with her early education in Paris and the creation of her own academy in Cirey, Voltaire was not a mere visitor to Émilie's countryside chateau, but her intimate and intellectual companion. Twelve years her senior, Voltaire was already a famous poet and playwright when he first fell for Émilie Du Châtelet in Paris in 1733. By the time they had met and began spending significant time together, Voltaire was perhaps the most famous writer in France. He had already written a wildly successful modern rendition of the Greek tragedy of Oedipus, an influential account of the age of King Louis XIV, and many poems and essays. He was a prolific author and met with much acclaim early

in his career. Eventually, he would become the leading writer of the
Enlightenment. As Frederick the Great once said, Voltaire's works
will last longer than the Louvre.[7]

Yet life with Voltaire was never simple. Indeed, drama seemed
to follow him wherever he went. By the time he met Du Châtelet,
he had already fallen out with the authorities several times, earn-
ing an expulsion from Paris on one occasion and jail time in the
Bastille on another. During an important sojourn in England in the
late 1720s, Voltaire managed to avoid controversy. But soon after
he returned to France and fell in love with Du Châtelet in the early
1730s, he landed in trouble once again. This time, the cause was his
Philosophical Letters, written to express his admiration for English
Enlightenment culture. Some readers took the text to promote
materialism about the soul; others thought it flirted with atheism.
Voltaire's ideas seemed heretical to the authorities, placing him in
danger again. The Parlement in Paris even had the book burned.

Despite the controversy surrounding Voltaire, Du Châtelet was
undeterred. In a move that would have profound consequences for
her life and for his, she appealed to the good graces of her husband,
hoping that he would see the benefit of helping France's leading
writer to avoid another imprisonment in Paris by granting him
refuge in the chateau in Cirey.[8] In a sign of the flexible social and
sexual arrangements for members of the high aristocracy, the
marquis agreed. So Voltaire fled to Cirey, where he spent several
months at the chateau overseeing extensive renovations before Du
Châtelet herself arrived. Perhaps because of Voltaire's high intellectual status, the marquis overlooked his lowly social one—after
all, Voltaire was widely celebrated, but he was merely bourgeois.
Once Du Châtelet joined her companion, Cirey became the center
of their lives together. She knew that she was fortunate. Not only
did Du Châtelet have a husband who never objected to her living
far from Paris in a chateau with Voltaire and numerous visitors, she
had found in Voltaire an intellectual partner who recognized her
talents.

During their days in Cirey, Du Châtelet and Voltaire each played the role of the academician. They debated the latest scientific and philosophical discoveries, exchanged extensive correspondence, solved equations, and eventually published their ideas through famous Parisian presses. They had some of the most sophisticated experimental equipment brought in from Paris and built one of the leading libraries in all of France in the chateau. Then within a few short years of one another, they each published major philosophical treatises focused on the sciences of the day. Voltaire published his *Elements of the Philosophy of Newton* in 1738, and Du Châtelet her magnum opus, *Institutions of Physics* (*Institutions physiques*), two years later. In the eighteenth century, the word "institutions" meant something like elements, principles, or perhaps foundations, so she was discussing the basic elements in physical science.[9] The pair quickly became the intellectual power couple of the era, serving as the subject of much gossip in Paris.

But there is an intriguing twist to their intellectually rich partnership. Despite their enduring love and their commitment to creating an atmosphere that would foster cutting-edge research and thought, Voltaire and Du Châtelet found themselves disagreeing about science and philosophy. Indeed, they disagreed profoundly. Even more remarkably, they allowed their intellectual disagreement to spill into the public sphere. They fostered a kind of dialogue between their two philosophical treatises. Voltaire's *Elements* came first, staking out his claim to being a major expositor of Newton's science. And Voltaire seemed to think at that time that Du Chatelet was on his side. But just two years later, Du Châtelet delicately noted in the preface to her *Institutions* that Voltaire's *Elements* had not fulfilled France's need for a "complete" treatise in physics. His text presented only Newton's ideas, as the title itself announced; it did not make its own original contribution. Instead of writing a commentary on Newton, Du Châtelet aimed to synthesize and analyze the latest knowledge in physics in her *Institutions*, along with its philosophical implications.[10]

Writing from the same chateau in the French countryside, they then continued their debate in the public realm, just like other academicians writing under a more official imprimatur. Voltaire replied to the first edition of the *Institutions* with a revised version of his *Elements* in 1741. Voltaire remained a fervent supporter of Newton, and he clearly thought the publication of Du Châtelet's much broader text meant that he had to defend his narrower one. In turn, Du Châtelet responded a year later with a revised *Institutions* that expanded the range of scientific thought covered in her text and clarified her original philosophical orientation.[11] With these publications, she had not merely participated extensively in Enlightenment academic life from her homegrown academy; she had joined a small intellectual European elite.

To the astonishment of many in her milieu, the ideas in Du Châtelet's *Institutions* spread quickly and widely through the intellectual channels normally reserved for men. After she revised the text for a second edition in 1742, it was translated into both German and Italian within one year, making it available to an even wider audience. It was then cited, debated, and praised by major figures in science, mathematics, and philosophy.[12] Her work was read from Prussia to Russia, from Italy to France, from Switzerland to England. It reached as far north as Sweden. Within a few short years, whole works were written to discuss her *Institutions*, and various savants published responses to her ideas in both academic journals and popular magazines.[13] Leading publications in French, German, and Italian carried reviews of her work.[14] It was not long before one of the Enlightenment's most important writers, Denis Diderot, called her "the illustrious Madame Du Châtelet" in one of his publications.[15]

It is difficult to overstate Du Châtelet's fame. The list of her interlocutors reads like a who's who of European intellectual life. It includes mathematicians like Johann Bernoulli and Jean D'Alembert; scientists like Georges-Louis Buffon and Pierre-Louis Maupertuis; philosophers like Immanuel Kant and Julien

La Mettrie; and writers like Francesco Algarotti and later J. W. Goethe. Within the first half of the 1740s, her work was praised by the Enlightenment's most famous mathematician, Leonard Euler of Basel, debated publicly by the leader of the Academy of Sciences in Paris, and denounced personally by Frederick the Great of Prussia. She was indeed *"the* woman *philosophe* of the first half of the eighteenth century,"[16] and philosophers continued discussing her ideas many years after her death.[17]

How did this happen? How could a young woman who was excluded from college and from the scientific academies throughout Europe, one who could not even walk into a popular Parisian café, have achieved such fame? How could she have garnered such widespread recognition at a time when women were so systematically excluded from intellectual life?

Du Châtelet and the "Revolution" in the Sciences

Despite his brilliance, which everyone recognized at a young age, Isaac Newton was a reluctant writer. He spent countless hours solving equations, calculating planetary trajectories, and performing chemical experiments, but he was hesitant to publish his results. When his first publications, announcing some experiments in optics, caused a stir in the 1670s, Newton's reticence increased. He could not tolerate the idea that anyone would doubt his conclusions. Newton's mathematical and scientific work continued furiously, but he published little. Those living in his small orbit in Cambridge admired his genius, and he quickly became the Lucasian Professor of Mathematics there, but few others were aware of his work. Indeed, if it were not for a famous visit from the astronomer Edmond Halley to Cambridge in 1684, Newton might never have published his magnum opus, the *Mathematical Principles of Natural Philosophy.* In this text, Newton unified an astonishing array of previous research, including Galileo's experiments on free fall; Kepler's analysis of the elliptical planetary orbits; Descartes's conception of the laws of motion; and the analysis of impact by Huygens, Wren, and Wallis. He also presented his groundbreaking theory of universal gravity, showing that everything from the fall of a leaf in the backyard to the tides in the ocean to the moon's orbit was due to the force of gravity. When the Royal Society in London published Newton's *Principia* in 1687, as his work was typically called, it revolutionized science. The story of the apple hardly does it justice.

Just as Newton was a reluctant writer, he was a reluctant revolutionary. In fact, he didn't consider himself to be a revolutionary at all. He played a key role in what we now call the Scientific Revolution, a movement that upended centuries of tradition in philosophy, physics, astronomy, and mathematics. But Newton actually regarded his results and methods in the terms of the Renaissance. He believed that the ancient Greeks discovered mathematical and philosophical secrets that were later lost. Through strenuous intellectual efforts, he had revived some of them. Although he famously said that he "stood on the shoulders of giants," he said precious little about the revolutionary modern science they created.[18] And he was not alone: none of the leaders of what we now call the Scientific Revolution, from Galileo in Italy to Descartes in France to Huygens in Holland, announced that they were contributing to a "revolution."[19]

In fact, Émilie Du Châtelet was the first person to proclaim the "revolution" in the sciences. She did so prominently in the preface to her most important work, the *Institutions* of 1740. Historians have attributed the notion to some men in her milieu, but she clearly scooped them by several years.[20] Her *Institutions* would catalogue many of the recent transformational developments in science. She cautioned that she would not "write here the history of the revolutions experienced by physics" because "to report them all would require a large book," but she provided the highlights, singling out Huygens and Kepler, Descartes and Galileo, Newton and Leibniz.[21] She echoed Newton's famous sentiment that he stood on the shoulders of these giants, giving him a special perch, but insisted that many figures contributed to the revolution. Their contributions merited as much attention as Newton's. For her, learning these developments was central to understanding how philosophy ought to evolve in the modern age. Du Châtelet's conception would soon become a leading idea of the Enlightenment.

Du Châtelet's notion of the "revolutions" in the sciences replaces the old trope that philosophy answers perennial questions. For her, philosophy does not inherit a series of ancient questions about truth, beauty, or justice, as if one's historical location is irrelevant. Instead, the first task of the philosopher is to situate herself historically. Knowledge has a history, and the philosopher must learn it. She proclaims that the revolution in the sciences was a key precursor to her historical moment. But how exactly did the recent revolution in astronomy and physics happen? How did thinkers like Copernicus, Galileo, or Newton surpass the efforts of pre-modern writers and achieve revolutionary new knowledge? These were Du Châtelet's questions, and they are more difficult to answer than one might think.

With many modern revolutions, whether in art, music, or politics, their leaders often developed a self-conception as revolutionaries. They were happy to proclaim what was radical about their work, explaining how they overturned generations of thinking about color patterns, perhaps, or symphonic compositions, or maybe the nature of legitimate government. But the figures in the revolution of the sciences had no such perspective. Much of the work in the seventeenth century led to Newton's revolutionary synthesis, yet Newton himself insisted that he was reviving ancient wisdom—if anything, he was an intellectual conservative. His reluctance to engage in disputes after the early 1670s, his aversion to any statement that might be considered controversial, did not help matters. He was often terse, at times just plain obscure, about his new methods. As a result, Du Châtelet understood that the first task of the philosopher was to ponder how the revolution in the sciences happened. Since the scientists themselves had not answered this question, it became a philosophical one.

It is practically a truism of modern life that every revolution moves through a few key stages. The heady days of pamphlets and protests proclaiming the injustices of the ancien régime lead to the first stage of a new government. Those early governing days eventually give way to the dissolution of the movement and squabbles among its leaders. Has any revolution led to a new structure without someone proclaiming that the ideals of the movement had now been forgotten or betrayed? The revolution in the sciences of the seventeenth century was no different. But in a sense, it was worse, at least from the point of view of the analyst attempting to capture its key developments. For even if one can establish the list of the revolution's leaders, one struggles to discern anything fundamental on which they agreed, even before the inevitable squabbles and proclamations of betrayal. Was experimentation and observation the key? That would certainly have pleased Galileo but can hardly be said to capture Descartes's approach. Perhaps the development of new mathematical techniques was essential. That would have been endorsed by Descartes and also by Leibniz, but ironically it leaves out Newton, who did not even employ the beautiful new techniques of his own calculus in his magnum opus! As a good son of the Renaissance, he stuck with the geometry of the ancients, baffling many mathematicians in later years.[22] And it wasn't long before Leibniz and Huygens charged Newton with betraying the new science by rejecting a consensus in thinking about causation in nature. Du Châtelet's task of characterizing the revolution may seem hopeless.

Du Châtelet's next insight is that the scientific revolution in fact lacked any unifying method or approach. It was aptly called a revolution, or a set of revolutions, because there was a revolutionary overthrow of the existing Aristotelian or "Scholastic" order in which the ideas of the "Schools" had been taught for generations. Indeed, that was perhaps the one area of agreement. But it was not accompanied by any consensus on the new methods that ought to replace the old. Instead, Du Châtelet proposes that the philosopher recognize the contributions that many thinkers made to the new sciences without insisting that they agreed on any single methodology. Indeed, in a way, she insists on the opposite. Right after explaining how Newton brilliantly used Kepler's description of the elliptical planetary orbits to help establish his new theory of gravity, she writes: "Physics is an immense building that surpasses the powers of a single man" (Du Châtelet, *Institutions*, 1742, XI, 12). Her architectural metaphor liberates us from attempting to find the essence of the revolution, the ideal or method that all the revolutionaries endorsed. After all, workers do not construct a building by engaging in the same activities, they engage in different activities in concert with one another. One lays the foundation with bricks and mortar, another raises a wall, a third paints it, and so on. The metaphors we use are just as illuminating as the fairy tales we tell.

The metaphor that the revolutionary new science is a great structure built by many hands prevents philosophers from attempting to discern the one true scientific method from the works of any single author. It suggests that one look for contributions wherever they may be. Unlike Voltaire, who decided that Newton alone had found the right method, the way to *the truth*, Du Châtelet insists that "each philosopher has seen something, and none has seen everything." And if a central figure in the revolution of the sciences, like Descartes or Newton, made mistakes, that was "because he was a man, and it is not given to a single man, nor to a single century, to know everything" (Du Châtelet, *Institutions*, 1742, V, 6). Therefore, we must search for wisdom in the works of the many figures who helped to build the new structure of physics. In the preface to the *Institutions*, Du Châtelet illustrates this point with a discussion of hypothetical reasoning in science. Many followers of Newton had taken one of his famous warnings about the dangers of hypotheses in science and promoted it as the essence of the scientific method. They called for a *ban* on hypotheses. The followers of Descartes, on the other hand, had long promoted the use of hypothetical reasoning to explain various natural phenomena. For her part, Du Châtelet argues that neither position is correct, although each contains wisdom. We should neither ban hypotheses nor run rampant with them. They have a useful, but limited, role to play in science. She expresses that idea through a continuation of her architectural metaphor. Hypotheses, she tells us, are as "necessary as the scaffolding on a house being built; it is true that when the building is completed, the scaffolding becomes useless, but it could not have been erected without its help" (Du Châtelet, *Institutions*, 1742, VIII, 9).

Du Châtelet's conception of science leads her to a distinctive notion of philosophy's task. Since the revolution in science did not have a single leader, since it was the work of many hands, the task of the philosopher reflecting on the creation of new scientific knowledge is to search for wisdom in various thinkers. Indeed, her reaction to the debate about hypotheses in science is characteristic of her approach throughout the *Institutions*. When confronted with a debate among the revolutionaries of the past, whether it concerns hypotheses, the nature of matter, the large-scale structure of space and time, or the shape of knowledge, Du Châtelet seeks to find the insights hidden in opposed positions. Rather than following the path of Voltaire, who promoted the ideas of a single heroic figure, and who often retold the story of Newton's apple, she argued that philosophy ought to adopt a more nuanced perspective when searching for the truth. Even when she clearly agrees with an influential figure on some pressing issue of the day—for instance, she eventually endorses Leibniz's ideas about space and time rather than Newton's—she still insists on finding some wisdom in the opposing view. She acknowledged that Newton had developed profound ideas about motion and its implications for space, even if his conception of the latter was ultimately flawed.

Du Châtelet's *Institutions* was a deeply influential work because she had found a way to capture a key element of her historical moment with her vision of the revolution in the sciences. Indeed, her idea that philosophy must situate itself historically vis-à-vis the recent revolution in the sciences became a defining element of the Enlightenment. So did her idea that the best view of the revolution is a pluralistic one that trumpets the many contributions of the revolutionaries without searching for their hidden agreements on method or ideas. Indeed, Du Châtelet's pluralistic conception is on full display in the most famous text of the whole Enlightenment, D'Alembert's *Preliminary Discourse to the Encyclopedia*. D'Alembert knew Du Châtelet's work well (although he never referred to her in that text). He nearly spoiled Du Châtelet's view by attributing the "revolution in physics" primarily to Newton. But he also gave the other key figures their due. In noting that the *Encyclopedia* would not merely represent a compendium of all knowledge presented in alphabetical form, but more importantly, a "reasoned dictionary" of such knowledge, D'Alembert gives considerable space to the figures who led to the Enlightenment. He provides a history of knowledge. In the *Preliminary Discourse*, an impressively concise text, he takes a full twenty pages to outline the accomplishments of Bacon, Descartes, Huygens, Newton, Locke, and Leibniz. Perhaps the list is unsurprising for a man who proclaimed that to live in the enlightened age is to live in an age of philosophy. Indeed, the enlightened thinkers often simply called themselves *philosophes*.[23] D'Alembert did not adopt Du Châtelet's architectural metaphor, but in the end, he promoted her pluralistic conception of the sciences.

The most famous philosopher in the Enlightenment continued in this same vein. In his own magnum opus, the *Critique of Pure Reason*, Immanuel Kant emphasized his understanding of his place in history right at the work's beginning, taking the notion of the revolution to new heights. As he noted dramatically in the preface to the second edition of 1787, his task was to create a revolution in philosophy that would mirror the recent revolution in the sciences. Indeed, he would revolutionize philosophy precisely by rendering it scientific for the first time. His historical narrative is a familiar one: it was not until "the ingenious Francis Bacon" that the study of nature became *scientific*. The "sudden revolution in the way of thinking" promulgated by Bacon inspires philosophy now. Whereas geometry had been set on the "secure path of a science" by Euclid, as had logic by Aristotle, the study of nature had not been scientific until the revolution caused by figures like Bacon and Galileo. Philosophy in Kant's hands would now follow suit.[24] Whereas the modern figures trumpeted in the *Critique* had little interest in their historical location and never proclaimed a revolution as such, Kant's philosophical revolution was oriented toward specifying the importance of his own. This famous intellectual and philosophical development, which brings us to the end of the eighteenth century, began with Du Châtelet's treatise in 1740, published when Kant was a young student living in Königsberg, then a reasonably obscure coastal city in Prussia. He read her work in the German translation.

If great thinkers like D'Alembert and Kant adopted Du Châtelet's framing of Enlightenment science and philosophy, why isn't she a household name like them? Why isn't her contribution part of every narrative of the Enlightenment? Despite her widespread intellectual influence on the major figures of her day, an influence they were happy to acknowledge on various occasions, there was another dynamic at play. Those very same figures would also seek to excise her influence from the *official* record of their movement. That record took the form of novel histories of modern philosophy. The *philosophes* expressed their historical location not only by specifying the key details of the scientific revolution but also by producing a new history of modern philosophy. They sought to chronicle the history of modern philosophy even while living through the modern era. And all of them sought to excise Du Châtelet from the emerging official history of philosophy.

The most important *modern* history of modern philosophy was written at the height of the Enlightenment by a German *Aufklärer* named Johann Jacob Brucker. Although he has been mostly forgotten today, Brucker became famous during his lifetime. Over the course of several years in the 1740s, he published an immense five-volume history, calling it *Historia Critica Philosophiae*. His effort was a "critical history of philosophy" because it focused on original sources, as later scholars would take to be *de rigeur*. The text became the key source for understanding the history of philosophy for the *philosophes*, from Diderot to D'Alembert to Kant. Brucker covered the entire history of philosophy, from ancient Hebrew and Egyptian civilization to the Greeks to the medieval period, right up to the "modern" era. Indeed, he chronicled the Enlightenment as it was happening around him. He discussed Bacon and Descartes, Newton and Locke, and even managed to reach his contemporary Christian Wolff, the most famous Prussian philosopher before Kant.[25] Brucker wrote the history of his own historical moment.

We may have forgotten the names of figures like Brucker, but we are still living in the Enlightenment's wake. When the *philosophes* articulated their own history, when they discussed the key figures in "modern" science and philosophy who brought them to their enlightened age, they bequeathed to us a conception of modern philosophy that we still embrace today.[26] Their conception of modern philosophy is perfectly familiar. Their emphasis on Bacon, Descartes, Newton, Leibniz, and Locke requires no explanation for today's readers—indeed, any student would recognize their names. We are no longer living in the Enlightenment, but our idea of modern philosophy and its heroes is an Enlightenment idea.

Reaching back to the source of this consensus in the Enlightenment, we find the original conception of philosophy's task as the analysis of the scientific revolution's implications in Du Châtelet's *Institutions*. The *Institutions* was read and discussed by the great thinkers of the century. Since Brucker had chosen to write the history of modern philosophy as it was happening around him, discussing the ideas of living philosophers, Du Châtelet had a real chance to join the modern philosophy canon. Since Brucker wrote about his contemporary, the philosopher Christian Wolff, he certainly *could* have included Du Châtelet as well. He *could* have added a woman to the modern philosophy canon, thereby ensuring that generations of readers would recognize her deep contributions to the Enlightenment and to modern philosophy. But he did not. No one else did, either. This is the story of why, and of what happened instead.

From Philosopher to "Mistress"?

If any woman stood a real chance of breaking into the modern philosophy canon, it was Émilie Du Châtelet. But eventually, her exclusion from the modern canon by figures like Brucker left her legacy open to misappropriation and distortion. Eventually, the very element that seemed like such good fortune, her years of participation in intellectual life, especially in her own academy in Cirey, sealed for her a different fate. So did her many years as Voltaire's intellectual companion. It is this fate that we find in numerous contemporary accounts of the Enlightenment rather than the astonishing story of her intellectual rise and the influence of her work. Du Châtelet helped to shape the narrative of Enlightenment science and philosophy, but the narrative of her own life, and of her influence on the Enlightenment, was written in very different terms. A new narrative, casting her in the role of Voltaire's sidekick, eventually eclipsed her fame and influence.

Examples of the eclipse of her intellectual stature by her romantic life abound in contemporary discussions. For instance, readers looking for an official description of the life and work of Émilie Du Châtelet might begin with a classic source like *Encyclopedia Britannica*. This is what we find in her entry:

> Gabrielle-Émilie Le Tonnelier de Breteuil, marquise du Châtelet, (born Dec. 17, 1706, Paris, France—died Sept. 10, 1749, Lunéville), French mathematician and physicist who was the mistress of Voltaire. . . . In 1738 Mme du Châtelet and Voltaire competed independently for a prize offered by the Academy of

Sciences for an essay on the nature of fire. Although the prize was won by the German mathematician Leonhard Euler, Mme du Châtelet's *Dissertation sur la nature et la propagation du feu* [Dissertation on the nature and propagation of fire] was published in 1744 at the Academy's expense. She wrote several other scientific treatises and many posthumously published works on philosophy and religion.[27]

Official sources like *Encyclopedia Britannica* rely on generations of scholarship; in this case, contemporary scholarship on the Enlightenment would be most relevant. In his influential book on the Enlightenment first published in 2015, the historian Anthony Pagden introduces Du Châtelet to his readers in this way:

> Voltaire had spent much of the 1730s and 1740s shut up with his mistress Gabrielle-Émilie, Marquise du Châtelet, in her country house at Cirey-sur-Blaise. Madame du Châtelet was a brilliant mathematician and physicist; the translator of Newton's *Principia Mathematica*, to which she added her own "algebraical commentary"; and the author of, among other things, a treatise on happiness.[28]

Nothing that Pagden says is *false*. She did indeed produce an analytical commentary on the *Principia*, thereby providing not only a modern-language version of Newton's Latin text but also a modern mathematical presentation to replace his old-fashioned geometric one. She did write a famous treatise on happiness. And indeed, she and Voltaire lived for many years at her home in Cirey, down in the Champagne region of France, far from the gossip and distractions in the capital. And yet Pagden also diminishes her work, calling her a "brilliant mathematician and physicist" without even mentioning her magnum opus *in those very fields*. Pagden's narrative ensures that Du Châtelet remains within a comfortable gendered category: a "brilliant" woman, to be sure, one who managed to translate the latest science from Latin and geometry into their modern cousins, French and analysis, but one with a derivative intellectual impact. In Pagden's narrative, she becomes a mere historical curiosity, certainly not someone who might disrupt our basic understanding of what the Enlightenment was all about. Perhaps that is the point.

Tracing the origins of Padgen's narrative through the contemporary literature leaves us with a depressingly static interpretive approach. Pagden emphasizes both that Du Châtelet was "strong-willed and independent" and that she was Voltaire's "mistress." The dynamic in Pagden's account echoes Du Châtelet's presence in one of his sources, Jonathan Israel's influential book *Radical Enlightenment*, first published in 2001. Israel introduces her to the reader like this:

> A woman with a formidable philosophical reputation for a time was Voltaire's mistress, Gabrielle-Émilie, marquise du Châtelet, whom he celebrated in print in 1738, as a paragon of female intellectual power, and a true disciple of Newton and of "truth." Furthermore, this "minerve de la France," as he calls her, not only shared his conversation, scientific experiments, and bed but soon rebelled against his uncompromising Newtonianism, demonstrating a spirited independence of mind.[29]

Once again, her magnum opus is never mentioned. Israel, in turn, relied in part on the most influential interpreter of the Enlightenment from a previous generation, Peter Gay. Writing in the 1960s, Gay introduces Du Châtelet as Voltaire's mistress and describes their time together in Cirey, but once again with no mention of her major philosophical work. Moving a bit further back into history, Israel and Gay rely on the French scholar Paul Hazard's *European Thought in the Eighteenth Century*, which was published right after the Second World War. Hazard doesn't say that she was Voltaire's "mistress"—Gay, Israel, and Pagden supply that nugget of information—but the approach is similar. Although he emphasizes their years in Cirey together, he also fails to mention that in Cirey, she wrote a major work on the foundations of physics. With Hazard, the trail runs cold: he provides no citations.[30]

Ironically, the constant refrain among professional historians for the past seventy-five years that Du Châtelet was Voltaire's "mistress" is itself questionable from a historical point of view. It is certainly true that the two of them were lovers for a time, housemates for longer, intellectual partners for longer still. But the idea of a "mistress," along with the concomitant notion of an illicit "affair," does not pass historical muster. As feminist historians explained long ago, in Du Châtelet's milieu, sexual freedom was accorded to aristocratic women, especially if they remained within the proper social circles and if the overall social system benefited men.[31] Indeed, the Marquis Du Châtelet explicitly approved the arrangement in the chateau in Cirey. It is therefore misleading to use contemporary terminology that carries connotations of illicit behavior. But contemporary historians cannot help but promote that idea, over and over again.[32] Perhaps the story is just too titillating to pass up.

More profoundly, the portrayal of Du Châtelet in these influential accounts of the Enlightenment also fails to reflect a generation of feminist scholarship stretching back to the 1970s.[33] This scholarship not only demonstrates the historical inaccuracy of portraying Du Châtelet as Voltaire's "mistress," it documents the deep and lasting influence of her thought, represented most clearly in her *Institutions*, a text that is often ignored today. That scholarship culminated in the recent work of Judith Zinsser, who not only analyzed Du Châtelet's numerous contributions to European intellectual life in the middle of the eighteenth century, but who also published a recent biography that corrected many portraits of Du Châtelet that subordinated her to Voltaire and his projects.[34] Zinsser's rich portrait of Du Châtelet's life would enable any scholar to understand the deeply misleading, if not downright inaccurate, portrayals of Du Châtelet in many works on the Enlightenment.

How did this happen? How did the most famous woman in intellectual life during the Enlightenment end up being someone's "mistress"? How did the source of a major consensus during the Enlightenment concerning the revolution in the sciences receive such a minor role in our histories? Feminist scholarship on Du Chatelet certainly represents significant intellectual progress toward correcting the historical record. Unlike in many cases, however, those scholars were not recovering a voice that was never recognized in history. On the contrary, Du Châtelet was famous during her lifetime. So the question is, how could she have become a famous philosopher during the middle of the eighteenth century, only to be reduced to the sidekick of some man in the twenty-first? How could she have achieved a high intellectual status in the middle of the eighteenth century at a time when the barriers facing women were much steeper than those in our own day, only to find herself written out of the history of philosophy in a supposedly more progressive era?

You would be forgiven for expecting a banal answer to this question. After all, haven't women always been excluded from our narratives of the history of science and philosophy? And haven't men received the credit for women's ideas since time immemorial? Why should Du Châtelet's idea of the revolution in the sciences be any different? Of course, *scholars* have long known about the philosophical work of women in modern Europe like Laura Bassi, Margaret Cavendish, Anna Maria van Schurman, and Princess Elisabeth, but the public still rarely hears their names.[35] Why should Émilie Du Châtelet be any different? Indeed, wouldn't we expect her to suffer the same fate as these other thinkers, finding herself written out of the dominant narratives of Enlightenment Europe? Wouldn't we expect the men in her orbit to take credit for her ideas?

If we dig deep enough into the historical record of the Enlightenment, we find an answer to the mystery of Du Châtelet's exclusion that is anything but trivial. We encounter an untold story not only of the Enlightenment's most famous woman but also of modern philosophy itself. Indeed, as luck would have it, Émilie Du Châtelet became the most famous woman in science and philosophy in Enlightenment Europe at precisely the moment when the *philosophes* first proclaimed the beginning of a new era in philosophy. The modern era. Suitably to this era, they proclaimed a new conception of the modern philosopher. When we dig deeply into the major Enlightenment sources, from the works of Voltaire to the writings of academicians in Berlin and Paris to the *Encyclopedia* of Diderot, we find something fascinating. Du Châtelet and her ideas threatened to upset a new conception of the modern philosopher proclaimed in her age.[36] She was not merely betrayed by later misogynist portrayals in recent times. Even as she rose to the highest levels of intellectual fame in eighteenth-century Europe, she was first betrayed by the Enlightenment itself. For the leading figures in her era, she posed a danger to the emerging narrative of their movement. She was present at the birth of the modern canon in philosophy, but because of the threat she posed, she was excluded at that very moment. This is her story.

2

What Was the Scientific Revolution?

Émilie Du Châtelet's idea of the revolution in the sciences became a defining feature of the Enlightenment. Soon after she published her main work, *Institutions of Physics*, intellectuals adopted her notion that the revolutionary knowledge of the new science should become a central topic for Enlightenment thought. And it became a prime inspiration for widely promoting enlightened ideas. But there was a complication. Some figures eventually resisted Du Châtelet's specific conception of science as a collaborative endeavor involving many cooperating figures, expressed most clearly in her metaphor that physics is an immense building constructed by many hands. The reason is that her conception conflicted with a growing desire to identify the *hero* of the revolution. The search for a hero fomented the notion that the revolution in science actually resulted from a single genius laboring alone. And there was really only one suitable candidate for the position of *the hero* of the revolution: Sir Isaac Newton. The story of watching an apple fall and quickly deducing a theory of gravity covering the whole universe perfectly captures their way of understanding him. No one denied the importance of Copernicus's research on the heliocentric model of the solar system, Galileo's experiments on free fall, or Huygens's ideas about collisions. But they were thought to be significant because they led to Newton's grand new idea that the universe was bound together by a single force. Even Newton admitted that he saw further because he stood on the shoulders of giants. But what really mattered was what Newton saw from his uniquely high perch.

The story of Newton's genius became a central notion of European intellectual and social life in the eighteenth century. Hyperbole was rampant. Leading figures in the Enlightenment did not merely trumpet Newton's scientific and mathematical prowess, his intellectual genius. They went much further. In his *Philosophical Letters*, Voltaire said that one might regard Newton, rather than say Caesar or Alexander the Great, as the greatest man who ever lived.[1] Others were a bit more measured. As a good son of the Enlightenment, Thomas Jefferson, who had served as ambassador to France before becoming president, contended that Newton and his fellow Englishmen Locke and Bacon were the *three* greatest men who ever lived.[2] But more often than not, Newton was singled out for praise that no one else would receive; as Edmond Halley had said, "No closer to the gods can any mortal rise." Perhaps Alexander Pope captured this hyperbolic attitude best with his famous couplet:

> Nature and Nature's Laws lay hid at Night
> God said, *Let Newton be!*, and All was
> Light.[3]

Although the Enlightenment philosophers and poets were helping to usher in a new secular age, they often could not resist biblical imagery to express their profound admiration of Newton's genius and his influence on modern culture. They had their hero and a conception of science to accompany him.

This widespread hero worship during the Enlightenment raised a problem. Unlike the work of earlier figures like Galileo, who was a brilliant writer and rhetorician, or of Descartes, who sought to reach a wide audience for his philosophy, Newton's own work was extremely obscure. Indeed, Newton's *Principia* is one of the most difficult scientific treatises ever written. Even if one could read Latin, very few mathematicians in the world could understand the intricate geometric arguments that he had employed in his new physics. As the famous Newtonian J. T. Desaguliers put it succinctly in *A Course of Experimental Philosophy*, "The Thoughts of being oblig'd to understand Mathematicks frighted a great many from the Newtonian Philosophy[.]"[4] They were *frighted* indeed. Even highly educated, prominent philosophers sympathetic to Newton's ideas, like John Locke, could not understand many of the geometric proofs and arguments in the *Principia*. (Locke purportedly asked the Dutch mathematician Huygens whether Newton's math checked out!) Newton had failed to make his science accessible, even to the educated public. That failure raised the question: how revolutionary could the new science be if almost no one understood it? The intellectual world of 1700 may have been completely different from the world of 1600, but if educated readers knew little about it, what difference did that make?

A great task of the Enlightenment was born: to spread the gospel of science in the vernacular. In the first few decades of the eighteenth century, countless works in English, Dutch, and Italian were published to describe Newton's triumph in terms that an educated public could understand. Even if these works used the old scholarly language of Latin or the new one of French, they would avoid Newton's daunting mathematics, solving Desaguliers's problem. They had titles like *An Introduction to Sir Isaac Newton's Philosophy*, *A View of Sir Isaac Newton's Philosophical Discoveries*, and even *Newtonianism for the Ladies*. They sought to reach educated publics throughout all of Europe, and as the last title suggests, they often explicitly aimed to reach intellectually minded women, who had been excluded from colleges and academies. The task of spreading the new science to the public was considered so crucial to the Enlightenment that many authors sought to break through the gender barrier to reach the widest readership. They were spreading the Newtonian gospel, but through a method that was barely envisioned by Newton himself.

Voltaire led the way. During his extended visit to England from May 1726 until the autumn of 1728, Voltaire attended Newton's funeral at Westminster Abbey, socialized with members of Princess Caroline of Wales's circle in London, and became close with Samuel Clarke, Newton's parish priest and friend.[5] Voltaire happily converted to Newtonianism and began to preach its gospel. His first foray was his *Philosophical Letters*—also called the *Letters from England*—in the early 1730s. It quickly landed him in hot water with the Parisian authorities for its controversial views—his insistence that England had enlightened ideas that would help bring traditional, not to say backward, France into a new century did not help matters. Despite the controversy, he remained undeterred. Four years later, he devoted an entire text to explicating Clarke and Newton's worldview, titling it *Elements of the Philosophy of Newton*. Voltaire wrote the *Elements* while living with Du Châtelet at her country chateau in Cirey. She helped him understand some of the intricacies of Newton's mathematical physics, a fact he was happy to acknowledge. She, too, was sympathetic to Newton's approach toward understanding the natural world, and equally ready to transcend the still dominant Cartesian attitudes of the Parisian Academy, as was her former tutor Maupertuis. In his famous poem to Du Châtelet that opens his *Elements*, Voltaire calls her a "disciple of Newton," the same honorific he bestowed on himself.[6] He hoped that this proclamation would ensure that Du Châtelet remained within the Newtonian fold (Figure 6).

Voltaire's hopes were dashed. Just two years after Voltaire published his popularization of Newton, Du Châtelet published the first edition of her own masterwork. She made it plain from the beginning that she would not play the role of Newton's disciple (Du Châtelet, *Institutions*, 1742, VI, 7):

> You can receive much instruction on this topic from the *Elements of the philosophy of Newton*, which appeared last year. And I would

omit what I have to tell you on this subject if its illustrious author had embraced a wider terrain. But he confined himself within such narrow limits that I did not believe I could dispense with speaking about it with you.

Was it merely Voltaire's narrow treatment of the subject that pushed her to publish her own account on the heels of his? Or was something deeper at play? Once again, she chose to be direct. In the very next sentence, she warns that one must avoid "the inevitable obstinacy to which the partisan spirit carries one," for it is "ridiculous in physics." One must instead search for the truth. Voltaire had not merely written an overly narrow account, he had also become a partisan for Newton. He had abandoned the search for truth, whatever its sources might be.

Du Châtelet was exactly right—Voltaire had indeed become a partisan for Newton's ideas. In fact, "partisan" is too weak a word. Voltaire himself said in a contemporaneous letter that Newton's philosophy is "the sole truth," and he told the Italian writer Francesco Algarotti that his commentary would present the "Newtonian catechism."[7] By 1743, when Voltaire had been elected a member of the Royal Society in London, his letter of thanks to the Society's president Martin Folkes could be mistaken for a religious tract. He writes of his time in England:

> My first masters in the free and learned country, were Shakespeare, Addison, Dryden, Pope; I made some steps afterwards in the temple of philosophy towards the altar of Newton. I was even so bold as to introduce into France some of his discoveries; but I was not only a confessor to his faith, I became a martyr.[8]

Even when writing to the most important science academy in the world, Voltaire believed that only religious imagery could express the depth of his devotion to Newton and his philosophy.

Du Châtelet rejected this hyperbolic attitude toward Newton. But she also rejected the spirit of discipleship more generally. She

wasn't merely contesting Voltaire's conception of the Scientific
Revolution, she was contesting his conception of the Enlightenment and of its philosophers. He had described her as another one
of Newton's "disciples," but she rejected that label, urging her readers to remain independent like her. If she was no disciple, Newton's
book was not the gospel. The two ideas went hand in hand.

Within just a few short years, then, two French intellectuals living in the same stone chateau in the countryside of Champagne
articulated two competing visions of science, philosophy, and the
Enlightenment. Voltaire's vision of science and of Newton's heroic
role in helping to make it a modern site of intellectual progress is
far more familiar today than Du Châtelet's alternative vision of science as a collaborative endeavor that exceeds the powers of even the
greatest genius.[9] Indeed, Voltaire did as much as anyone to promote
the story of a young Newton discovering the theory of gravity just
by watching an apple fall on his mother's farm. Du Châtelet's vision
of scientific knowledge is not so easily promoted by a simple tale,
and hardly anyone in Europe during the eighteenth century could
compete with Voltaire's wit, his knack for finding the right *bon mots*
to capture some complex thought. So perhaps it's not surprising
that his vision of the Enlightenment and of Newton's role within
it eventually eclipsed hers. But what happens if we rethink the historical record with Du Châtelet's vision of the Scientific Revolution
as a collaborative effort in mind? Does her approach change our
understanding of how science and philosophy evolved during the
early days of the Enlightenment? If we ignore the apple and bring
Newton back down to earth, what happens?

Was Newton the Hero of the Scientific Revolution?

In order to recover the historical record of Newton's actual reception, we have to wade through a thicket of narratives about his

genius, his influence on European life, his status as the greatest figure of the age of reason. It is of course true that if we survey the whole eighteenth century, Newton's influence was immense.[10] Not only did he inspire much of the mathematical and scientific work of the Enlightenment, his success in understanding nature prompted figures in other fields, from geology to psychology to economics, to find a new means of achieving scientific knowledge. Everyone from writers like Voltaire in France to economists like Adam Smith in Scotland to leading figures like Benjamin Franklin in America were self-proclaimed Newtonians.[11] Yet we must forget about all of these developments, despite their historical and intellectual significance, and return to the origin of the story. We have to recapture the moment when Newton first announced his scientific ideas. So, what first happened after Edmond Halley visited Newton in Cambridge in 1684 and he published his magnum opus, the *Mathematical Principles of Natural Philosophy*, three years later? How did the intellectual world react?

Soon after the Royal Society in London published Newton's *Principia*, he sent signed copies to two key thinkers, G. W. Leibniz in Prussia and Christian Huygens in Holland. Newton regarded them as the leading mathematicians in his day. At the time, some scholars thought they might be the only two people alive who could understand all of Newton's mathematical proofs.

Gottfried Wilhelm Leibniz is known to high school students around the world as the co-discoverer with Newton of what we now call the integral and differential calculus. Indeed, Leibniz's notation and approach to the calculus eclipsed Newton's, which was quickly considered idiosyncratic (few people today would know what a "fluxion" is).[12] Leibniz was also a prodigious and capacious thinker. In addition to his extensive and deep research in mathematics, Leibniz wrote about metaphysics, theology, natural science, history, diplomacy, and numerous other topics. To accompany his influential publications during his lifetime, he left behind a trove of manuscripts totaling thousands of pages—scholars in Hanover,

Germany, are still poring over those texts, as they have done for decades.

For his part, Christiaan Huygens is less known today than Leibniz, but Newton—who like many geniuses was rather stingy with praise—said that he was a "master."[13] Born to a prominent family in Holland, the young Huygens exhibited a keen interest in science and mathematics. After a youthful period as a committed Cartesian philosopher, Huygens eventually conducted his own experimental and mathematical research on motion and the laws of impact, publishing his work in the Royal Society's *Philosophical Transactions*. He followed that influential account, one cited by Newton in his *Principia*, with a brilliant exposition of gravity and its study through the workings of the pendulum in 1673. If anyone could understand Newton's work in those days, it was Leibniz and Huygens.

When they received Newton's *Principia* in the post, both Huygens and Leibniz read it carefully and with great interest. Both were enormously impressed with its scope and reach, the sophistication of its mathematics, and its immense implications for natural philosophy. They understood that Newton's theory of universal gravity was a profound and challenging new conception of the natural world. But neither accepted it.

What was the problem? Neither Huygens nor Leibniz thought that Newton had made any mathematical error, or an error in reasoning. Instead, they agreed that Newton had made something like a philosophical mistake. They focused on the most startling aspect of Newton's theory. According to the *Principia*, the free fall of bodies, the tides, the motion of the moon, and the planetary orbits, are all caused by the force of gravity. Just as a ball that I drop falls to the ground by the force of gravity, so too the moon traces its constant path around the earth by that same force. Indeed, one of Newton's greatest feats of imagination was to use the latest empirical information and then to imagine what would happen if the moon itself were to approach the earth and then fall toward its surface. It would drop much like that ball that fell from my hand, he reasoned.

Newton's imagination was incredibly fertile. He also proclaimed that this same force of gravity explained why the satellites of Jupiter maintained their orbits, why the earth orbited the sun, and so on. It was this conception of gravity that troubled Huygens and Leibniz. How could the gravitational force between the earth and the sun, which are millions of miles apart, keep the earth in its orbit? Newton implied that the sun acted directly on the earth, but how could it do so from such an immense distance? Neither Huygens nor Leibniz could accept that idea.

Like so many thinkers during the Scientific Revolution—including Galileo, Descartes, and Boyle—Leibniz and Huygens endorsed what was then called the "mechanical philosophy."[14] They assumed that all change within nature is due to the impacts that material bodies make on one another. They concluded that Newton's theory erred because it failed to provide a "mechanism" underlying gravity. Surely, the sun could accelerate the earth, maintaining its orbit, only through some kind of mechanism. Newton himself had explained his three laws of motion, along with his controversial idea of a "centripetal force," with simple examples like a stone whirled around in a sling. The sling holds onto the stone, preventing it from flying off along the tangent to its orbit, perhaps as you swing it over your head, Olympics style. If you let go, the stone goes flying. Newton grew up on a farm in the English countryside, and he gave other such examples: water swirling around in a bucket, a horse pulling a stone across a field, and so on. Now, one could imagine a giant rope extending from the center of the sun to the earth, with the earth flying around the sun as a result. But Newton was asking his readers to remove the rope! We can think of gravity as *like* a rope that holds the earth in its orbit as it accelerates around the sun, day in and day out. It's a nice way of thinking. But surely, it cannot be *literally* true: without the rope, there's nothing *physical* holding the earth in place. There's no mechanism.

So, Huygens and Leibniz objected to Newton's most important idea in physics. A few years after reading Newton's *Principia*,

Huygens published an influential essay in 1690, making his criticism succinctly. Newton is a brilliant mathematician, Huygens said, but even after hearing about his theory of universal gravity, we must still search for "an intelligible cause" of the planetary orbits. Simply proclaiming that *gravity itself* explains them is just not understandable.[15] A year earlier, Leibniz had made much the same point: after reading and taking notes on the *Principia*, Leibniz published an essay in the famous journal *Acta Eruditorum*. An imposing piece in Latin with sophisticated mathematics, Leibniz's "Essay on the Causes of Celestial Motions" argued that attributing the planetary orbits to gravity was a mere *façon de parler*. There must be some mechanism to explain the motions of the planets—he favored an old Cartesian idea, a vortex. A massive, imperceptible, swirling fluid carried the planets around the sun, and Leibniz believed he could make the mathematics of that idea work out.[16] That may sound rather fabulous to modern ears, but Leibniz and Huygens thought they stood on solid ground: for nearly a century, leading European thinkers had endorsed the mechanical philosophy. They were convinced that there must be some mechanism underlying gravity.

Du Châtelet's vision of science as a collaborative endeavor encourages us to look past the stories of Newton's genius by searching for the initial reaction to his work among the intellectuals he himself respected the most. And as a matter of historical fact, the turn into the eighteenth century was characterized by a profound dispute about the new science involving many leading thinkers in Europe. Indeed, influential figures continued to proclaim for the next fifty years that some mechanism for gravity, as for electricity, magnetism, or any force of nature, had to be found. They were not satisfied with Newton's non-mechanistic approach. His work was not the gospel.

The most important mathematician after the age of Newton and Leibniz, Leonard Euler, was one of the most prominent mechanistic thinkers. Born in Basel in 1707, Euler was a mathematical prodigy with a capacious appetite for solving scientific, technological, and mathematical problems. He was the first person to use the new calculus systematically in rational mechanics, and he eventually published hundreds of technical papers, more than any other eighteenth-century figure. He was like an academy of sciences unto himself, making contributions to acoustics, astronomy, hydrodynamics, optics, and numerous branches of mathematics from analysis to number theory. For many years, he held prominent positions in the academies of St. Petersburg and Berlin.[17] Although Euler accepted the mathematical rigor of Newton's law of gravity, he continued to argue in the middle of the eighteenth century that gravity's action must involve some mechanism.[18] Euler's name is often mentioned along with figures like Euclid and Gauss, so Newton would surely have respected his work. If we insist on viewing Newton as the hero of the new science, these reactions among leading thinkers become perplexing.

Of course, Voltaire and his colleagues were too smart to let a few facts get in the way of a compelling narrative. They had a ready-made reaction to the resistance that Newton's theory of gravity had felt. Certainly, old-fashioned, conservative, often "Cartesian," thinkers were resistant to the profound implications of Newton's new science, they would note. What did you expect? Influential philosophers and scientists, protecting their influence through traditional institutions like scientific academies, always resist revolutionary developments. They irrationally resisted Newton, thereby impeding the progress of the Enlightenment. That is why Voltaire and other intellectuals took it upon themselves to spread the Newtonian gospel. If Leibniz and Huygens rejected Newton's reasoning, so much the worse for them: they were on the wrong side of history.

There is no doubt that Voltaire's story of conservative thinkers resisting the immense progress represented by Newton's new discoveries was a compelling one. He was aware that amongst Newton's steadfast supporters in England, there were bound to be disagreements. But they were trivial in his eyes. Voltaire saw a single gospel and a coterie of disciples. In his *Letters from England*, and especially in his *Elements of the Philosophy of Newton,* he did not distinguish the views of Newton from those of his follower Clarke, or even from those of his friend John Locke.[19] For instance, Voltaire says that space is a property of God, a view presented by Clarke but actually denied by Newton; and he attributes to Newton Locke's famous idea of adding "solidity" to the Cartesian view of matter.[20] With the goal of overcoming resistance to the new science ever in his mind, Voltaire used every idea and quotation at his disposal to spread what he regarded as the Newtonian gospel. If the leader himself had been reticent to tackle philosophical topics, he would help himself to the ideas of Clarke and Locke to fill in the details. Perhaps they disagreed on subtleties, points of emphasis, the right formulation of some claim. But for Voltaire, they all presented the same "philosophy," which he was now promoting.

In her *Institutions,* Du Châtelet presented a strikingly different picture. Where Voltaire saw a single coherent philosophy emanating from Newton's London, she saw deep disagreements among Newton's acolytes. They did not disagree over finding the right turn of phrase, the best way to explain Newton's ideas to the masses, or the best means of responding to its various Continental critics like Leibniz and Huygens. She argued instead that they debated what Newton's theory of gravity really meant. The *Institutions* reflects this recognition throughout. Whereas Voltaire sees a group of English philosophers all reading from the same hymnal, Du Châtelet sees a dispute about what the gospel really says. Whereas Voltaire quotes Newton, Clarke, and Locke indifferently, she carefully distinguishes Newton's own published views from those of his various followers, not to mention those of Locke. To smooth over these differences—taking the various disciples to speak in a single voice on behalf of the "great man"—is to miss the true disputes within science at the time. But it is also to commit a sin that Du Châtelet identifies in the preface to the *Institutions.* She writes (Du Châtelet, *Institutions,* 1742, X, 11): "I advise you not to carry respect for the greatest men to the point of idolatry, as do the majority of their disciples." She cautions against taking one's respect for Newton to the point of "idolatry," which implies a problem with becoming his disciple. Her borrowing of religious imagery was clearly apt because her housemate and partner had already declared his discipleship.

Once again, viewing the historical record through the lens provided by Du Châtelet helps us to see science and philosophy in a new light. And if we view history through her lens, we naturally encounter the question: was she right that there were profound disagreements among Newton's advocates? And if so, why did they disagree so strongly?

Disputes in the House of Newton

Newton's *Mathematical Principles of Natural Philosophy* is immensely complex, but its basic scheme is reasonably clear. It begins with a brief preface, some definitions followed by a discussion of space and time, and then a treatment of the three laws of motion. It then has three books: in the first, Newton considers various kinds of possible motions without worrying about resistance; in the second, he considers motion within resisting media (e.g., water); and in the final book, he discusses "the system of the world," using extensive observational data from astronomy to analyze the motions of the planets. Whether the planets travel freely through the solar system or must traverse some kind of medium, like an ether or a vortex, was an open question at the time.

In the first seven propositions of Book III, Newton articulates a series of increasingly general conclusions about the force he had studied in the greatest depth, namely, gravity. We proceed from considering Jupiter and its satellites to the planets orbiting the sun to the moon orbiting the earth until we reach the proposition with greatest generality. That proposition proclaims: "Gravity is in all bodies universally, and is proportional to the quantity of matter in each."[21] The latter half of this conclusion was the result of considerable empirical work on Newton's part. His discovery that the force of gravity is proportional to the mass—what he called the "quantity of matter"–of a body was a key aspect of his startlingly novel conception of many phenomena in nature that were previously conceived of as disparate. The former half of the conclusion—that *gravity is in all bodies universally*—was met with some skepticism. After all, although Newton used sophisticated new techniques— like taking an average of measurements concerning the same phenomenon from different observatories—and considered the best astronomical data available in his day, he had no information about anything beyond the solar system. So, how did he know that gravity is in all bodies in the universe?

There was also a problem with more pedestrian examples covered by Newton's law of gravity, such as falling rocks and swaying pendulums. As some of his contemporaries noted, Newton says that gravity is proportional to the mass of both the attracting body (like the Earth) and the attracted body (like the pendulum in his experiments). He could show that it was the mass in the attracted bob of a pendulum that affected the gravity acting on it, but he had no means of showing that the Earth's mass (as the attracting body) also affected the strength of the force. Newton's solution to this problem was to cite his third law of motion, noting that the actions of the attracted body and of the attracting body on one another are equal and opposite. But that solution was controversial. In order to apply the third law of motion to cases of "attraction," as when one studies a pendulum's behavior to understand the gravitational interaction between it and the Earth, one must assume that the two bodies are acting directly on one another. But many philosophers and mathematicians had long since argued that these bodies may actually be interacting with something in between them, like a vortex or an ether. So it could be an unwarranted assumption to say that the bodies are acting *directly* on one another.[22]

A supporter of Newton would view these issues as reflecting skepticism toward his philosophy promoted by figures like Huygens and Leibniz. Their instinct would likely be to defend his conclusions. As important as they were, these issues masked an even more fundamental question, one that Du Châtelet emphasizes in many places in her *Institutions*. Leaving aside skeptical reactions to the law of universal gravity, the more basic question is, what exactly is Newton claiming about gravity? Is he saying that all bodies have a certain *property* called gravity? If so, was he suggesting that *matter as such* has this property?[23] Was he really saying that he had discovered something about matter no one had ever imagined? Rather than focusing on the resistance to Newton's ideas, Du Châtelet emphasized the importance of taking these questions seriously as deep questions within physics.

Newton himself recognized that his theory of gravity could be inherently confusing, even for sympathetic readers. So he and his circle of supporters in London, Cambridge, and Oxford decided in 1712 that a second edition of the *Principia* would be helpful. Alas, Newton did not alter most of the mathematical discussions in the text. But he did acknowledge to his friends Samuel Clarke and Richard Bentley that his philosophy still needed further public support and clarification. Newton and his circle chose Roger Cotes, a highly respected young mathematician and philosopher in England, to edit the second edition, expanding on some elements of Newton's philosophy. In those days, Cotes was one of the few people Newton respected intellectually. When Cotes died tragically at thirty-three after a severe fever, Newton tersely remarked: "If he had lived, we might have known something."[24]

For the new edition of the *Principia* edited by Cotes, Newton added a section called the *Regulae philosophandi*, or "Rules for philosophizing." This brief section tackled issues familiar to any well-educated student of philosophy. It represented one of Newton's attempts to clarify some of his main ideas (he also sought new clarity with the General Scholium). The third of Newton's rules reads as follows:[25]

Those qualities of bodies that cannot be intended and remitted and that belong to all bodies on which experiments can be made should be taken as qualities of all bodies universally. . . . [I]f it is universally established by experiments and astronomical observations that all bodies on or near the earth gravitate toward the earth, and do so in proportion to the quantity of matter in each body, and that the moon gravitates toward the earth in proportion to the quantity of its matter . . . it will have to be concluded by this third rule that all bodies gravitate toward one another . . . . Yet I am by no means affirming that gravity is essential to matter. By inherent force I understand only the force of inertia. This is immutable. [*Attamen gravitatem corporibus essentialem esse minime affirmo. Per vim insitam intelligo solam vim inertiae. Haec immutabilis est.*] Gravity is diminished as bodies recede from the earth.

Newton suggests that he has the appropriate kind of empirical evidence to conclude that gravity is in all bodies. He emphasizes that the kind of inductive inference that undergirds this conclusion is analogous to other kinds of inductive inference that had been employed to considerable effect by the great mechanical philosophers of the modern era.[26]

The last few lines of the quotation above, however, reflect Newton's awareness that in addition to a question about the empirical evidence required for a certain type of inductive inference, there was a prior issue, the question of how to *understand* what Proposition Seven means in the first place. Evidently, the claim that *gravity is in all bodies universally* does not mean *gravity is essential to matter.* This implies that some readers would endorse this interpretation of Newton's theory. Why else would he deny it? In presenting this clarification, Newton's denial of a possible interpretation of his theory's conclusion is predicated on the notion that the concepts involved in the denial are clear to his readers. Perhaps here more than anywhere in the *Principia*, we find a limitation of Newton's cautious approach toward broaching broad philosophical issues. Rather than providing any clarification, Newton uses the notion of an *essence* without further ado.

The idea of an essence is one of the most important in all of metaphysics. But which concept of an essence did Newton have in mind? Since at least Aristotle, philosophers have debated what essences are; there has never been any consensus on the issue. So what did Newton mean here? And why did he assume that someone might read him along those lines in the first place?

Newton's famously cautious approach toward traditional metaphysics was not the sole cause of his readers' confusion. Contending that gravity is universal—or as Newton sometimes puts it, saying that *all bodies gravitate toward one another*[27]—seems unlike other universal claims. For instance, if a philosopher says, "All bodies are extended," as Descartes did, then the claim is clear enough: all bodies are three-dimensional bits of matter. Similarly, if a philosopher says, "All bodies move," or maybe, "All bodies are moving," one has no trouble understanding the idea. Of course, one might dispute it, deny that we could know it to be true, etc., but those reactions rely on understanding it in the first place. The problem for Newton is that gravity is not antecedently understood to be the kind of item— such as a property—whose status can be contemplated by friends and foes alike. And it is for this reason, in turn, that interpreters of Newton were frustrated by the discussion in Rule 3, which focused on the empirical evidence for the inductive inference in question. In a way, Newton defended the idea *that* something is *universal* without really specifying *what it is* that is said to be universal in the first place. Confusion remained.

Perhaps with these issues in mind, Roger Cotes used his extensive editor's preface to broach traditional philosophical questions that Newton evaded, even in the new sections of his text. Cotes understood that one could rehearse the argument for universal gravity, detailing the impressive array of empirical evidence that Newton used in its support, but one would ultimately have to clarify what the theory of gravity *meant*. He tried to do so by using a concept that Newton himself carefully avoided in his section on the rules for philosophizing. In a key passage, Cotes writes:

> Thus all bodies for which we have observations are heavy; and from this we conclude that all bodies universally are heavy, even those for which we do not have observations. If anyone were to say that the bodies of the fixed stars are not heavy, since their gravity has not yet been observed, then by the same argument one would be able to say that they are neither extended nor mobile nor impenetrable, since these properties of the fixed stars have not yet been observed. Need I go on? Among the primary qualities of all bodies universally, either gravity will have a place, or extension, mobility, and impenetrability will not. And the nature of things either will be correctly explained by the gravity of bodies or will not be correctly explained by the extension, mobility, and impenetrability of bodies.[28]

Cotes rushed in where Newton feared to tread. Using one of the most prominent conceptual innovations of the seventeenth century, one employed to great effect by everyone from Galileo to Descartes to Boyle to Locke, Cotes declares that Newton should really be understood as having discovered that *gravity is a primary quality*.[29] That is, he claims that it is just like extension, a feature that all material things have. It is just like the other qualities that the mechanical philosophers had studied throughout the Scientific Revolution. Cotes was clever: if there was anything that philosophers understood, it was the idea of a primary quality of a body, a quality that all material things have.

In the event, Cotes's maneuver failed to convince many readers. Although the idea of a primary quality was perfectly clear and widely accepted in the early Enlightenment, it was nonetheless difficult to see how *gravity* could be one. And ironically, that was due to reasons found in Newton's own book. In the opening Definitions,

Newton had described gravity as an example of a certain kind of force.[30] In Definition Four, Newton introduces the notion of an impressed force, a *vis impressa*, for the first time. He then adds in Definition Five that gravity (along with magnetism) is an example of an impressed force (viz., the kind of impressed force that is centripetal). This means that gravity is presented by Newton as "an action exerted on a body to change its state either of resting or of moving uniformly straightforward." His addendum to Definition Four is also significant: "This force consists solely in the action and does not remain in a body after the action has ceased."[31] So here's the problem: if gravity is an action exerted on a body, it is confusing to think of it as a primary quality. The standard primary qualities— like extension and impenetrability—are properties of a thing. They are basic properties that all material things are supposed to have. But Newton says here that gravity, like any impressed force, is not a feature in that way because it does not remain in the body after the action has ceased. Indeed, an action does not seem like a property at all. It's just the wrong kind of item.

When Cotes's argument failed to convince many readers of the *Principia*, one of Newton's other ardent defenders, Samuel Clarke, tried to figure out a different solution to the problem of explaining Newton's most important idea. Since his days as a student at Cambridge in the late seventeenth century, Clarke had been an early and keen advocate for Newtonianism. He eventually made many contributions to the public dissemination of Newton's ideas, including by translating Newton's *Opticks* into Latin in 1706—English was too obscure a language then to be of much use. A philosopher and theologian, Clarke became a member of Newton's inner circle during his London years. The two were actually neighbors for a time. Although Clarke was a somewhat unorthodox theologian, which may have prevented him from rising high in the Anglican Church, he nonetheless served as rector of St. James Westminster, a prominent position in the capital.[32] It's fair to say that he was a public intellectual at that time and sensitive to the many political, theological, and philosophical aspects of Newton's ideas. Secure in the knowledge that neither Cotes nor Newton himself had succeeded in explaining the new theory of gravity to a wider public, Clarke adopted an entirely different conception of that theory. He would soon have a prominent venue in which to present that conception.

Just as Cotes was chosen to write a long editor's preface to the second edition of the *Principia* in 1713, broaching the philosophical topics Newton eschewed, Clarke was chosen to represent Newton and his philosophy in what would become one of the most famous disputes of the entire eighteenth century. The new edition of the *Principia* did little to quell the various philosophical objections to Newton's ideas that had been presented by Leibniz and his many followers in Continental Europe. And Leibniz sought to broaden the audience for his disagreements with Newton. So just two years after Cotes edited the new version of Newton's most important text, Leibniz sent an incendiary letter to Princess Caroline of Wales. Rather than using articles and new editions of texts to air various disagreements, Leibniz was trying to provoke the English into a direct and public debate.

Leibniz's choice of Princess Caroline is doubly significant. She was an influential royal figure at the time, one married to the son of King George I of England. (She would eventually become the grandmother of King George III, who oversaw the "loss" of the colonies during the American Revolution.) And just as important, Caroline was an important intellectual ally of Leibniz: she was a fan of his earlier philosophical work, especially his *Theodicy*, which tries to reconcile human evil with God's goodness.[33] Leibniz imagined that Caroline might be sympathetic to his ideas. A deft political thinker, he also guessed that if his letter to Caroline decried the state of intellectual life in the British Isles, it would demand a response from the highest levels of society. It would provoke an open debate.

Leibniz's gambit worked. After receiving his brief and accusatory letter in late 1715, one that attributed a decline in English religion to Newton's influence, Caroline gathered together the most important members of Newton's circle in London. The circle was central to intellectual life: by this time, Newton had been knighted by Queen Anne and was president of the Royal Society. He was the public face of British science. Despite the enormous stakes in replying to Leibniz, however, Newton's reticence to engage in debates and to clarify his ideas for the wider public remained as strong as ever. Happily, it turns out that Caroline was not only intellectually close to Leibniz at this time, she had also become a friend of Clarke. So in the end, it was decided that although Newton would be regularly consulted, Clarke would take it upon himself to reply to Leibniz's letter. The correspondence between Leibniz and Clarke eventually grew to more than a hundred pages, it was published and translated many times, and it soon became one of the most influential philosophical exchanges of the Enlightenment.

Leibniz and Clarke spent page after page debating everything from the meaning of various philosophical terms to the implications of Newton's theory of gravity to the true nature of God's creation of the world. There was hardly any important notion that they could not find some means of debating. As the correspondence dragged on for months, it became decidedly repetitive. Near the end of Clarke's fifth and final letter to Leibniz, written in late October of 1716, he attempts one last time to clarify what Newton's theory of gravity really means:

> It is very unreasonable to call (sec. 113) *attraction* a miracle and an unphilosophical term, after it has been so distinctly declared that by that term we do not mean to express the cause of bodies tending toward each other, but barely the effect or the phenomenon itself, and the laws or proportions of that tendency discovered by experience, what is or is not the cause of it. . . . The phenomenon itself, the attraction, gravitation, or tendency of bodies toward each other (or whatever other name you please to call it by), and the laws or proportions of that tendency, are now sufficiently known by observations and experiments.[34]

For Clarke, gravity isn't a primary quality, and it isn't the cause of motions, it is really just a "tendency" toward motion that bodies have. One with a certain law expressing it. That's all. So what was all the fuss about? Obviously, Clarke concluded, Leibniz was being just plain unreasonable in insisting that Newton's theory was "unphilosophical."

But as with Cotes's attempt to explain Newton's ideas just a few years earlier, Clarke's explanation was not terribly convincing. Once again, it was hard for many readers to see how Clarke's conception fit with the basic points made by Newton in the *Principia* itself. If one returns again to Definition Four and then ponders the theory of gravity, the plain meaning of Newton's text is this: a particular action exerted on a body to accelerate it affects all bodies. It says nothing about a "tendency" toward motion that bodies have, or a quality that they all share. It's hard to avoid the conclusion that both Cotes and Clarke tried to explain Newton's ideas by evading the plain meaning of his own text.

Throughout her *Institutions*, Du Châtelet emphasizes that Newton and his followers could never agree on how best to understand the most important conclusion of his new science. They might all concur that Newton's *Principia* was the gospel, but they were like the leaders of religious factions who could not agree on the meaning of their shared text. One is reminded of fundamental disagreements about the Trinity among Protestants and Catholics in this era. And like the participants in those famous religious disputes, Newton and his closest friends in England never came to an agreement before his death as an old man in 1727.

Partisans like Voltaire had an entirely different approach. They would emphasize how Newton's critics, like Huygens or Leibniz, were deliberately misreading the *Principia*, or quibbling about the precise formulation of his profound new theory of gravity. Voltaire frequently quoted from or paraphrased Clarke as speaking for Newton, so he might underscore Clarke's insistence that Leibniz was being "very unreasonable" in his objections. But Du Châtelet was alive to a deeper disagreement, one that appears clearly if one ignores Newton's avowed critics to focus on his strongest supporters. Clearly, Clarke, Cotes, and Newton could not agree on the proper characterization of the most profound conclusion of his new physics. Is gravity an action, a primary quality, or just some kind of tendency or motion? By refraining from adopting the stance of the disciple, who must paper over such differences to preach the gospel, Du Châtelet was in a position to understand the importance of these disputes.

Indeed, the problems not only ran deep within the Newtonian camp, but even within the man himself. We now know that Newton struggled mightily to find the right characterization of gravity. That struggle occupied him for many years, as illustrated by a famous epistolary episode from years earlier. In 1692, Richard Bentley, the future master of Newton's alma mater Trinity College, was chosen to give the first Boyle lectures concerning Christianity and the new science. The lectures had been endowed in Robert Boyle's will the year before—Boyle was not only a famous scientist, but one of the richest men in all of England at the time—and would quickly become a major venue for promoting Newton's ideas to the general public.[35] (Clarke gave some famous lectures in the series years later.) Bentley was a young churchman, an already famous classicist, and a recent convert to Newtonianism. He was one of many Englishmen devoted to showing the compatibility of Christianity and the new science. And he would play a key role in spreading the gospel of Newtonianism through popular works.

When Bentley was preparing the text of his Boyle lectures for publication, he corresponded extensively with Newton in the hopes of clarifying various philosophical and theological implications of his theories.[36] Although they were originally private, the letters were first published in the eighteenth century and have since become a major source for our understanding of Newton's interpretation of his own science. Typically, this correspondence is discussed in the context of ongoing debates concerning Newton's apparently vexed attitude toward action at distance and his divergence from the mechanical philosophy.[37] But it is also remarkable for the window it provides into Newton's own struggle to understand gravity. In reply to one of Bentley's letters, here is what Newton says:

> It is inconceivable that inanimate brute matter should, without the mediation of something else, which is not material, operate upon and affect other matter without mutual contact, as it must be, if gravitation in the sense of Epicurus, be essential and inherent in it. And this is one reason why I desired you would not ascribe innate gravity to me. That gravity should be innate, inherent, and essential to matter, so that one body may act upon another at a distance through a vacuum without the mediation of anything else, by and through which their action and force may be conveyed from one to the other, is to me so great an absurdity, that I believe no man who has in philosophical matters a competent faculty of thinking can ever fall into it (Newton to Bentley, 25 February 1692).[38]

Newton was well aware that some of his readers, perhaps even a supporter like Bentley himself, might inadvertently attribute to him a construal of universal gravity he wished to eschew. In particular, he recognized that one might understand the idea that gravity is in all bodies to mean that gravity is a *property* of all bodies. And if it is a property of all bodies, perhaps it's part of their essence. Newton blocks this interpretation with his forceful warning. Alas, his blocking maneuver does not clarify a prior question. What do you mean by *innate, inherent,* and *essential*? Are these terms synonymous? If so, why use all of them? Is it just for emphasis?[39] Alas, even in private correspondence with a sympathetic supporter, Newton failed to clarify his understanding of gravity: he never explained what he meant by these terms.

One might think that this criticism of Newton is not really fair. After all, maybe Newton and his various supporters could not agree on how to understand gravity because it is a special case.

It is incredibly complicated to determine why this force acts on all bodies in the universe, unlike every other force, and seemingly across vast distances. In fact, one may reasonably think that no one really understood gravity until Einstein's general theory of relativity proclaimed in 1915 that it involved the curvature of space-time itself. It is hardly fair to blame Newton for failing to grasp this idea, or even its possibility. After all, Einstein relied on non-Euclidean geometry, which was not discovered until the work of Gauss, Bolyai, and Lobachevskii in the nineteenth century.[40] Although they were obviously geniuses, Newton and Leibniz lacked the conceptual understanding even to raise the question of whether space is *curved* or not. Gravity is indeed a rather special case.

It is precisely the mysterious nature of gravity that Du Châtelet acknowledges in her *Institutions* in a way that Newton's disciples rarely did. From her point of view, the best conclusion that we can reach is this: in all honesty, we do not yet know precisely what to say about the nature of gravity.[41] She thought that no one could say with any confidence how gravity ought to be understood. We can avoid philosophically problematic interpretations of Newton's theory that overreach in one way or another, and avoiding philosophical extremes in the interpretation of science is itself a kind of progress. Yet we must not be overconfident about how much progress we have made, for the exact nature of gravity is still unknown. It is far better for science and philosophy to acknowledge their limits than to embrace pretensions to knowledge. Newton was indeed a genius, one with great insight. He made immense progress in helping humanity to understand the forces of nature. But if we idolize him, and think of him as the hero of science, then we cannot rest with Du Châtelet's acceptance of uncertainty. For how can Newton be a hero if he and his greatest fans cannot even agree on what he exactly accomplished? The idolization pushes us to figure out his theory of gravity once and for all. It leads to a distortion of scientific knowledge.

Du Châtelet's insistence that we must not idolize Newton as the singular genius of the revolution helps us to recognize that his understanding of gravity, as significant as it was in many ways, was not unique. It was not the sole site of major philosophical and scientific disputes in the Enlightenment. Indeed, more basic questions about the forces of nature, questions that a standard historical narrative would regard as having been settled by Newton himself, continued to animate science and philosophy well into the eighteenth century. And as with the debate about gravity, it was not merely a bunch of minor figures who raised those basic questions; it was the leading thinkers of the era. It was precisely the kind of person, like a Huygens or Cotes, who even the great Newton would have respected.

Was It Newton's Physics or Euler's?

Today, students learning basic physics are taught that Newton wrote down three laws of motion. The first law, also known as the law of inertia, had a rich legacy: textbooks often mention Galileo's studies of motion before Newton's day, a lineage underscored by Newton himself in the *Principia*. But in fact, Descartes was the first philosopher to publish the law of inertia. He did so in the form of two laws of motion in a text that Newton studied extensively as a young man, the *Principles of Philosophy* of 1644. So Newton was quite aware that the law of inertia was not original with his work. But his second law of motion *was* original, not least because it involved a novel concept, *mass*, first presented in the *Principia* itself in 1687. Descartes had described the quantity of matter, but he took a body's volume to be its measure. Newton replaced that unhelpful notion with the fertile notion of mass, a measure of a body's resistance to acceleration. That idea took fruition in the second law of motion, which stated that force is equal to mass times acceleration. At least, that is how students around the world learn the second law: they learn "$f = ma$."

However, it was in fact the leading mathematician in the generation after Newton and Leibniz, Leonhard Euler, who used the new analysis to transform the second law of motion from a statement concerning a proportion between force, mass, and acceleration into the modern equation, "f = ma." As shocking as it may sound to any high school student cramming for a physics test, Isaac Newton never wrote down "f = ma."[42] Indeed, he did not present *any* of his laws as equations. Just as Newton presented the arguments and derivations of his *Principia* in geometric form, paying respect to the methods of antiquity he highly valued, he also presented the laws of motion in the traditional form of statements about proportions. So as a matter of historical fact, what is attributed to Newton as an idea that was well established by, say, 1700 is in fact something that was fully developed by Euler several decades later. The same thing has been said of the calculus.[43]

With due respect to Euler, is this historical correction more than mere quibbling? Perhaps it's important in certain contexts to be as precise as possible about the historical development of modern science, but is it really misleading for students to learn that Newton's second law is "f = ma"? After all, isn't that basically what Newton meant? We can give credit where credit is due, in this case to Euler, without wondering why anyone called them *Newton's laws* in the first place.

The point is well taken. But let's step back and ask, "What exactly did Newton mean by a force in the first place?" That is, what did that *f* in what would become the famous equation really mean? Now, things get interesting once again. Newton introduced the concept of mass in his *Principia*, and he thought of mass as a measure of a body's resistance to acceleration. But that is only half the story; it's the half that has made its way into the textbooks. The real situation in Du Châtelet's era, the one confronted by leading thinkers like Euler, is more complex, and also more interesting.

Here's the other half of the story. Newton believed that it was especially important that ordinary material bodies have a property in virtue of which they resist acceleration. He emphasized the importance of that resistance, and resistance seemed like an *action*.

It did not seem like a property, but instead something that a body *does*. He had already defined forces as actions: the canonical notion of a force, which he called a "vis impressa"—an idea reflected to this day in our phrase, X *impresses* a force on Y—is the notion of an action. This idea then led Newton to say the following in his third Definition in the *Principia*:[44]

> Definition Three
> Inherent force of matter is the power of resisting by which every body, so far as it is able, perseveres in its state either of resting or of moving uniformly straight forward.
>   This force is always proportional to the body and does not differ in any way from the inertia of the mass except in the manner in which it is conceived. Because of the inertia of matter, every body is only with difficulty put out of its state either of resting or of moving. Consequently, inherent force may also be called by the very significant name of force of inertia.

If bodies resist acceleration because they have mass, and that resistance is an action, well then, we should say that the mass of a body is a force of resistance. Newton's famous idea of the "vis inertiae," the force of inertia, was born. Newton was a cautious and careful writer: we must pay attention when he says that something is "very significant." However, this idea never made it into the textbooks. Why not?

Once again, it was Euler who made a key intervention. But this time, his reaction cannot be categorized as merely tidying up Newton's results, as when he transformed statements about proportionalities into modern equations. For in this case, Euler *rejected* one of Newton's principal ideas, contending that there was a sense in which Newton's concept of force was confused. This move certainly aimed for the heart of Newton's science.

For a number of years, Euler himself had used Newton's notion of the "force of inertia." For instance, he pondered the notion in an

important letter he wrote to Du Châtelet.[45] But then in a famous
paper, "Research on the Origin of Forces," published by the Berlin
Academy of Sciences in 1752, he finally announced his conclusion
that the idea was actually a mistake. He writes:

> With respect to this definition of the term "force," I remark that
> it is very inappropriate to call inertia the force of inertia. For,
> since the effect of inertia consists in the conservation of the same
> state, and that of forces in changing the state of bodies, it is clear
> that these two effects are directly contrary to one another and
> that inertia is something that is entirely opposed to the idea of
> forces. This remark seems more than a little necessary because
> this denomination has contributed more than a little to confusion
> in the theory of the first principles of body and of motion. For
> in most of the books that treat this subject, one finds so many
> obscurities and contradictions that one is obliged to renounce
> them altogether, when one wishes to apply oneself successfully to
> the study of mechanics [.][46]

The typically staid Euler thought that science, to which he had
already contributed greatly with his 1736 treatise *Mechanics*, faced
"obscurities" and even "contradictions" so long as its practitioners
employed the notion of the force of inertia. In his view, forces are
in a sense the very opposite of inertia: one is the cause of a body's
acceleration, the other its resistance to it. So the notion of a force of
inertia should be expunged from science once and for all.

On the question of inertia, history went with Euler. Indeed,
Euler's argument was *so* successful that later interpreters could not
even understand Newton as saying that mass is a kind of force. Any
student in a high school physics class today would be corrected if
she tried to say that mass is a kind of force.

But history is often ironic. Before Euler had rejected Newton's
idea of the "force of inertia" as a confusion, and before the textbooks had fallen in line with Euler's understanding, Newton's own

idea spread far and wide. Indeed, Newton's discussion of the force of inertia circulated more widely than many of his principal arguments in the *Principia*, for he discussed that controversial notion in a much more popular text, his *Opticks*.

Everything about the *Opticks* ensured it would become a popular work. Unlike the *Principia*, which was written in Latin and in complex geometry, the *Opticks* was written in English, contained little mathematics, and eventually included a series of provocative appendices. Called "Queries," these appendices involve a wide-ranging discussion of scientific, philosophical, even religious topics. For readers who did not wish to wade through Newton's detailed descriptions of his optical experiments, they could skip right to the "Queries," where they would find discussions of numerous topics. Newton discussed everything from the existence of atoms to the basis of fermentation to God's creation of the world. Just as the force of inertia appears unchanged in all three editions of the *Principia*, Newton uses the notion to great effect in the most famous Query of them all, the thirty-odd-page one with which he ended his popular work.

In Query 31 to the *Opticks*, Newton tells us that "God in the beginning" formed matter into particles with various properties, including the kinds of properties emphasized by the mechanical philosophy, the so-called primary qualities. These particles will never break, "no ordinary Power being able to divide what God himself made one in the first Creation." Partly in response to the mechanist claim that he had revived "occult qualities" in his physics, he then adds:[47]

It seems to me farther, that these Particles have not only a Vis inertiae, accompanied with such passive Laws of Motion as naturally result from that Force, but also that they are moved by certain active Principles, such as is that of Gravity, and that which causes Fermentation, and the Cohesion of Bodies. These Principles I consider, not as occult Qualities, supposed to result

from the specifick Forms of Things, but as general Laws of Nature,
by which the Things themselves are form'd; their Truth appearing
to us by Phaenomena, though their Causes be not yet discover'd.

When expressing his understanding of God's creation of matter,
of the material particles with properties that underlie all natural
phenomena, Newton returns again to the *vis inertiae*, calling it a
"force" from which the laws of motion result. This concept is therefore no mere slip of the pen, no mere residue from earlier modes
of thinking about powers from late Renaissance philosophy or the
like. Instead, Newton employs the force of inertia to express the
content of his laws of motion: material bodies following the laws of
motion resist attempts to accelerate them. And he insists, whether
writing in Latin or English, that this should be understood as a
kind of force.

Obviously, Newton was perfectly well aware that if mass is a force
of resistance, it cannot be a force in the same sense in which gravity
or electricity or magnetism is a force. That is why he describes the
former as a kind of "passive" principle in Query 31, and gravity an
"active" one. If one were to start off with a large number of material
particles separated from one another in empty space, then in virtue of their *passive* "force" of inertia, nothing would happen. They
would just sit there. However, if one were to add the *active* principle
of gravity to the mix, then the bodies would gravitate toward one
another (however minutely). Something would happen. But until
the end of his life in 1727, whether speaking to the mathematical
elite or the general public, Newton insisted that both are genuine
types of force. In challenging this idea, therefore, Euler was challenging something near and dear to Newton's heart, a notion that
had a wide-ranging impact during the Enlightenment, for the queries to the *Opticks* were easily the most read of all of Newton's works
in the eighteenth century.[48] And because the *Opticks* was such a
popular work, it would take many years, perhaps even decades,
before Euler's conception would replace Newton's.

The process whereby Euler's attitude replaced Newton's not only took many years, but it also involved many twists and turns among leading *philosophes*. A prominent example involves the mathematician Jean D'Alembert. In the first edition of his most famous work in physics, the *Treatise on Dynamics* (1743), D'Alembert said that he would attempt to reduce all of mechanics to three principles: "the force of inertia, compound motion, and equilibrium." The first item was no slip of the pen: he didn't mean a law of motion or the principle of inertia. For he said in the very first chapter of part one of the work that he calls it the "force of inertia" in fact "with Mr. Newton." He added that he regarded this as a *property* of bodies, the property in virtue of which, as Newton had said in the Queries to the *Opticks*, bodies follow the laws of motion.[49] Years later, in the summer of 1757, in volume seven of the first Paris edition of the *Encyclopedia*, D'Alembert's entry "Force d'inertie" once again discusses the force of inertia as a property of bodies. As always, D'Alembert expresses his skepticism about the notion of force, or power (*puissance*), but he assures his readers that the "force of inertia" is really a property of bodies, so this idea need not make use of any obscure or "metaphysical" notion like that of force or power.[50]

Hence, if we focus on two of the greatest mathematicians in Enlightenment Europe in the generation after Newton, Leibniz and Huygens, we find that they reacted to his work in diametrically opposed ways.[51] For his part, Euler argues that Newton's conception of forces is confusing, insisting that the "force of inertia" should be jettisoned in favor of the idea that "impressed force" is the only genuine force in nature. This is a clear notion, one appearing in the laws of motion. But D'Alembert argued the opposite! It was the notion of a force that was obscure, so he tried to rid physics of forces altogether. In contrast, he regarded the idea of a "force of inertia," which is properly understood as a property of matter, as perfectly clear.[52] So, even by the middle of the eighteenth century, there was no consensus on the basic elements of the new physics.[53] As Du Châtelet had already wisely proclaimed, "Physics is an immense building that surpasses the powers of a single man," so it should come as no surprise that the task for a French philosopher reflecting on the development of physics during the Scientific Revolution cannot be to interpret and promote the words of one person. Instead, one must survey the architectural plan of a building built by many hands.

As Du Châtelet made clear to her readers, the elements of physics include not only ideas about matter and the forces of nature but also about the space and time in which matter moves under the influence of those forces. And she indicated something that disciples of Newton's would try mightily to hide: if anything, Newton's view of space and time was even more controversial than his theory of gravity and his conception of the forces of nature. Why so? Generations later, Einstein described that view in his typically pithy way: "It is characteristic of Newtonian physics that it has to ascribe independent and real existence to space and time as well as to matter[.]"[54] That is, Newton regarded space and time as real things. Numerous philosophers and contributors to science in the eighteenth century could not swallow that idea. Understanding why they were so resistant to the notion helps us to grasp another key aspect of the complexity of science and philosophy during the Enlightenment. It also highlights the errors of insisting that Newton was the hero of the revolution.

Newton's Absolute Space

In his magnum opus, before making complex geometric arguments about the motions of bodies under various conditions, and even before stating his three laws of motion, Newton presented the basic terminology of his text in a set of definitions. That's where he introduced the notion of mass, along with the more controversial idea of the force of inertia. Then in the Scholium appended to those definitions, he took a different tack. Rather than defining additional terminology, he noted that everyone knows something about space, time, and motion. So he would not *define* space, time, and motion, or the words that refer to them; he would help readers to see the difference between thinking about these things in the way that ordinary people do, and thinking about them like a physicist. This maneuver was wise. Whereas ordinary folks at this time had never heard of mass, they had obviously thought about things like motion. Anyone who ever rode a horse or sat in a carriage had thought about motion. So, the task is not to introduce a new technical concept; it is to guide readers in liberating themselves from the ordinary way of thinking about motion so that they can think about it *mathematically*. But how might that work?

If you were living in London when Newton published his *Principia*, you might have taken a ride across town in a carriage. When you arrived at a dinner party, you might have entered the home, removed your cap and coat, and mentioned that the road was bumpy, thick with cows and horses, or especially muddy. Your trip across London involved going from one part of town to another, so Newton suggests that you would use an idea of *relative motion*. According to that idea, to move is to change your *relation* to your origin by approaching your destination. Newton had no objection to the idea of relative motion. If you want to arrive at a London dinner party on time, it's a perfectly good idea. You may not really be thinking much about space, but if you had to say something about it, say on your trip home from the dinner party, you might note that you are moving by crossing a certain space in a certain amount of time. What is that space? In this case, it's the city of London. Newton would call this an idea of relative space. London itself is such a space, since it's defined in terms of relations: it's the city that is bisected by the Thames, with the Houses of Parliament along the North Bank and what is now the Tate Modern along the South.

Suppose the dinner parties in London are growing boring, so you decide to take a holiday in Paris. You travel down to the southern coast at Dover and then hop on a ship bound for Calais. As you sit on the deck of your ship, your companion tells you: "Don't go anywhere, I'll be right back—I want to see the portside view." It would be daft to reply: "I'm on the deck of a moving ship, of course I'm going somewhere! Isn't that what we're paying them for?" Obviously, your companion was employing an idea of relative motion. Relative to the ship, one could stay stationary along the top deck, even if the ship itself is sailing across the sea. Newton himself discusses such a ship. He then pulls back from the scene, noting that this same change in perspective can be made at a higher level: just as you are stationary on a moving ship, you can be on a stationary ship at port, moving with the earth's rotation. In an ordinary context, say when strolling on deck, thinking about the motion of the ship is irrelevant; in another, say when contemplating the solar system, the motion of the ship and even of the earth itself could be relevant.

Well then, why didn't Newton simply pull back from an ordinary perspective and employ a more capacious conception of relative motion? Just as we can ignore the ship's motion when standing on deck, we can consider its motion when approaching the port in Calais. And just as we can ignore the motion of the earth, say when sailing home from a grand holiday in Paris, we can consider its motion, say, when gazing at the moon through a telescope. Why not simply expand the reach of the relative idea? Isn't the physicist thinking about motion from a broader perspective than our couple on the ship's deck? Can't we do our planetary science from a grandiose, but ultimately *relative*, point of view? Thus far, it does not seem that a "mathematical" perspective is even needed.

Newton's reasoning continued. One problem is that it's not so easy to scale up to the level of the earth itself. After all, we know that we're moving in a carriage, or on a ship, by feeling bumps in the road, or seeing the water sloshing against the hull. But the earth doesn't change its relation to anything in such a way that we can detect its motion. For centuries, astronomers have gazed at the stars, thinking that the heavens are rotating in a great arc around the earth. Copernicus's breakthrough was of monumental importance during the Scientific Revolution, but he certainly couldn't just point to the sky to prove his theory! And although Copernicus had an immense influence on the course of modern science, the question of the earth's motion was not yet settled when Newton wrote in 1687.

But Newton saw a deeper problem as well. The problem is not easy to see if we think about trips across the English Channel, but it becomes apparent if we imagine two objects moving in outer space. Newton knew that his physics would have to apply to bodies generally, to comets and satellites and falling objects, so he would have to think about motion in an expansive and unified way. Imagine two comets in our solar system. For them to be in "relative" motion is just for them to change their relation. That can happen if one comet moves toward its stationary companion, or if they both move. But these situations are obviously different. If one comet moves toward a resting twin, then we must find the cause of its motion; yet if the situation is reversed, even though that may keep the same relative motion, we should seek the cause in the other comet. So, relative motion is not a helpful concept if we seek the *causes* of motion. We have to determine which comet is *really* moving, and then infer what forces are acting on that comet. We require a concept of a kind of motion that is *not relative*. The idea of *absolute* motion was born.

The idea of "absolute" motion may seem confusing. Isn't motion an inherently relativistic idea? In a sense it is, and Newton doesn't deny it. For that reason, the idea of absolute motion can seem odd, like the non-relative version of a relative thing. What Newton means by "absolute," however, is not *exactly* "non-relative," but rather "not relative to any object," like a ship, a port, or even the Earth itself. That is, when we talk about a comet's absolute motion, we are not discussing its changing relations to another object. The idea of motion is still an idea about changing relations, however, so what Newton means by absolute motion is: changing relations to something other than another object.

Now, if there were some stationary body, say in the center of the solar system, or maybe even the center of the galaxy, then we could define absolute motion as a change in relations to that body. That would be very handy. Alas, there may be no such stationary element. And even if there were, there's no guarantee that we could *detect* it, which would make the concept of absolute motion rather unhelpful. Coherent, it's true, but pretty useless.

At this juncture, when matters seem desperate, Newton helps himself to an idea that every geometer knows and loves: the idea of Euclidean space. He says: absolute motion is non-relative in the sense that it involves changing relations to space itself. That is why he calls this a "mathematical," rather than a "common," point of view. We're asked to conceive of the universe of objects as being embedded in a space which is studied in Euclidean geometry. The absolute motions of any objects within the universe involve a change in place within that space. He called that "absolute" space, so absolute motion is motion with respect to absolute space.

The patient reader now may lose patience. We were just told that even if there were some stationary body to which we could refer all motions, we might not be able to perceive it. But surely absolute space isn't any better! After all, we're talking about an imperceptible, homogeneous, three-dimensional magnitude first studied by Euclid. That idea does not seem any more helpful than our imaginary stationary body. Both concepts of motion might be coherent, but neither seems useful.

Newton anticipates this objection and answers it brilliantly. He does not deny that absolute space is imperceptible; however, absolute motion has one great benefit that relative motion lacks, viz., it can have perceptible "effects." To explain himself, Newton thought back to his life on the farm as a young man. His example became one of the most famous in the history of physics. Suppose you have a bucket full of warm milk, just filled from old Betsy. If you hold the full bucket from a rope, twist the rope many times, and then let the rope go, the bucket will slowly begin to turn as the rope untwists. At first, the milk moves little as the bucket begins to turn, but gradually, it spins along with the bucket. As the bucket spins faster and faster, the milk inside it will spin faster as well, adopting a concave shape on its surface. That is Newton's "effect." The concave surface of the milk indicates that it is truly in motion—it has absolute motion, and not merely relative motion. Why? Because as the milk spins around, the bucket spins around with it, so the relative motion of the milk is eventually nil. It isn't changing its relation to the bucket. However, its surface indicates that it is truly moving, so it has absolute motion. The fact that we cannot perceive space itself doesn't matter; the milk's surface is all we need.

Despite his clever examples, his patient explanations, and his entreaties, many philosophers still rejected the idea of absolute space. Buckets of milk and sailing ships were one thing, but the idea that the world of material things is embedded in an infinite, imperceptible, three-dimensional Euclidean magnitude was something else altogether. It was one thing for a mathematician to say, for example, how a point moves through Euclidean space to describe a certain curve, and then to study that curve. That was an abstract case with roots in antiquity, and Newton may have called his notion of space "mathematical" to acknowledge such ancient discussions. However, he was not merely talking about abstract cases. He was saying that nature itself is actually embedded in an infinite Euclidean space! He planned to use the structure of that space to articulate how actual bodies truly move under certain forces. But how could philosophers accept the idea, as Einstein notes, that in addition to all the matter in the universe, there is also an infinite, causally inert, three-dimensional magnitude all around us? Newton built a reputation for avoiding tricky metaphysical topics, preferring to focus on empirically tractable, or mathematically solvable, problems. But if we consider the concept of absolute space, we must admit that few modern philosophers had dreamed of anything more extravagant.

As one might expect, it is precisely here that Voltaire and Du Châtelet part ways. If one is presenting Newton's philosophy, then one must defend the controversial idea of absolute space as best one can, just as one must settle once and for all on some understanding of Newton's theory of gravity. But that was not Du Châtelet's project. She decided instead to present the state of physics in 1740 from a broad perspective rather than from the point of view of a disciple of Newton. That is why she acknowledged the controversial status of absolute space. As she had already expressed in the preface to the *Institutions*, one of her goals was to present the ideas of many thinkers, including, of course, Newton, but also those of his great rivals G. W. Leibniz and Christian Wolff (the latter was soon to be a star of Brucker's influential history of modern philosophy). As she outlines, Leibniz's skepticism about Newton's conception of absolute space became influential in the early eighteenth century. However, rather than taking up Clarke's side in the dispute, as Voltaire had done, Du Châtelet presented Leibniz's arguments as a serious challenge to Newton's conception of space and time. Indeed, like many eighteenth-century philosophers, Du Châtelet concluded that Leibniz was right to reject Newton's view of space as extravagant. But even then, she did not rest. For she refused to act as anyone's disciple, including Leibniz's. She always had another lesson in mind. She pushed deeper by recognizing that the debate between Leibniz and Clarke about absolute space reflected a more basic dispute about physics and philosophy. Du Châtelet's treatment of that dispute represents one of her most important insights.

Du Châtelet's Insight

Ever the geometer, Newton had begun his *Principia* with what he called "Axiomata, sive leges motus," that is, axioms or laws of motion. Today, students just learn about Newton's *laws*, but it is significant that he also called them *axioms*. In noting that his three laws of motion were *axioms*, he was signaling that they would serve as the fundamental principles in his system. Whether one thinks of an axiom as a self-evident starting point for reasoning, or simply as an assumption that a system builder makes, he presented them as the bedrock of his new science. There would be no more fundamental principle to which Newton would appeal.

To no one's surprise, the other greatest geometer in this era, Leibniz, rejected Newton's approach. He regarded a philosophical principle, rather than a law of nature, as his "axiom." The two camps would have trouble agreeing on what we might call the *theorems* of physics, since they disputed its *axioms*. As his own axiom, Leibniz chose the Principle of Sufficient Reason, the claim that everything has a reason why it is so and not otherwise. Du Châtelet highlighted the importance of Leibniz's principle already in her preface and made considerable use of it throughout her *Institutions*. This causal principle had also been used to great effect by some of the seventeenth-century's leading metaphysical system builders, such as Spinoza.

In his dispute with Clarke, however, Leibniz sought primarily to employ the Principle of Sufficient Reason as a cudgel. He argued that Newton's conception of absolute space led to a violation of the principle. The idea was this: if it were true that space is absolute, then it would also be true that space would exist even if no matter existed. And if completely empty space could exist, then it would follow that if God were to contemplate creating some matter somewhere within that space, there could be no reason for God to choose some region over another. After all, independently of the matter that exists, space itself is homogeneous—all of its regions are perfectly alike. So even an omnipotent, omniscient being could not formulate a reason for choosing one region over another, say, when deciding where to create the earth.[55] And as the principle says, there must be a reason why everything is the way it is rather than some other way. Since Leibniz takes the principle as an axiom, the notion of absolute space, however useful it might be for thinking about motion and force, must be jettisoned.

Leibniz's argument against the Newtonian view of absolute space might seem quaint, or at least confusing. Newton was making an argument in physics, after all, so to bring God into the discussion is really just to change the subject, isn't it? At least, that is likely how it would seem today. And as it turned out, Clarke rejected Leibniz's argument anyway, using a clever maneuver involving a distinct interpretation of the principle of sufficient reason, one whereby it did not have the consequences for God's decision making outlined by Leibniz. That move can seem just as puzzling to us. But these twists and turns are not what really matters about the Leibniz-Clarke correspondence. Indeed, Du Châtelet's approach toward the dispute helps us to recognize that there was in fact a deeper philosophical issue underlying this debate about space and the principle of sufficient reason. And that deeper issue helps one to understand how science and philosophy were intertwined during the early Enlightenment.

As a mathematician, Newton would take seriously any argument showing that some claim or proposition led to a violation of one of the axioms in a system. He would reject any notion, e.g., that a material body could accelerate without any force being impressed on it, since that would violate one of his laws (axioms). The problem was not that Newton and Leibniz thought about geometry or reasoning differently; the problem was that they disagreed on the axioms for physics. For his part, Newton never even mentioned the principle of sufficient reason in the *Principia*, not even to reject it. He simply ignored the basis of Leibniz's criticism. This produced an intriguing asymmetry in their dispute: whereas Leibniz endorsed the principle of inertia, but regarded the principle of sufficient reason as more fundamental—an axiom to inertia's status as a "theorem," we might say—Newton ignored the Leibnizian axiom. For this reason, although Newton's controversial conception of absolute space helped to generate one of the most influential philosophical debates of the Enlightenment, Newton himself was in no position to engage in the dispute. In this light, the choice of Clarke as Leibniz's respondent makes good sense: unlike Newton, Clarke certainly took the principle of sufficient reason seriously, even if he wished to contest Leibniz's version of it. They could at least debate the issue.

A defender of Newton's philosophy faces a choice at this point. One could ignore the principle of sufficient reason, as Newton himself had done, and attempt to defend the idea of absolute space on empirical, conceptual, or other grounds. Alternatively, one could defend Newton as Clarke had done by contesting Leibniz's specific construal of the principle in question. Either way, one would be apt to miss the deeper point at hand: what precisely are the axioms of physics? An overly narrow construal of the debate about absolute space would focus on various arguments about absolute motion or the like. But it would miss the deeper question of whether physics ought to take the laws of motion as its axioms, à la Newton, or whether it ought to regard the principle of sufficient reason as an axiom, à la Leibniz. By defending Newton with his own interpretation of the principle, Clarke had in fact taken a different perspective than Newton himself, taking up supposedly Newtonian positions on Leibnizian ground! Another dispute within the house of Newton.

This is Du Châtelet's lesson for us: the real dispute here concerns not only gravity, the forces of nature, and absolute space; it concerns the deeper issue of which principles science should use to understand nature. To characterize the state of physics circa 1740, then, one must not only describe the debate about absolute space; one must highlight the potential importance of the principle of sufficient reason by emphasizing the question of which principles should be taken as the most fundamental in science. If we regard Newton's own attitude toward principles like that of sufficient reason as a guide to eighteenth-century physics and philosophy, we would expect that the principle would be simply ignored after Leibniz's death in 1716. After all, Newton lived on and always ignored the principle. But history tells us otherwise. Indeed, many leading thinkers of the Enlightenment—from Wolff and Kant in Prussia, to Maupertuis in France, to Euler in St. Petersburg—regarded metaphysical principles like that of sufficient reason as fundamentally important. Few major thinkers simply ignored the principle, as Newton had. This is true even in the case of the eighteenth-century's greatest *critic* of metaphysics, David Hume. Despite his significant credentials as a proponent of the "experimental method of reasoning" associated with Boyle and Newton, signified in the very subtitle of his *Treatise of Human Nature*—published the same year as Du Châtelet's *Institutions*—Hume spilled considerable ink arguing against causal principles like the principle of sufficient reason. Ironically, that was a decidedly non-Newtonian approach: even after Leibniz's criticisms, Newton did not even *reject* the principle of sufficient reason. After Hume supposedly awoke him from his "dogmatic slumber" as a young philosopher, Kant defended causal principles in his *Critique of Pure Reason* against Hume's brilliant criticisms.

So, philosophers throughout the whole Enlightenment agreed on a deep question that Newton had eschewed. Should the axioms of science be principles that hail from the internal development of physics, like the law of inertia, or should they be principles like the principle of sufficient reason, which hail from philosophy? Du Châtelet's refusal to serve as Newton's disciple meant that she was alive to this crucial eighteenth-century debate. On this key issue, Newton and his disciples (like Voltaire) missed the boat, one that Du Châtelet caught.

Once again, the great mathematician Euler played a central role. Even when defending Newton on the concept of absolute space, which he thought was crucial for science, he embraced philosophical questions Newton had eschewed. In 1748, Euler responded to the Leibniz-Clarke dispute by highlighting the centrality of this dispute over axioms. Leibniz had shown that it was possible to regard a basic principle of metaphysics as conflicting with a prominent concept of the new physics. Euler decided to tackle this problem directly by arguing that Leibniz had misunderstood the epistemic priority of the principles involved. From Euler's point of view, by this time the law of inertia had received widespread support from mathematicians and physicists throughout the learned world—if anything could be regarded as a bedrock principle of the new physics, that would be it. (The law of universal gravity, as we have seen, continued to provoke substantial debate.) In contrast, no principle of metaphysics had received such widespread support, and in any case, Leibniz, Clarke, and many others had disputed their meaning. Euler concluded that the law of inertia has epistemic priority over principles of metaphysics.

After this resolution of the axiom problem, Euler defended Newton on the grounds that the physicist must regard space as absolute because of the law of inertia. His basic argument went roughly like this. The law of inertia picks out uniform rectilinear motion as a special case. This presupposes, in turn, that there is some meaning to the idea of sameness of direction. After all, if it's an axiom that a body moving uniformly in a straight line will continue doing so until a force is impressed on it, there had better be a clear meaning to "straight line." But, Euler argued, if space were not absolute, if it were just the network of relations among material things, as Leibniz and his followers had been arguing for years, then there would be no meaning to "straight line." The reason is that any set of objects we might employ to define a straight line could also move. Therefore, the law of inertia requires us to use the concept of absolute space in physics. In this way, Euler had embraced a philosophical maneuver by arguing that we should give the law of inertia epistemic priority over a principle like that of sufficient reason. In the end, even when Euler defended a Newtonian idea, he did so by making a decidedly non-Newtonian move.[56]

To a contemporary reader, these questions about space, time, matter, and force are *obviously* questions in physics. If you want to understand the nature of matter, the forces acting between material bodies, the large-scale structure of space and time, read a physics textbook. During the Enlightenment, however, there were not only debates about matter, the structure of space, and the forces of nature, there were also debates about whether physics or philosophy would answer questions about such topics. Indeed, that was one of the deepest issues guiding the Enlightenment's discussion of the foundations of physics. And that was not Newton's idea of a worthwhile discussion. Thus, although some historians might still contend that the eighteenth century saw the rise of what Thomas Kuhn would call the Newtonian "paradigm" in the sciences—a more measured cousin of the notion that Newton was the hero of the Scientific Revolution—in fact, the debate about the foundations of physics, which occupied nearly all the major mathematicians and philosophers of the era, was not a *Newtonian* debate. Many thinkers embraced Newton's physics, but they often rejected his conception of its relation to the rest of knowledge.

The Enlightenment was not the effect of spreading the British gospel of Newton and Locke throughout the Continent, causing a cultural shift toward science and away from superstition. Partisans like Voltaire may have seen things in that way, and it makes for a compelling narrative that became widespread years later. But if we review the historical facts, the leading mathematicians of the era, such as D'Alembert and Euler, were not reading from the Newtonian hymnal any more than their great predecessors Leibniz and Huygens had been. The Enlightenment was not a time of growing consensus about what we would now call the "Newtonian paradigm"; it was an age in which intellectual and cultural progress was made through foundational debates about space, time, matter, and forces, but also about the basic principles of knowledge. It was precisely the *lack* of consensus that made science and philosophy during the Enlightenment so rich and interesting.

It was in this rich intellectual milieu that an aristocrat in Paris, one known to all the leading thinkers of the day, decided to raise her voice. Having studied mathematics and physics, Latin and English; having conducted experiments on light and fire; having analyzed the latest work published by the Paris Academy of Sciences, Émilie Du Châtelet decided to write a book. Now we know why she gave it the title, *Foundations of Physics*.

3

Du Châtelet's Vision of Science and Philosophy

Ever since Aristotle's Latin commentators named one of his books
physica and the other *metaphysica*, philosophers have pondered
their relation. The commentators gave his books those names
because the metaphysics came *after* the physics. The implication
was that we first learn about nature, and then ponder the results.
Philosophical reflection unconstrained by empirical information is
of little use, mere armchair speculation. Some have called this broad
approach "empiricism," so it's not surprising that Aristotle is often
regarded as the first empiricist. As sensible as this approach might
seem, other philosophers questioned it. In the post-Aristotelian
world of Descartes, some argued that although empirical information about nature is crucial, the goal of science must be to explain
natural phenomena, and explanations require descriptions of
causal processes. So philosophy must first articulate a commitment
to some basic causal principle, like *ex nihilo, nihil fit* (out of nothing comes nothing), or maybe the Principle of Sufficient Reason.
Such principles were often regarded as non-empirical because they
guided empirical research in the first place. Some have called this
broad approach "rationalism," so it's not surprising that Descartes
is considered one of the leading rationalists. Although Descartes

succeeded in vanquishing Aristotle in science with the publication of his *Principles of Philosophy* in 1644,[1] the wider dispute between these two orientations continued. With his empirically grounded "axioms" or laws of nature, Newton furthered the first tradition;[2] with his use of the principle of sufficient reason as a fundamental "axiom," Leibniz embraced the second.

When Émilie Du Châtelet published her magnum opus in 1740, she sought to do justice to each tradition. In choosing the title, *Institutions de physiques*, which means *Foundations of Physics*—or more literally, *Institutions of Physics*—she may have been implying that physics requires a foundation of some kind. Many Enlightenment thinkers were at least sympathetic to the idea, often traced to Descartes, that physics required in particular a metaphysical foundation. It's debatable whether that was her intention. But she made it clear right from the start that the "institutions" or elements of physics would include classic metaphysical topics such as the principles of knowledge, the existence of God, and the nature of essences. So the question is, what do such issues have to do with physics? Du Châtelet makes the bold pronouncement early in her text that they have everything to do with it.

Du Châtelet opens chapter 3 of her *Institutions* like this (1742, §32):

> There are perhaps no words with a less fixed meaning, and to which those who use them attach ideas more different, than those of essence, attribute and mode. I believe therefore that it is necessary to give you here a very precise idea of what one should understand by these words, for on the true notion of essence, modes and attributes depends the most important truths of metaphysics and many of physics.

She makes the same point about space's importance for both physics and metaphysics (1742, §72), concluding that truths in physics, metaphysics, and geometry are interconnected (1742, preface, XI).

The conceptual overlap of these disciplines is a central theme of her work. If you study Aristotle's *Metaphysics*, you will find the idea of an essence. The same is true if you read Descartes's *Meditations*, designed to loosen Aristotle's grip on philosophy. But how might a truth in physics be connected with this idea?

The most successful element of the Scientific Revolution, Newton's theory of universal gravity, bequeathed to philosophers a deep question. In saying that gravity affects all matter, had Newton discovered that gravity is part of the *essence* of matter? (His follower Cotes certainly seemed to think so, even if Newton himself denied it.) Du Châtelet understood the importance of this question, recognizing that one cannot answer it unless one first clarifies what essences are. Newton's physics raised this question, but didn't answer it. She made it clear in her own work and in her translation of Newton's *Principia* that his precise phrasing left the issue open.[3] And Newton's supporters did not settle this issue: if one were to read Newton and then Bentley, Clarke, and Cotes, one would find answers that range all over the place.

Du Châtelet seeks to solve this problem. She argues that essential properties have two aspects. First, the essential properties of a body are what make it *the thing it is*. So for instance, a triangle is essentially a three-sided figure. She also notes, second, that essential features must be *intrinsic* to their bearer. This means, e.g., that triangles have three sides independently of any relations they might have to other figures.[4] A triangle might be larger or smaller than another triangle, or congruent with one, etc., but its nature as a triangle does not depend on any relations it may have. Even when following traditional lines of thought, Du Châtelet's insight appears: many philosophers in this time did not distinguish between these two ideas.[5]

But Du Châtelet was not engaged in a philosophical enterprise in which the goal is to articulate a conception of essences in the *abstract*. Her goal instead was to discuss essences in order to clarify aspects of the new science, including Newton's theory of universal gravity. So now the question is, does that theory proclaim that gravity is essential to matter? Her answer is: well, that depends. If we assume that essential features are intrinsic, then we would be saying that gravity is an intrinsic feature of all bodies. So the question is, how plausible is that idea? She proceeds by applying her analysis from chapter 3 to basic questions about "Newtonian attraction" raised in chapter 16, writing (Du Châtelet, *Institutions*, 1742, §396):

> One cannot say that God could know what would happen to the body on the present supposition because the attraction, according to the Newtonians, is a property that he has given to all matter, so God could not have foreseen what must happen as a consequence of this property. For, besides the fact that this supposition is inadmissible by the doctrine of essences in Chapter 3, the attraction moves bodies with a certain velocity and in a certain direction. Now this direction and this velocity are variables, because they depend on the position and the mass of the attracted body and on its distance from the attracting body.

Thinking of gravity as an intrinsic feature is difficult. The reason is that it varies with its bearer's distance from other bodies—gravity weakens as bodies grow distant. Amazingly, one body's gravitational pull also varies with the mass of the body it attracts. It therefore seems to be a relational feature: if I take two bodies and alter one of them, I alter the gravity of the other. I can even make it disappear by zapping one of the bodies out of existence. She says "according to the Newtonians" here because she is careful not to attribute this view to Newton, who cautiously avoided it. She knew that one could not simply attribute the ideas of his followers to Newton himself.

However, Du Châtelet recognizes that this is not the end of the dialectic. Suppose one wishes to know whether gravity is essential to matter in the other sense, namely, whether it helps to make material things what they are. Some might find that suggestion attractive. After all, if Newton is right that *all* material bodies in the universe gravitate, is it much of a stretch to say that gravity helps to make something material in the first place? That was precisely the idea that Roger Cotes presented in his famous preface to Newton's *Principia*, arguing that gravity is one of the primary qualities of matter. With the discussion of essences under her belt, Du Châtelet tackles this issue. She argues that one must return to the reasoning that led Newton to assert universal gravity in the first place. In his argument in Book III of the *Principia*, Newton treated the space between the planets, and between, e.g., Jupiter and its satellites, *as if* it were empty of matter. He did not *prove* that it is empty of matter, he simply assumed it. So perhaps it isn't empty of matter. In particular, many thinkers at the time wondered whether there might be some kind of medium among bodies, like an ether. Newton himself discusses the ether in the Queries to the *Opticks* (especially Queries 18–21). Such an ether could exist, and it would not disrupt his reasoning about universal gravity as long as it provides negligible resistance to motion. (Substantial resistance to motion might be detected by careful observation.) With this as background, Du Châtelet then argues as follows: gravity acts on all bodies in proportion to their masses; there may be some non-massive medium like an ether between bodies, and it is perfectly possible that gravity depends on that medium. Therefore, Newton's theory does not prove that gravity is essential to matter.[6]

We can illustrate the basis of Du Châtelet's reasoning with a simple example. If you imagine a rock existing independently of the ether, the rock would still be a material thing, even if it is not heavy, that is, even if it does not gravitate toward anything else. After all, if a rock isn't a piece of matter, what is? Thus, we cannot say that according to Newton's physics, gravity makes material things the things that they are. For all we know, there could be matter that *doesn't* gravitate. Newton's physics had not settled that question.[7]

The proper perspective, therefore, is to admit our ignorance on this issue: we simply do not know whether there could be material things that are somehow not affected by gravity. It's beyond our knowledge. Expressing humility appropriately is a hallmark of Du Châtelet's approach.

Once again, Du Châtelet understood that this conclusion is not the end of the dialectic. If one could not turn to Newton or Cotes for clarification, perhaps succor could be found among some of Newton's English followers. Since the days of Voltaire's *Philosophical Letters* of 1734, many French Newtonians had regarded Locke's philosophy as the best metaphysical supplement to Newton's theory. Whereas Newton had been reluctant to broach metaphysical topics, such as the essence of matter, Locke tackled them directly.[8] We find this narrative in D'Alembert's *Preliminary Discourse to the Encyclopedia*, where he trumpeted Newton's "revolution" in physics in tandem with praising Locke:[9]

> With respect to metaphysics, it seems that Newton had not entirely neglected it. He was too great a philosopher not to sense that it is the base of our knowledge, and that in it alone clear and exact notions about everything must be sought. Indeed, the works of this profound geometer make it apparent that he had succeeded in constructing such notions concerning the principal objects that occupied him. However, he abstained almost totally from discussing metaphysics in his best-known writings; we can hardly learn what he thought concerning the different objects of that science, except in the works of his disciples. . . . What Newton had not dared to do, or perhaps would have found impossible, Locke took up and executed with success. One might say that he created metaphysics almost as Newton created physics.

D'Alembert gets a bit carried away here, ending with some serious hyperbole. Metaphysics has existed since at least Aristotle; it was hardly created by Locke. But the broader point is this: by mid-century, at least among the proponents of the early French Enlightenment, there was a consensus that Newton's non-metaphysical approach to science could be supplemented with Locke's new approach to metaphysics.[10] He was given pride of place next to Newton. Why so?

Although he had praised Newton—along with Boyle and Huygens—as one of the great scientists of the age in the preface to his *Essay*, Locke said little about Newtonian science in the rest of his magnum opus. That is not surprising for a text largely written in the 1670s. But years later, he did address the question of universal gravity in an important discussion with Bishop Edward Stillingfleet, an influential figure at the time and a mentor to Newton's avid supporter Richard Bentley. The bishop had presented Locke with several objections to his views, often because he was potentially in danger of undermining the Anglican idea of the Trinity.[11] In reply to some of the bishop's queries, Locke wrote the following about a passage from his most important work, the *Essay Concerning Human Understanding*:

> It is true, I say, that "bodies operate by impulse and nothing else." And so I thought when I writ it, and can yet conceive no other way of their operation. But I am since convinced by the judicious Mr. Newton's incomparable book, that it is too bold a presumption to limit God's power, in this point, by my narrow conceptions. The gravitation of matter toward matter by ways inconceivable to me, is not only a demonstration that God can, if he pleases, put into bodies, powers and ways of operations, above what can be derived from our idea of body, or can be explained by what we know of matter, but also an unquestionable and every where visible instance, that he has done so. And therefore in the next edition of my book, I shall take care to have that passage rectified.[12]

The concern is Locke's defense of the mechanical philosophy via the idea that bodies operate by "impulse" alone. That idea, in turn, might rule out Newton's notion that gravity acts on all bodies: impulse does not appear to be involved, since Newton specifies no mechanism. Locke's suggestion that God has superadded gravity to matter implies that gravity is not essential to it: God has added gravity to what matter is *as such*, namely, extended solid stuff. So, God does not alter what matter is, but rather adds a "power" to it. We cannot conceive how matter gravitates toward other matter, Locke admits, but we know that it does so. Elsewhere Locke calls Newton's "admirable discovery" that "all bodies gravitate to one another" nothing less than "the basis of natural philosophy," another name for science in that era.[13] Locke's prominence in the French Enlightenment, his prominent appearance in the *Preliminary Discourse* and in Voltaire's influential writings, assured him center stage for years to come.

Locke's solution to Newton's problem raises a deep question, one that a grandiose reading would regard as a new pillar of modernity. It concerns the relation between science and religion. Here is a philosopher saying, "The new science has convinced me that God himself has added the property of gravity to all bodies; I don't really understand what it means to say that matter gravitates toward other matter, but if science tells me that it does, then it does." Locke was not making an old-fashioned theological point by claiming that God can act in mysterious ways. He was making a *modern* claim about science's authority. It is science, not religion, that proves to us that God must have acted in a mysterious way. Science was not merely authoritative vis-à-vis theology. A major philosopher was also proclaiming its authority over his own domain. Rather than insisting that science's conclusions about nature must be subjected to rational scrutiny, Locke argues that Newton must be right, even if we cannot really understand what he is saying.

Locke's maneuver avoids problems with asserting that gravity is essential to matter, but at a price that Du Châtelet thought was too high. As always, she is precise. She ensures that readers understand her criticisms of Locke without thinking that she is criticizing Newton himself, who never endorsed the idea of superaddition, despite his years as Locke's close friend and religious confidante. (The bishop was right to worry: both Locke and Newton had serious doubts about the Trinity.) She goes for the root of Locke's idea, arguing against the notion of *superaddition* generally. In the same correspondence, Locke had also famously informed Bishop Stillingfleet that although we cannot understand how matter thinks, God must have superadded thought to us, since we *do* think and we are of course (at least partly) material.

In chapter 3 of her *Institutions*, Du Châtelet rejects Locke's doctrine writ large (1742, §47):

> It follows furthermore from what we said about the foundation of the attributes that they are incommunicable: for having their sufficient reason in the essence, it is impossible to transport them elsewhere. And one cannot find in a subject any except those that follow from its essence. This ends the famous dispute among the philosophers whether God could have given thought to matter. For the philosophers who contend that it is not impossible that matter could think all acknowledge that matter as such, that is to say, matter as extended and impenetrable, cannot form a thought. But they say, *God has perhaps given matter the attribute of thought, even if it does not have it by its essence, and thus, just as one does not know what it pleased God to do, one cannot know whether what thinks in us is matter or not.* [italics in original]

For Du Châtelet, any claim concerning a thing's features ought to be intelligible to us given our understanding of that thing's essence. In case her readers were not steeped in the Locke-Stillingfleet correspondence, she makes the connection to the interpretation of Newton explicit in the next section:

> This single truth of the immutability of essences bans from Philosophy all precarious hypotheses in one stroke and all the monsters arising from the human imagination, which have so impeded the progress of the sciences and of the human mind. Such are the primitive forces of the Scholastics that were to be found in matter

with no other reason than the will of God. Such would be attraction if one wanted to make it a property of matter. Such is, finally, as I said (§47), the idea of the celebrated Locke on the possibility of thinking matter.

Locke is saddled with the idea that we cannot grasp how matter acts on matter, just as we cannot grasp how matter thinks. We simply declare that God's unfathomable power has made it so. Du Châtelet's discussion helps to clarify an implication of Locke's view of superaddition. Locke thinks that gravity is a (non-essential) "property" of matter. It is a separate property because it would not reduce to matter's other properties: it must be superadded, since an extended solid substance will not gravitate on its own. That idea is akin in Du Châtelet's mind to a Scholastic force, a power of a body that is "primitive" in the sense that it does not reduce to its other features. She could not follow her fellow French *philosophes* in trumpeting Locke's philosophy because it would leave a primary conclusion of Enlightenment science no better than a mystery.

Locke tells Bishop Stillingfleet that the *Principia* has convinced him that all bodies have a certain property established by God himself. But Locke does not explain why he understands Newton's theory as proclaiming that material bodies have a certain *property* in the first place. As we have seen, Newton himself does not make that claim in the *Principia*. Instead, Newton says that gravity is a centripetal force, which is a kind of impressed force, an action exerted on a body to accelerate it. Why think of that action as a *property*?

Of course, Newton himself understood this problem. In one of his only attempts to present a popularization of the *Principia*, he tries once again to explain himself. In his posthumous *Treatise of the System of the World*, a book that Du Châtelet read, he struggles to clarify his most famous idea:

> And though the mutual actions of two Planets may be distinguished and considered as two, by which each attracts the other;

yet as those actions are intermediate, they do not make two, but one operation between two terms. Two bodies may be mutually attracted, each to the other, by the contraction of a cord interposed. There is a double cause of action, to wit, the disposition of both bodies, as well as a double action in so far as the action is considered as upon two bodies: But as betwixt two bodies it is but one single one. It is not one action by which the Sun attracts Jupiter, and another by which Jupiter attracts the Sun: But it is one action by which the Sun and Jupiter mutually endeavor to approach each the other.[14]

Even in this more popular account, Newton avoids declaring that gravity is a property. He *also* avoids the path of Cotes (it is a primary quality), of Clarke (it is a tendency to motion), and finally of Locke (it is superadded by God). But once again, the cost is pretty high. Readers of the *Principia* would likely have thought that according to Newton, Jupiter acts on its satellites, and they act on Jupiter; the Sun acts on the Earth, and vice versa. In this popular text, however, Newton says that what he *really* means is that between each and every pair of bodies in the universe, there is a *single* action. That makes it even more difficult to construe universal gravity as a property that each body has, *for it cannot even be construed as an action that each body makes.*[15] What does it mean to say that two bodies perform the same action? Newton leaves his readers wondering. Locke was right about one thing: gravity is mysterious indeed.

Du Châtelet was wise to follow the intricacies of interpreting the new science of gravity wherever they led. She was also wise to insist that Locke did not speak for Newton, nor did Clarke. Indeed, as she noted, even Newton did not speak for his fellow Newtonians! Instead, they each sought their own means of understanding a profoundly new scientific theory. Finally, she was wise to avoid taking any of their routes to understanding gravity. Newton made astonishing progress in science by discovering his law. But philosophers, including even that rare moment when Newton tried to explain himself in his posthumous *Treatise*, erred in thinking that this discovery alone enabled them to say what gravity really is. Instead, Du Châtelet argues that as of the middle of the century, science had not yet progressed enough to address that issue. Knowing the law of gravity is hugely important. But it does not tell us that gravity is essential to matter, a special property given to matter by God, or a mysterious action that exists between each pair of bodies. The only rational move for an Enlightenment philosopher is to encourage further research, avoiding speculation.[16] That position reflects the intellectual state of affairs of her day, but it would have been a rather uncomfortable place for a disciple to find himself.

Hypotheses in Science

In tandem with her rejection of discipleship, Du Châtelet decided to make the avoidance of speculation—something that can be especially difficult for philosophers—into a keystone of her new methodology. That is why she provides an entire chapter on hypotheses in her *Institutions* right after discussing essences. Indeed, she quickly shows how speculation was rampant in the early Enlightenment. It was not merely the Newtonians or the followers of Locke who were guilty; it was their opponents as well.

What exactly did Du Châtelet think a "hypothesis" was? It involved speculation, a claim that transcends the available empirical evidence. But it had another key component as well (Du Châtelet, *Institutions*, 1742, §69): "A hypothesis is a supposition that explains a phenomenon." Or at least, purports to explain it. Thus, hypotheses are speculative explanations of natural phenomena. As was common in the day, she thinks that we explain a phenomenon by articulating what caused it.[17] So in her mind, hypotheses are speculative causal explanations of natural phenomena. They are therefore intended to achieve one of the main goals of science.

How were Newton's opponents guilty of speculation? The leading alternative to Newton's theory of gravity, both in his own day (Descartes, Leibniz) and well into the Enlightenment (Euler), was the so-called vortex theory of planetary motion. The vortex theory proposed a mechanism where Newton lacked one. The idea is that the planets are carried through their orbits by imperceptible swirling fluids, called vortices.[18] The vortex theory was first proposed by Descartes in 1644, but even after Newton's *Principia* was published, it received a hearty endorsement from none other than Leibniz. Although Leibniz was certainly no Cartesian—indeed, in 1686 he made his name in physics in part by publishing a short essay on Cartesian "errors" in physics—he was a thoroughgoing mechanist just like Descartes. And after reading the copy of the *Principia* that Newton sent him in 1688, Leibniz remained convinced that there must be some mechanism underlying gravity. Surely, *gravity alone* cannot cause the planetary orbits; there must be some mechanism whereby the moon orbits the earth, the earth the sun, and so on. So in 1689, Leibniz promoted a vortex theory that would update Descartes's by trying to account for Kepler's laws, as Newton's theory had done, and by using more sophisticated mathematics. In particular, Leibniz argued "by hypothesis" (*ex hypothesi*) that a planetary vortex must be in motion, accounting for the relevant orbit. His faith in the mechanical philosophy assured him that his hypothesis was a reasonable one.

Newton read Leibniz's vortex essay, but he was having none of it. Once again, he used the second edition of his *Principia* in 1713 to clarify and defend his controversial theory. In addition to the Rules of Philosophizing, Newton also added a kind of general appendix to the whole work. He called it the General Scholium, and it was not long before it became a hugely influential text. In this new section, Newton famously begins by informing his readers that the vortex theory is "beset by many difficulties." In addition to the difficulty of accounting for Kepler's laws, observations had shown that comets take "eccentric" paths through the solar system, which would seem to rule out a swirling fluid surrounding the planets that the comets pass through at various angles. The fluid would disrupt the comets' paths. Vorticists might agree that their theory faced many difficulties, but they could fall back on their mechanist faith: surely a hypothesis that must account for empirical data, however difficult that might be, is superior to the declaration that the planets act on one another directly across empty space with no mechanism! Newton did not have any overarching commitment on a par with the mechanical philosophy; so in lieu of one, he made a methodological pronouncement. In the General Scholium, he writes, "Thus far I have explained the phenomena of the heavens and of our sea by the force of gravity," but he had not assigned any mechanism to gravity. Gravity acts in direct proportion to the masses of the bodies and inverse proportion to the square of their spatial separation. Then he adds (Newton 1999, 943): "I have not as yet been able to deduce from phenomena the reason for these properties of gravity, and I feign no hypotheses [*hypotheses non fingo*]." The vorticists were on shaky empirical ground, but more significantly, they employed an illicit methodology in physics. Leibniz and his followers had "feigned" their vortex hypothesis—they had no evidence for it. Since Newton had made so few comments about methodology over the years, his followers took this pithy phrase and made it the heart of their enterprise. From now on, a principal rule of the new science would be to ban hypothetical reasoning from physics altogether. D'Alembert highlights that very issue in his *Preliminary Discourse*.

The true creativity in Du Châtelet's *Institutions* is evident in her reaction to this impasse. She did not write a chapter on hypotheses in order to argue that they ought to be banished from physics. Neither did she write it to suggest that the vortex theory was on solid ground after all. Instead, she sought a middle ground between these two extreme positions. The extremes were clear: whereas Descartes and Leibniz had erred by allowing their faith in mechanisms to justify their vortex theory without empirical evidence, Newton's followers had overreacted to that mistake by banning hypothetical reasoning altogether. She writes (Du Châtelet, *Institutions*, 1742, §55) that Descartes "gave the whole learned world a taste for hypotheses" and that as a result, "the books of philosophy, which should have been collections of truths, were filled with fables and reveries." Nonetheless, "the disciples of M. Newton have fallen into the opposite excess," for they "rose up against hypotheses and tried to render them suspect and ridiculous" for philosophers. Neither extreme is justified, according to Du Châtelet.

But if the hypothesis of the vortex theory has not been proven, which was one of the most central hypotheses in physics at the time, then why is it wrong to say that hypotheses in general are suspect? To answer this question, Du Châtelet cleverly chooses another example from science, a less controversial one from pre-Newtonian science. She writes (Du Châtelet, *Institutions*, 1742, §57) that hypothetical reasoning has been indispensable in astronomy, for if "to calculate the path of the celestial bodies, astronomers had waited for the true theory of the planets, we would have no astronomy now." The paths were too complex to have been a promising avenue for science. Instead, astronomy first considered the Ptolemaic or geocentric hypothesis of the solar system, working with its complex models of eccentricities for generations; only later did the Copernican hypothesis of heliocentrism receive substantial attention. Indeed, in her even more extensive recounting of astronomy's history in her posthumously published commentary, the *Short Exposition of the System of the World* (*Exposition Abregée du Système du Monde*), appended to her translation of Newton's *Principia*, she notes that before Ptolemy, the Babylonians and then Pythagoras defended a heliocentric model, so in fact their hypothesis was eventually replaced with Ptolemy's and then his by Copernicus's. In sum, she thinks that proposing, refining, and ultimately rejecting hypotheses has been an essential aspect of the development of astronomy. It has helped to build the house of physics. It would therefore be rash to banish hypothetical reasoning altogether, because the Ptolemaic and later the Copernican hypothesis were extremely useful in helping astronomy to progress.[19]

If hypotheses can be useful, but can also be taken too far, what precisely is the methodological middle ground between the followers of Leibniz and of Newton? If we look at astronomy's success, we see that, first of all, science can propose a hypothesis in order to see if observations and experiments can be made that might cohere with it. So the vortex theorist is well within his rights to propose vortices in order to see, for instance, whether Newton was right that they would disturb the observed paths of comets. If the hypothesis is consistent with the "facts" as they are understood at the time, then it can continue to be studied. Indeed, the more information that is found to be consistent with a hypothesis, the more probable it becomes. But one cannot follow the mechanists and conclude that it must therefore be *true*. As she says, "hypotheses are made only in order to discover the truth; they must not be passed off as the truth itself" (Du Châtelet, *Institutions*, 1742, §62). If "contrary" observations or experiments are found, then the hypothesis should be rejected, or at least suitably modified (Du Châtelet, *Institutions*, 1742, §64). But Newton's followers err when they hyperbolically proceed from using empirical evidence to undermine a particular hypothesis to concluding that hypothetical reasoning *in general* is flawed. Moreover, such reasoning should not bother them, she argues, because hypotheses are only "probable propositions": the Newtonians ought to respect a mechanistic theory of some aspect of nature if it's presented as merely probable, given the available evidence.

At the very end of her chapter on hypotheses, Du Châtelet hints at her overall approach to philosophical conflict. As a general rule, she proposes that one adopt a middle ground between philosophical extremes. But she also begins to diagnose why philosophers adopt extreme positions in the first place. If one studies the "revolution" in science of the past century, one finds that many "good hypotheses" have been proposed to advance science. She mentions thinkers like Copernicus, Kepler, Huygens, Leibniz, and even "M. Newton himself." This last name gives us pause, which her use of the word "himself" anticipates. Hadn't Newton banished hypotheses from physics? In fact, she knew that he had merely proclaimed that in the case of gravity, he would feign no hypothesis. He was not proposing a *general* methodology. Indeed, he had presented hypotheses for analysis on other occasions. For instance, he had suggested in the Queries to the *Opticks* that there might be an ether filling space, a suggestion that he then tried to analyze by inferring what empirical consequences an ether might have. (Indeed, Michaelson and Morley were still trying to detect an ether in the late nineteenth century, right before Einstein's revolutionary announcement of the special theory of relativity in 1905.) As she had already said at the chapter's beginning, it was not Newton but "above all his disciples" who fell into excess.[20] Du Châtelet suggests once again that philosophers should not become disciples of a great thinker. We must learn of their discoveries— philosophy must reflect on the revolution in the sciences that had just occurred—but we must not follow them blindly. To be a good philosopher, she thinks, one must avoid becoming a disciple; one must avoid the zealous attitude of the follower.[21] Now we can begin to see the import of a remark that she had made already in the preface, where she writes to her reader: "I advise you not to carry respect for the greatest men to the point of idolatry, as do the majority of their disciples." This is a principal theme of her text.[22] It highlights the deep philosophical problem with Voltaire's attitude as Newton's disciple, underscoring the profound difference between his approach and her *Institutions*.

A Novel Approach to Questions about Space

Advising one's readers to avoid idolatry, to avoid extreme philosophical views adopted by the disciples of great men, is all well and good.

Advising us to think for ourselves rather than merely following the teaching of "great men" certainly seems wise. So does the idea of searching for middle ground between philosophical extremes. But in practice, things can get dicey. Du Châtelet had seemed to solve the problem of hypotheses in a way that ought to have satisfied at least the reasonable members of the two competing camps. But not every debate in Enlightenment science was like that. Indeed, the very next chapter after the discussion of hypotheses in her *Institutions* concerns space. As everyone in the early Enlightenment knew, there was a vociferous debate about space between the followers of Newton and those of Leibniz. Whereas Newton had proclaimed that space and time are structures that exist independent of matter, Leibniz had bemoaned this metaphysically extravagant view, contending that space and time are nothing but the orders of relations among material bodies. In this case, it's not obvious that the zealous disciples of these two great philosophers were to blame. After all, space is either independent of matter, or it isn't. Where is the middle ground?

Just as important, the debate about space and time expressed in the Leibniz-Clarke correspondence, which ended with Leibniz's death in 1716, set the stage not only for the rest of the Enlightenment but for the rest of history as well. Even today, when we discuss quantum field theory or the general theory of relativity, theories which could not even have been imagined in the Enlightenment, philosophers still ask whether space-time points exist, or whether only material things and their relations do. The mathematics is sophisticated and the physical theories are novel, but the basic framework has changed little.[23] The question of how one could find middle ground here is therefore especially pressing. But it seems like an elusive goal.

Du Châtelet begins her discussion of space as one would expect, paying homage to Newton, Leibniz, and Clarke. She contends that Newton's extravagant conception of absolute space is indeed incompatible with the principle of sufficient reason (Du Châtelet,

Institutions, 1742, §§73–74). Leibniz was right. But even after endorsing Leibniz's criticism of Clarke and Newton, she quickly shows that she will also avoid becoming his disciple. She indicates that their debate is not the only framing of questions about space and time that she wishes to entertain. She also aims to ponder a deeper question. It is perfectly sensible to ask whether there are some general philosophical grounds for rejecting the idea of absolute space, such as the principle of sufficient reason, just as it is sensible to ask whether there are good reasons from within physics itself to embrace that idea, such as the law of inertia. We find the former move in Leibniz's oeuvre and the latter in Euler's. This then raises the question of which axioms one will endorse: if physics supplies the axioms, then perhaps we must endorse absolute space, as Euler argued; if metaphysics does, then perhaps Leibniz was right after all. But there's also another philosophical issue here. Regardless of how compelling any argument against absolute space using a metaphysical principle like that of sufficient reason might be, and no matter how compelling a counter-argument using a physical principle like the law of inertia might also be, Du Châtelet argued that in the case of space, there was another factor to consider. Intriguingly, she thought that factor was human psychology.

When analyzing the role of human psychology in our understanding of space, Du Châtelet emphasizes the importance of imagination and perception. One can grasp that importance with a simple case. Suppose I look around my office, see that it is cluttered with books and papers, and daydream about a more organized space. No more lost student papers! If I go home at night and imagine what my newly arranged office might look like, I might picture the desk full of papers, and slowly, one by one, remove each paper from its surface until I envision a beautifully clear desk. If I were committed to an even more radical rearrangement, perhaps one where I removed everything from the office so that it could be repainted, I might also imagine that the desk, the chair and the shelves are removed as well. I could picture an empty office.

What if we take things one step further? What if we're consider-ing a massive renovation, so I don't imagine an empty office, I imag-ine a truly blank slate? That is, what if I start with a slate so blank that literally nothing is on it yet, not even the floor of the office? What am I imagining when I imagine this blank slate? The answer is obvious: I'm imagining nothing. But as Du Châtelet cleverly notes, that isn't *quite* right. In fact, imagining nothing in this case actually means imagining empty space. That is, I'm not imagining *nothing*, I'm imagining *a space filled by nothing*.

This case reflects an intriguing fact about human psychology. If I wish to begin with a blank slate, and then imagine a newly stained wood floor for my office, newly painted walls, a newly cleared desk, etc., that's no problem. However, if I've been steeped in the Leibniz-Clarke debate about space and time, as every mathematician and philosopher in the Enlightenment had been, and if I believe that Leibniz won that debate, then a problem arises. If it's true that space is relative—if it is nothing but the order of relations among things like tables and chairs—then presumably I should be able to imagine *no space* by imagining *no objects*. After all, if there are no objects, there are no relations, and if there are no relations, there is no space. But Du Châtelet says I cannot do that. I do not imagine *no space*, I imagine *empty space*. It seems that I can imagine the disappearance of anything, but somehow space just sticks around. No disciple of Leibniz's would highlight this embarrassing fact.

One might still wonder, why exactly does Du Châtelet highlight it? As always, she avoids adopting the perspective of the disciple. A follower of Newton's might embrace her discussion, arguing that it conclusively shows that Leibniz was wrong after all. But that move would presuppose that a fact about human psychology rests on the same epistemic level as items like the principle of sufficient reason and the law of inertia.[24] Du Châtelet is too clever to make that assumption. She also knows that neither side would accept that idea: Leibniz's followers would argue that metaphysics and its principle of sufficient reason has priority over human psychology, and their opponents that physics has the priority. And perhaps each side would have a point. What, then, does this fact about human psychology really tell us? For Du Châtelet, it explains why a certain picture of space is compelling. She writes that it will "help us discover the source of the illusions that have been presented about the nature of space" (Du Châtelet, *Institutions*, 1742, §77). More precisely, because of the way imagination and perception work, space *seems* to be exactly like Newton said it was. Since we seem unable to imagine the disappearance of space itself, it seems to be a vast, independent entity. It seems to be absolute. This is a philosophical error, she thinks, but one that rests deeply within our psychology.

Moreover, she argues that metaphysics is distinct from other disciplinary realms, especially mathematics, because its lack of any agreed-upon technical language—like those used in algebra or the calculus—presses us to rely upon our imagination.[25] And that, in turn, can lead us astray in thinking about space, a topic of continuing interest in metaphysics. The upshot is clear: although Leibniz and his followers have the correct conception of space itself, Newton's conception is more attractive because of the way that our psychology works.

Du Châtelet's treatment of space is distinctive. Her discussion of psychology highlights her profound disagreement with Christian Wolff's metaphysical views, to which her own ideas have sometimes been compared. Indeed, Wolff himself had hoped that Du Châtelet would become his first influential follower in France. In his *German Metaphysics*—first published in 1720, republished many times, and sent to Du Châtelet and Voltaire by Frederick the Great of Prussia in a French translation in 1736—Wolff had insisted that our representation of space reflects the way that space really is. We *represent* space to be an order of objects, he argued, and in fact it *is* such an order, as Leibniz had already argued in his correspondence with Clarke.[26] The contrast with Du Châtelet is instructive: she argues that we in fact represent space as a being in itself, and not merely as the order of objects. That is, Leibniz's view is actually correct, but

Newton's conception *seems* to be the correct one. That fact means that Newton's view will always be attractive, even if it's mistaken.

Du Châtelet's approach enables us to avoid adopting a position in a debate involving two radically opposed positions. Rather than merely proclaiming that Leibniz is right about the nature of space because of the principle of sufficient reason and leaving it at that, Du Châtelet goes to great lengths to show that the Newtonian position seems compelling, for what we would call deep psychological reasons. This may not satisfy Newton's followers, but that is not her goal; instead, she wishes to find a middle ground between extremes, and when that is not feasible, to deal respectfully with each side. There is therefore a lesson here for Leibniz's followers as well: whereas a zealous disciple of the great German mathematician like Wolff would have endorsed the argument against Newton to vanquish a rival, Du Châtelet spent considerable energy analyzing the deep-seated well of Newton's views within human psychology. A partisan would never waste so much energy trying to find the wellspring of an opposing view.[27]

Despite its merits, this solution to the problem of space may still seem unsatisfying. After all, once we bracket the effect of human psychology, we still face the question: who is *right* about space and time? To answer that, we must answer the question of epistemic priority: will physics or metaphysics have priority here? Will we end up with absolute space because physics needs it, or reject it because it runs afoul of metaphysics? In an intriguing twist, Du Châtelet suggests that we may not have to face this question. Unlike Newton in 1687, and Euler in 1748, Du Châtelet resists the idea that in order to make sense of true motion, and of the law of inertia, it is best to postulate absolute space.

In chapter 11 of her *Institutions*, Du Châtelet discusses motion in considerable depth, arguing that although some relational theories of motion, such as Descartes's, are inadequate for various reasons, we should nonetheless try to avoid Newton's conception of absolute space due to its well-known metaphysical extravagance.

She proposes an elegant solution: we can try to find something to play the role of absolute space without declaring that space itself—an infinite, Euclidean magnitude—exists independently of matter. Her idea is that we try to use the fixed stars as a kind of reference, instead of absolute space. If we do so, we can still distinguish "relative" motion from "absolute" motion by defining the latter as motion with respect to the fixed stars. It is tempting to regard absolute motion as motion with respect to space itself and to regard space as an independent and autonomous being, as we have seen, but we can avoid conceiving of space in that way by proposing that absolute motion is motion with respect to the fixed stars. Whether this idea works in detail is an open question.[28] But the idea illustrates her method of seeking common ground. If a dispute between physics and metaphysics can be avoided, say by finding a solution to a problem in physics that does not raise the hackles of the metaphysician, then we can avoid the problem of epistemic priority. This will become a hallmark of her approach throughout the text, and it is one of the most distinctive aspects of her philosophy.

The more one follows these threads of reasoning through the *Institutions*, the more one encounters a prominent attitude toward philosophical conflict. Find a middle ground when you can, but in all cases, attempt to reduce conflict by dealing respectfully with each side of a dispute. In order to do so, one must relinquish the mantle of the partisan, adopting that of the independent thinker. As we read her text, we must always return to the sage words of the preface. Philosophy in her age self-consciously reflects on the revolution in the sciences effected by the works of several "great men," and we must respect their work, but we must never "carry respect for the greatest men to the point of idolatry." To endorse Leibniz's use of the principle of sufficient reason on the nature of space and time without carefully considering the underpinnings of the opposing view would be to carry respect too far, turning from a philosopher using her own reason into a disciple proclaiming the truth of the leader's ideas.

The Nature of Matter

After dealing with space and time, Du Châtelet spends several
chapters in the *Institutions* discussing the nature of matter. We
should read them with a renewed focus on potential philosophical conflicts, searching for her suggestions about the best means
for avoiding them. Just as one can consider the relation between
a physicist's question about space and a philosopher's, one can
consider a parallel relation between the way mathematicians think
about the divisibility of matter and the way the physicist does. Since
matter occupies space, and since geometry indicates that space is
infinitely divisible, philosophers and physicists have pondered
whether matter must also be. In discussing space, Du Châtelet
indicates that because of the human imagination, space appears to
be the homogeneous, autonomous, infinitely divisible being that
Newton describes. However, for Du Châtelet, that notion of space
is really a mere abstraction, not a real being. Geometry studies this
abstract thing rather than a real being; it is perfectly appropriate to
use geometrical reasoning when considering space itself. But that
same reasoning should not be applied to *matter*, to real things in the
world. She draws out this point in chapter 9 (Du Châtelet, *Institutions*, 1742, §168):

> Most philosophers, having confused the abstractions of our mind
> with physical body, have wanted to demonstrate the divisibility of
> matter to infinity by the reasoning of geometers on the divisibility
> of lines that can be pushed to infinity. But they could have avoided
> all the difficulties that this divisibility involved if they had been
> sure never to have applied the reasoning that one employs for the
> divisibility of geometrical bodies to natural and physical bodies.

Because space is nothing but an abstraction studied in geometry,
one can reason about its infinite divisibility, along with that of the

geometrical figures inhabiting it. But such reasoning does not apply to material things like tables and chairs. Since geometry and physics concern different domains, they need not conflict on the question of divisibility, so their approaches need not be reconciled after all. But does that mean that physics has the final word on real beings like tables and chairs, planets and comets? Does philosophy have no role in analyzing such things? Knowing that such questions will arise, Du Châtelet does not shy away from discussing potential conflicts about the nature of matter. For instance, she notes that since antiquity, both physics and metaphysics have asked questions about matter, its constitution, and its divisibility. After all, atomism was an ancient doctrine developed by thinkers like Democritus, one that was famously revived during the Scientific Revolution by figures like Galileo and then embraced by Newton, who discussed it in the Queries to his *Opticks*. Many philosophers knew that questions about matter might be answered differently by physics and metaphysics. Numerous clever maneuvers were then proposed to handle this apparent conflict. The various maneuvers made in Du Châtelet's milieu underscore the creativity of her approach.

One of the most prominent maneuvers was made by Immanuel Kant. Born in a small coastal city in Prussia called Königsberg, Kant famously spent his whole life there, save a brief sojourn as a tutor in a nearby town and a few forays into a regional forest.[29] After entering the local university in 1740, Kant quickly distinguished himself as a brilliant young thinker and writer. Although he never left Königsberg and its environs, he sought to establish a name for himself in the Republic of Letters by publishing essays on a wide range of topics. He also entered several essay competitions run by the Berlin Academy. His papers concerned topics in metaphysics, ethics, theology, and many aspects of natural science. In 1770, having finally received the university professorship he had long sought, Kant fell silent. He worked for a full decade on what would become his most famous work, the *Critique of Pure Reason*, publishing it in 1781. He then saw great fame and influence during the last two decades of his life. All of nineteenth-century German science and philosophy was created in his wake, often by self-proclaimed "Kantians."[30]

In the mid-1750s, Kant entered an essay competition run by the Berlin Academy concerning the nature of matter. The result is a short piece now commonly known as the "Physical Monadology." In this essay, he suggested that philosophers and mathematicians could have their cake and eat it, too. They could endorse geometry's idea that space is infinitely divisible, think of matter as existing within that space, and yet still insist that matter consists of fundamental constituents that are not divisible. This seemingly impossible feat is pulled off in the following clever way. First, we can conceive of matter as consisting of indivisible particles, which Kant called "monads" following the view of Leibniz and Wolff. Then, we can conceive of the monads as exuding a divisible shell of force within space. Now, since the shell is divisible, space remains divisible in just the way that the geometers have said. However, since the monad that exudes the force shell is just a point—it is not three-dimensional—it itself is *not* divisible. Physical processes could break through the shell, but nothing could divide the monad itself because it is not extended.[31]

Kant's elegant solution involving the distinct conceptions of matter in geometry (akin to physics for him) and in metaphysics presupposed that these distinct disciplines operated in the same domain. That notion may puzzle contemporary readers. Isn't a question about non-extended substances, like monads, a classic topic in metaphysics? Why would it be of any concern to physics or mathematics? The question is perfectly reasonable from our point of view, but it is anachronistic. The sentiment underlying it does not reflect Du Châtelet's and Kant's intellectual milieu. In fact, the Berlin Academy of Sciences, one of the leading scientific institutions in the world at the time, had already proposed a prize essay competition on the question of monads (using Leibniz's terminology) in 1746–47. The Academy proposed one again in 1755—apparently, the problem had not been solved the first time around!—and that's when Kant wrote his piece.

The Berlin Academy's prize competition generated an intense and sometimes personal debate. The debate involved figures like Samuel Formey and Samuel König, both self-professed Leibnizians, but also leading mathematicians like Euler[32] and supposedly anti-metaphysical philosophers like Condillac in France.[33] For instance, König submitted an essay defending monads, and then Euler broke the rules of the Academy as one of its competition judges by anonymously writing an essay against monads. Then Formey responded anonymously to Euler by defending them.[34] The many German-speaking scholars who followed Wolff were outraged when Euler broke the Academy's norms by publishing his thinly veiled anonymous attack on monadic theory during the time of the monad competition. The topic was clearly considered to be of great importance in the sciences.

For his part, Euler made the same assumption as Kant: he took physics and metaphysics to be tackling the same questions, which reflects what he took to be the aptness of the scientific academy focusing on metaphysics. Euler argued in particular that the laws of motion explain all natural phenomena and that the law of inertia specifically undermines the possibility of monads. The reason is that many philosophers, following Leibniz's lead from years earlier, conceived of monads as bearing internal principles of change. Since many monadists ascribed inherent forces or principles of change to these entities, Euler argued that they could be "self-moving," in violation of the law of inertia.[35] The details are not as important as the overarching point here: Euler conceived of metaphysics and physics as occupying the same intellectual domain. Therefore, they must be rendered consistent, in this case, by the former jettisoning ideas that conflict with those of the latter.

It is therefore remarkable that in her discussions of matter in the *Institutions* (chapters 7–9), Du Châtelet presents a distinctive view by arguing that in fact the conflict in these topics is imaginary.

For her, physics and metaphysics, like geometry and physics, can operate in distinct domains. She argues that from the perspective of metaphysics, matter does in fact consist of fundamental points, which she calls "simple beings." These beings are *simple* in the sense that they are not three-dimensional; they are like mathematical points. Leaving aside her reasons for postulating these beings for a moment, she insists that this idea need not worry the physicist. It should make no difference to physics whether the world ultimately consists of simple beings, for if there were such things, they would never be empirically detected. A non-extended being will not interact with any instruments, it will not reflect light or sound waves, etc. So, simple beings are simply irrelevant to physics, and the laws of physics apply to things in nature, not to objects of metaphysics. There is no conflict here after all. Kant's "physical monadology" and Euler's refutation of monads each attempt to resolve an illusory conflict.

But is it *really* illusory? Doesn't the physicist ask the question of whether there are ultimate constituents of matter, just as the philosopher does? Aren't physicists interested in whether atoms, or something else, compose ordinary material things like tables or even planets?

Du Châtelet's answer to these questions lies in considering her reason for endorsing simple beings, which also illustrates the broader contours of her approach in the *Institutions*. As a philosopher who endorses the principle of sufficient reason, she rejects the notion that matter is just a brute fact. That is, she thinks that everything must have a rational explanation, including the existence of matter.[36] This does not pose a problem because the philosopher's limitless demand for rational explanations has no parallel within physics. She insists that the physicist ("Physicien") can ignore this argument, for it answers a question she does not ask. It is apt for physics to take matter as a brute fact. For physics, the world is full of matter moving around in space and time under various forces— the goal is to figure out how that works. So the physicist's idea that material bodies like tables and chairs consist of tiny particles is perfectly acceptable. Only philosophy must avoid brute facts.[37]

As usual, that last point is not quite the end of the dialectic. For what if physics and metaphysics disagree on the question of whether there are any brute facts? Then doesn't the conflict dissipate, only to remerge? Intriguingly, Du Châtelet does not think so. Although physics may be unconcerned by brute facts, such as the existence of matter, or the specific character of the laws of nature, it does not *demand* them. To take a famous eighteenth-century example: there may be no explanation for the fact that gravity grows weaker as material things get farther apart (it goes as $1/r^2$). It might just turn out, as far as physics is concerned, that that's the way the world is. Perhaps we will learn the reason for this feature, but perhaps we will not. However, physicists studying gravity were certainly not committed to the idea that it *must* be a brute fact, i.e., that no explanation could ever be found. After all, it could have turned out that Newton's speculations about the ether in the Queries to his *Opticks* were correct and that an ether was empirically discovered. (Again, many scientists remained curious about the ether well into the nineteenth century.) The properties of that ether, in turn, may very well have eventually allowed science to explain why the gravitational force varies as $1/r^2$, rather than, e.g., as $1/r^3$. Indeed, the century's greatest mathematician, Euler, wondered about that very idea. So, Du Châtelet concludes, the conflict can be avoided after all.

The idea of "monads" or simple beings, so hotly contested in the eighteenth century, can seem odd today. But it does have parallels with a contemporary scientific idea. Consider our conception of subatomic particles. When I lean against my desk, it *seems* like it has a large, solid surface. However, in reality the desk is mostly empty space—it consists of countless particles like electrons, which zip around at unimaginable speeds. It turns out that when one puts together enormous numbers of electrons and other particles in certain arrangements, they will be perceived by us to be a solid thing like a desk. Similarly, Du Châtelet can explain our failure to perceive simple beings by noting that lots of them put together are perceived by us *as* solid tables. Just as electrons are fundamentally different from the things they constitute—they lack definite momentum and position and were famously said by the physicist Richard Feynman to be best understood as "probability clouds"[38]—so too are simple beings. Obviously, electrons are posited because of empirical physics, and simple beings are not, but the other parallel remains. This point presses critics to clarify their objection: if the claim is that simple beings are not part of an empirical theory, Du Châtelet would agree; they are not intended to be. Indeed, that is a feature, rather than a bug, of her approach. If the claim is that we rebel against the idea of simple beings because we cannot imagine such things, she would agree again—indeed, she says so explicitly. And nowadays we would add: we cannot imagine electrons, either.

As one might suspect, however, this is still not quite the end of the dialectic, as Du Châtelet herself knew well. The problem is that many philosophers had attempted over the years to use pure reasoning to undermine atomism, a famous theory in science with ancient roots. If philosophers make *that* move, then the conflict concerning the divisibility of matter disappears, only to reemerge yet again on yet another intellectual terrain. Such a philosophical move would disrupt a physics that deals with atoms. Du Châtelet's solution to this problem is elegant. She agrees that physics may endorse atomism because it focuses on the empirical question of how far material bodies can be divided. But in that case, she thinks that the philosopher should recognize that atomism is an answer to an empirical question, not a philosophical one. In pondering matter's divisibility, physics will stop with particles of some kind, maybe atoms; metaphysics will consider the possibility of something else entirely, namely, non-extended beings.

In her final lesson on matter at the end of chapter 9, where she notes that a physicist would be wasting her time pondering the possibility of something that could not be detected, she writes (Du Châtelet, *Institutions*, 1742, §183):

> One can conclude from all that has been said in this chapter that although it is very important in metaphysics (Métaphysique) to know that there can be no physical atoms and that all extension is in the end composed of simple beings, nonetheless these questions have only a remote influence on experimental physics (Physique expérimentale). Therefore the physicist (le Physicien) can abstract from the differing sentiments of philosophers on the elements of matter without causing any error in his experiments and his explications, for they will never reach simple beings or atoms.

Du Chatelet's solution is to endorse a division of labor. The physicist can ignore the monadic theory of the philosopher because it will have no import for her experiments and explanations of natural phenomena. If physics wishes to endorse atomic theory, that is fine. The philosopher is then free to propose a different idea in metaphysics. The question of matter's divisibility can be approached through the lens of physics, or that of metaphysics; to change the figure, when they ask that question, they speak with different voices.[39] Conflicts can be avoided.

But what precisely did Du Châtelet mean when she said that, "in the end" all matter is comprised of simple beings? Is that a subtle form of cheating, noting that when science tires of questions about matter's divisibility, the philosopher can jump in and proclaim that *ultimately*, there *really are* simple beings? Du Châtelet is not fudging or cheating here; she's being honest: science deals with nature, with the world around us, taking matter as a brute fact. For physics, it turns out that the world is full of matter—the task is to study it. If it turns out that it's made up of tiny particles, or atoms, then so be it. For philosophy, however, the existence of matter cannot be regarded as a brute fact, so atomism is not a satisfying view. The reason is that atomism would try to explain the world of extended things like tables and chairs by saying that microscopic extended things, called atoms, exist. And that's no explanation, because then we would want to know, well, why do microscopic extended things exist? And atomism cannot answer that question—a physicist can endorse atomism as long as she doesn't think it answers this *philosophical* question. Atomism would be an answer to a distinct question, such as, what are the smallest units into which we could divide matter, or, what are the smallest perceivable bits of matter, or perhaps, what are the smallest things that will interact with our lab equipment?[40] Those are physical questions. The philosopher is not focused on such questions, so she can ignore their answers.[41] In this way, Du Châtelet once again manages to dissolve the potential conflict between science and philosophy.

A Vision of Harmony between Science and Philosophy

Do these various threads within the *Institutions* come together? It seems difficult to find a unifying theme in Du Châtelet's discussions of space, time, matter, monads, gravity, forces, and the like. In the case of *gravity*, physics *requires* a foray into the metaphysics of essences, but in the case of *space*, physics does *not* require such a foray; instead, we appeal to human psychology. In the case of *matter*, physics and metaphysics operate in different domains, so neither seems to require a foray into the other, as long as they don't interfere with one another. One may despair at finding a common thread. Indeed, one may even despair at finding the right metaphor for her text's disparate elements. The theme of avoiding discipleship and the extremes that it produces runs through the whole *Institutions*, but is there any overarching conception of science and philosophy to accompany it?

Indeed, there is. Underlying this seeming diversity in the *Institutions*, there is in fact a unity. Du Châtelet suggests it already in the preface to the *Institutions,* writing: "Many truths of physics, metaphysics and geometry are obviously connected with one another" (Du Châtelet, *Institutions,* 1742, XII, 13). Simply put, for Du Châtelet, *science and philosophy ought to be in harmony.* In the case of essences and gravity, harmony is best promoted by appealing to analyses in metaphysics so that we can achieve clarity in physics. In the case of matter, we promote harmony by recognizing that science and philosophy ask different questions. And similarly, the discussion of space reminds us of the wisdom in the preface: when we carry our respect for great men too far, becoming their disciples, we harden our philosophical views, promoting conflict. Indeed, the disciple seeks conflict, hoping to vanquish his leader's foes. We ought instead to resist discipleship. We ought to think for ourselves precisely by reanalyzing old debates to see if they can be construed in a way that avoids conflict between science and philosophy.

This view is original and compelling. Some mathematicians and philosophers in the Enlightenment argued that physics has a kind of epistemic priority, and that metaphysics can be simply ignored. For them, the laws of nature are the axioms of the new system; these laws, along with the existence of matter and universal gravity, may all be brute facts. It is only one's allegiance to an outmoded metaphysics that may convince one that a deeper explanation is needed, they said. Others argued that metaphysics has epistemic priority and that physics must comply with its demands. For them, the principle of sufficient reason is the axiom of the new system, not the laws of nature; indeed, these laws, along with the existence of matter, must bear a rational explanation. There can be no brute facts. It is only one's attempt to turn the new physical theory into the gospel, or a grandiose *Weltanschauung,* that convinces one that deeper explanations are no longer needed. For Du Châtelet, both approaches are mistaken. Neither physics nor metaphysics has epistemic priority. Neither *requires* such priority unless we assume that they occupy the same domain and therefore must come into conflict. The task is clear: when analyzing essences and matter, space and time, hypotheses and reasoning, we ought to find the underlying harmony between science and philosophy. If they can be shown to be harmonious, then neither need assume authority over the other. Neither need dominate the other.

The metaphor of harmony captures each aspect of the *Institutions*. There are cases in which physics sings alone, and cases in which philosophy does; when they both sing, the goal is to be harmonious. Du Châtelet does not think that they must sing together all the time—there are cases in which science takes the stage where philosophy may be silent; later, the roles might reverse. In the last chapters of the *Institutions*, we find discussions of the pendulum and the inclined plane: these are historically important topics in physics, but of no concern to metaphysics. Similarly, she opens the text with a discussion of the existence of God, one of the oldest metaphysical questions, but one of little concern to physics. Then there are topics that concern both physics and metaphysics, including matter's divisibility, where harmony is achieved by recognizing their distinct approaches. In other cases, they should seek a harmonious chorus.

Du Châtelet began her *Institutions* with the contrast, ever present in the France of her day, between the Cartesian and the Newtonian systems. Whereas Descartes saw basic metaphysical notions as the foundation of physics, Newton rejected that approach, contending that physics could progress without wasting time on old-fashioned philosophy. Du Châtelet understood the dialectic between them, but self-consciously chose a distinct path. She transcended the debate about the epistemic statuses of physics and metaphysics by proclaiming that the question of priority is rendered moot if we seek to promote harmony between them. Unlike Descartes, she does not think that metaphysical principles, including central notions like *essence*, or our knowledge of the divine, are the foundation of physics. But she also resisted the implication that such a reaction to Descartes must mean that she endorses Newton's alternative picture. For, in order to grasp what the law of universal gravity really tells us about matter, we require an analysis of essences, something Newton himself sought to avoid. Neither system is correct, but each contains wisdom.

These examples may suggest a simpler interpretation. Perhaps Du Châtelet is simply saying that neither physics nor metaphysics garners epistemic priority because they do not conflict, and they do not conflict, in turn, because they view the world from radically distinct perspectives. The idea is reminiscent of the famous biologist Stephen Jay Gould's NOMA hypothesis. Science and religion need not conflict, Gould argued, because they inhabit "non-overlapping magisteria" (or NOMA). Science studies the age of rocks, religion the rock of ages; science explicates the heavens, religion lights the path to Heaven, as Gould pithily says in a book published in the late twentieth century.[42] To continue with my own metaphor, if Du Châtelet thinks they need not conflict with one another, why not embrace the idea of two voices, singing on their own, leaving each to find its tune? It is precisely here that Du Châtelet's originality is clearest. As she explicates already in chapter 3, on essences, it turns out that physics and metaphysics cannot ignore one another: the most successful physical theory of the age, Newton's theory of universal gravity, requires an exploration of metaphysics to clarify its potential proclamations about matter's essence. Therefore, although the two disciplines must respect their boundaries, they do need one another.

Novel views like Du Châtelet's take time to grasp, and they often provoke quibbling along the way. That reaction can be interpretively useful, pressing us to re-read the text, finding a new meaning within seemingly innocuous passages. My metaphor may provoke skepticism. To achieve harmony, of course, we require at least two voices or instruments working together. Du Châtelet does indeed argue that physics needs a discussion of essences from philosophy. But one may still wonder, does philosophy really need physics? Couldn't philosophy focus on the principles of knowledge, the existence of God, the nature of essences, etc., without ever worrying about the nature of electricity, the swing of the pendulum, or the force of gravity? She has advised philosophers to ignore atomism rather than arguing against it; why not go one step further and advise them to ignore physics and its problems altogether? In that case, the metaphor of harmony would not be apt.

If we take Du Châtelet's advice and think for ourselves, even about her work, we can rethink the *Institutions* with this question in mind. But to do so sensibly, we must remember its historical context, a lesson reflected in the preface to the *Institutions*. In particular, we must consider the scope of science in the early Enlightenment. Despite their numerous differences, prominent texts in this era had one thing in common: they exhibited a vast scope, tackling a huge range of natural phenomena. They discussed topics in astronomy, the laws of motion, aspects of human physiology, the nature of minerals in the earth, meteorological phenomena, heat, light, plants, and animals, and much else besides. The reason is that at this time, physics was often conceived of as *the general science of matter*, that is, a science that dealt with the entire material world, from plants and animals to human beings to the planets and the stars. (Most scientific specialization in Europe would come later.) This approach ran from the seventeenth until deep into the eighteenth century.[43]

The broad conception of physics in modern thought is evident in numerous texts that Du Châtelet and her interpreters studied. For instance, we see it in Descartes's *Principles of Philosophy*, and also in the treatise to which Du Châtelet compares her own in her preface, the *Treatise on Physics* of Jacques Rohault, a self-proclaimed Cartesian whose ideas were influential in the early eighteenth century.[44] A diverse group embraced this vision of physics, including figures who were often on opposite sides of various disputes. For instance, we find it embraced by Wolff,[45] the most famous follower of Leibniz in the early Enlightenment, but also in Wilhelm s'Gravesande's *An Introduction to Sir Isaac Newton's Philosophy*.[46] We find it in well-known experimentalists like Joseph Privat de Molières, and also in the famous thinker Nicholas Hartsoeker.[47] These authors employed physics to explain *all* of nature.

The contrast with Du Châtelet's text is sharp. Whereas these predecessors and interlocutors sought to explain everything under the sun, not to mention the sun itself, Du Châtelet narrowed her focus dramatically. She said little to nothing about heat and light, minerals and the earth, the weather and the growth of plants. Instead, she focused on classic questions about space, time, matter, and forces. And even when discussing dynamics, she emphasized those forces which she thought were best understood at the time, such as gravity. To discuss *all* the forces of nature—like electricity, magnetism, etc.—would have required speculation of a type she rejected. Her discussion of hypotheses had already warned against that. Of course, her interests were as wide-ranging as her contemporaries'. She ran numerous experiments with Voltaire at her chateau in Cirey, published an essay on the nature of fire, composed another one on optics, read widely in experimental physics. But her commitment to her methodology prevented her from *speculating* about such things. Her text has a far narrower scope than its cousins.

These facts help to highlight Du Châtelet's distinctiveness, especially if we remember why her peers embraced a general science of nature in the first place. They often did so because they endorsed overarching metaphysical conceptions of the world undergirding the use of physics to explicate all of nature. The clearest example of such a conception is the mechanical philosophy, which was widely shared among philosophers throughout the Scientific Revolution and the Enlightenment. A deep metaphysical commitment to mechanisms gave philosophers faith that *all* of nature is explicable in terms of matter and motion. They did not have scant evidence for vortices swirling around the planets; they had no evidence whatever! Instead, they had faith in mechanism, a faith that inspired speculation.

In contrast, Du Châtelet has no such grandiose commitment. She makes no deep commitment to the mechanical philosophy.[48]

When we read through the entire *Institutions* and compare it to the physics of her day, the contrast is stark: she has substantially constrained metaphysics through physics. If metaphysics were free to roam unconstrained, as happened to many of the mechanical philosophers, then the harmony she sought would dissipate. If metaphysics involves a general commitment to something like the mechanical philosophy, then physics could in principle explain any natural phenomenon through reference solely to matter and motion. She does not deny that the mechanical philosophy is very fruitful, but she cautions that one must not invent matter and motion when trying to explain parts of nature (Du Châtelet, *Institutions*, 1742, §182). As she knew, the best physics of the day suggested that such inventions were hopeless: no one yet understood electricity or magnetism or heat as Newton had understood gravity. No law governing any of these phenomena had yet been found; more empirical research would be required. As Du Châtelet reminds us time and again, physics is an empirical discipline. It cannot achieve harmony with metaphysics if the latter engages in wild speculation. Just as metaphysics will constrain physics by saying, e.g., that we cannot accept purported explanations of phenomena that violate the principle of sufficient reason, so too will physics constrain metaphysics by saying, e.g., that we cannot abide mechanist speculations about natural phenomena that haven't yet been empirically analyzed. To achieve harmony, we must keep both voices within the right range.

Du Châtelet thinks that just as physics must on occasion look to metaphysics for assistance, the converse is also true. Suppose I am particularly enamored of the mechanical philosophy and therefore believe that, in principle, any natural phenomenon can be explained by referring to the impacts that material particles make on one another. I would be in good company: such an overarching view was embraced by a wide range of figures in this period, including Hobbes, Boyle, Hooke, Galileo, Locke, Descartes, Huygens. In the early Enlightenment, many thinkers with such an attitude then sat down to write hundreds of pages of explanations using only matter and motion, "explaining" lightning or fog, the moon's orbit or the tides, the circulation of the blood or the way frogs jump. Du Châtelet recommends a distinct course: check with the best physics to determine if your metaphysical conception is leading you astray. Do these many explanations involve a series of hypotheses? Or do they involve extensive experimentation, the careful analysis of empirical evidence, and an attempt to discover new laws of nature? If we embrace extensive hypothetical reasoning with little empirical support, then our metaphysics has led us astray.

When Du Châtelet rejects the mechanical philosophy as a broad metaphysical conception in chapter 9, she (characteristically) analyzes the revolution in the sciences for pertinent examples. She notes that in fact much of modern physics has not been limited to mechanical explanations, which make use only of the figure, size, and situation of particles. Instead, physics will often refer to other qualities, e.g., elasticity or heat, without considering whether these are mechanically explicable. One of her examples is this: the famous scientist Robert Boyle explained the phenomenon of his air pump by referring to air's elasticity without proposing a further "mechanical" explanation of elasticity itself, i.e., without reducing elasticity to the size, shape and motion of air particles.[49] Her discussion of hypotheses in chapter 4 is also especially relevant here: one may propose a hypothesis according to which, e.g., the elasticity of the air is reducible to mechanical features of air particles, but only to propose experiments, perhaps with corrections to the hypothesis on the basis of experimental data. This can be entertained only as a probable idea, not as the final answer.

Yet old habits die hard. Readers like Voltaire, enamored of the idea that Du Châtelet was really a "Newtonian" at heart, might be tempted to make a last-ditch rescue for their interpretation of her text. Perhaps she was really a Newtonian who rejected the mechanical philosophy and thereby constrained her conception of physics appropriately. But in fact, Du Châtelet is just as critical of Newtonians who run amok with a new worldview centered on principles of "attraction" as she is of the mechanists. She chastises Newtonians who speculate that electricity or fermentation or the cohesion of bodies can be explained by *attraction*.[50] She criticizes the Newtonians concerning the explanation of bodily cohesion in chapter 10 (Du Châtelet, *Institutions*, 1742, §205), and then explains in greater depth in chapter 16 how some disciples of Newton use a principle of attraction to explain not only cohesion but also chemical effects, aspects of light, etc. They even invented a new law whereby the attraction may diminish as $1/r^3$ rather than $1/r^2$ (Du Châtelet, *Institutions*, 1742, §389). Despite their status as self-identified "Newtonians," these thinkers engage in just the kind of hypothetical reasoning and speculation that one finds in the mechanists. Du Châtelet is just as skeptical of attempts to say that magnetism involves the exchange of specially shaped particles as she is of claims that it actually involves some inherent principle of attraction. Speculation is speculation.

Intriguingly, one of Du Châtelet's own earlier, unpublished works highlights the fact that her argument against the Newtonians can also be seen as an act of self-criticism. In her unpublished *Essay on Optics*, she herself had apparently adopted the mantle of the disciple. The essay was long thought lost but was recently discovered by the scholar Fritz Nagel among the papers of the Bernoulli archive in Switzerland. Having visited the famous "academy of science" at Du Châtelet's chateau in Cirey, Johann Bernoulli took a complete copy of the essay back to Basel with him.[51] It then rested in the archives for two centuries.

In her *Essay on Optics*, Du Châtelet writes the following:

> All areas of physics owe a great deal to M. Newton, but there is none he extended more than optics; it may be said that he created and perfected the part of this science of which colors are the object. Truth is one—and once it is discovered, there is nothing

more but to follow it. Thus I dare say that anyone who wishes to explain the nature of light and colors, without conforming to Newton's discoveries, will go astray. Indeed, the more one wishes to deepen the causes of opacity and transparence, the more one ought to study the treatise on optics of that great man. (*Essai sur l'optique*, 230r)

Her role as a disciple in this text is clear: her job is to recognize that Newton, the "great man," has found the truth, and then to spread the gospel. Reflecting that attitude, she spends much of the *Essay* using the principle of attraction to "explain" various optical phenomena, much as Voltaire does in his *Elements of the Philosophy of Newton*.[52]

The contrast between the method in Du Châtelet's unpublished essay on optics and the approach in the *Institutions* is clear. That fact was recognized by no less a figure than Goethe years after her death.[53] Du Châtelet may very well have planned to discuss optics in the proposed second volume of her *Institutions*—the second edition proclaimed the new version of the text to be merely "volume one"—but her approach to that science would obviously have been radically different. No more discipleship.

Is this really the end of the story? Did Du Châtelet really jettison speculation altogether? After all, she opens her text with a rather traditional discussion of God's existence. And isn't that a case in which metaphysics involves some pretty wild speculation? It would certainly seem so to many readers today. As a result, one's skepticism may return. One might ask, you are saying that she refused to speculate whether elasticity, or electricity, involved the exchange of little particles, and yet she was happy to discuss the divine being? What are we to make of that?

This is a natural question. Yet here we do not encounter the limits of our interpretation but rather of our often limited understanding of a historical moment radically different from our own. Although atheism did exist in the early modern period and gained steam during the Enlightenment—one hears a lot about Hobbes and Spinoza, and later David Hume—there is no doubt that throughout the eighteenth century, nearly all of the major philosophers, as well as the leading mathematicians and physicists, took the existence of God for granted. They often simply assumed that God's existence could be demonstrated through one means or another. Many *philosophes* who criticized religion, or ridiculed the Bible, were still deists.[54] The list of such thinkers would include many major thinkers of the Enlightenment, even those on opposites sides of nearly every other issue, like Leibniz and Locke, Euler and Voltaire, Maupertuis and Wolff. Yet for her part, Du Châtelet insisted that although metaphysics can establish the existence of the divine being as the creator of the universe, that notion cannot be used to derive any truths within physics. We cannot abide that kind of speculation. Metaphysics must adjust its voice to sing in harmony with its partner.[55]

If physics constrains its sister discipline, what kind of metaphysics does one have? Du Châtelet's metaphysics emphasizes *methodology* and an attendant epistemic modesty. Leaving aside the existence of the divine being, which plays little further role in the text, we find a discussion of epistemic principles—especially the principle of contradiction and the principle of sufficient reason—and then a discussion of essences and of hypotheses. Du Châtelet's metaphysics is not grandiose; we find here not an *esprit de système*, but rather the *esprit systématique* trumpeted by the *philosophes*. The mechanical philosophy was an all-encompassing system, a comprehensive conception of nature that promoted speculation about a wide range of topics where a wise physicist would preach caution. The philosophy of "attraction" promoted by Newton's disciples was similarly grandiose. In contrast, Du Châtelet's metaphysics focuses on topics that are especially fruitful for science, restricting itself largely to areas in which science has made substantial progress, especially concerning the nature of forces like gravity.

Du Châtelet's thought is reflective of her milieu, but also reflects self-awareness of her moment in history. The physics of many figures in her milieu—including Rohault, Wolff, Molières, Hartsoeker, and others—is comprehensive, something akin to a final theory that attempts to explain everything under the sun. This conception of physics lacks awareness of its place in history. Anyone surveying European science in the early Enlightenment should have been quite aware that great progress had been made in many areas, including the understanding of gravity, the rules of impact, the laws of motion, the nature of light, etc. However, science had made little progress in understanding a wide range of topics in physics, including heat, electricity, and magnetism, not to mention topics in what we now call meteorology, chemistry, geology, and human physiology.[56] Du Châtelet recognizes this epistemic situation, presenting a conception of physics that is explicitly aware of its place in history. In lieu of attempting to present a final theory of nature, which would perforce involve substantial speculation about a wide range of topics, she presents a methodologically rich conception. She says: we do not yet understand much about nature, but the "revolution" of the past century enables us to grasp some of the *methods* to follow if we want to learn more. We are in no position to present a final theory of nature, but perhaps we now have the methods to take us toward one.

The wisdom of the *Institutions'* preface is salient once more. It is not only "great men" who have disciples, but their ideas. A man can become an idol, but so can his theory. The idol of the early days of the "revolution" was the mechanical philosophy, one heartily endorsed by nearly every influential thinker one can mention, from Galileo to Boyle to Descartes to Huygens to Locke. These moderns rejected Scholasticism's supposedly irrational devotion to Aristotle, as Jacob Brucker would later emphasize in his history of philosophy.

But eventually, their followers took the new mechanical philosophy and placed it on its own pedestal. The proponents of mechanistic thinking eventually convinced themselves that they could write a complete physics of nature using only matter and motion. If they were concerned at times by the wild speculation that proposing mechanisms for everything must involve, they were comforted by their faith in the system. And then years later, in the heady final days of the "revolution," Newton challenged the dominance of the mechanical philosophy. He analyzed the forces of nature without worrying whether they involved any mechanisms. The mechanist disciples were aghast. Before long, Newton had his own acolytes. Some of them took his cautious remark about the cause of gravity, *hypotheses non fingo* ("I feign no hypotheses"), and magnified it into a general ban on hypothetical reasoning. Others took the opposite tack, taking speculative remarks in the Queries to the *Opticks* about attraction to be the new gospel. It was not long before they had replaced faith in mechanisms with faith in hidden "attractive principles" that could supposedly explain everything in nature. Either way, many Newtonians acted like disciples—as often happens, they simply interpreted the gospel differently. Devotion to mechanism, or to its Newtonian rival, produced extensive conflicts, hiding the unbridled speculation that now undergirded so much of physics.

In the *Institutions*, Du Châtelet bemoans these excesses. She warns against extreme positions concerning any number of philosophical topics, most especially hypothetical reasoning. She tries to resolve conflicts between various methods and ideas in both science and philosophy. But perhaps her greatest originality lies in her effort to diagnose the intellectual situation that causes thinkers to adopt extreme positions and to promote conflict in the first place. Her caveat in the book's opening that one must remain autonomous and avoid becoming a mere disciple reverberates throughout the whole text. The tendency to idolize "great men" like Descartes, Leibniz, and Newton produces mere followers, and then extreme positions flourish, as she saw all around her. Unlike so many early Enlightenment figures, she refuses to become a disciple and warns her readers against falling under the spell of some leading thinker. For the men in her milieu, it was that attitude and that advice to her readers which made her so dangerous.

FIGURE 1 Portrait of Émilie Du Châtelet. © The Trustees of
the British Museum.

FIGURE 2 Photograph of Place des Vosges. © Andrew Janiak.

FIGURE 3 Photograph of Notre Dame
Cathedral. © Adela Deanova.

FIGURE 4 Du Châtelet's château. © Château de Cirey.

FIGURE 5 Frontispiece to Algarotti work,
Venice, 1737, depicting Algarotti explaining
things to Du Châtelet at her chateau.

FIGURE 6 Frontispiece to Voltaire work, Amsterdam, 1738, depicting Du Châtelet holding a mirror that reflects Newton's heavenly light down to Voltaire.

INSTITUTIONS

DE

PHYSIQUE.

A PARIS,
Chez PRAULT fils, Quai de Conty; vis-à-vis la
descente du Pont-Neuf, à la Charité.

M. DCC. XL.
Avec Approbation & Privilége du Roi.

FIGURE 7 Title page, *Institutions de physique*, Paris, 1740.

FIGURE 8 Title page of Mairan, Letter in reply to Du Châtelet's *Institutions*, Paris, 1741.

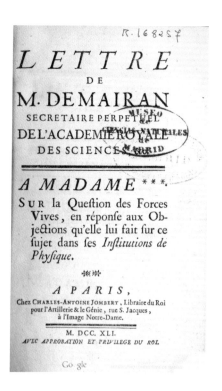

LETTRE
DE
M. DE MAIRAN
SECRETAIRE PERPETUEL
DE L'ACADEMIE ROYALE
DES SCIENCES

A MADAME ***.

SUR la Question des Forces Vives, en réponse aux Objections qu'elle lui fait sur ce sujet dans ses *Institutions de Physique*.

A PARIS,

Chez CHARLES-ANTOINE JOMBERT, Libraire du Roi pour l'Artillerie & le Génie, rue S. Jacques, à l'Image Notre-Dame.

M. DCC. XLI.
AVEC APPROBATION ET PRIVILEGE DU ROI.

Google

RÉPONSE

DE MADAME ***

A la Lettre que M. De Mairan, Secretaire perpetuel de l'Academie Royale des Sciences, lui a écrite le 18. Fevrier 1741. sur la question des forces vives.

A Bruxelles, chez FOPPENS 1741.

FIGURE 9 Title page of Du Châtelet, Response to Mairan, Brussels, 1741.

INSTITUTIONS
PHYSIQUES
DE MADAME LA MARQUISE
DU CHASTELLET

adressées à Mr. son Fils.

Nouvelle Edition, corrigée & augmentée,
considerablement par l'Auteur.

TOME PREMIER.

A AMSTERDAM,
AUX DEPENS DE LA COMPAGNIE.
M DCC XLII.

FIGURE 10 Title page, *Institutions physiques*, Amsterdam, 1742.

Der
Frau Marquisinn
von **Chaſtellet**

Naturlehre

an Ihren Sohn
Erſter Theil
nach der zweyten Franzöſiſchen Ausgabe
überſetzet

von

Wolf Balthaſar Adolph von Steinwehr
Königl. Preuß. Hofrath, der Hiſtorie, und Alterthümer,
wie auch des Natur⸗ und Völkerrechtes Prof. Publ. Ord. auf der
Univerſität zu Frankfurth an der Oder, derſelben Biblio⸗
thecario, und der Königl. Preußiſchen Societet der
Wiſſenſchaften Mitgliede.

Mit allergnädigſten Privilegio.

Halle und Leipzig
In der Rengeriſchen Buchhandlung
1 7 4 3.

FIGURE 11 Title page, *Naturlehre*, Halle and Leipzig, 1743.

INSTITUZIONI
DI FISICA
di Madama la MARCHESA
DU CHASTELLET
INDIRITTE A SUO FIGLIUOLO.

Traduzione dal Linguaggio Francese
nel Toscano,

Accresciuta con LA DISSERTAZIONE
SOPRA LE FORZE MOTRICI
DI M. DE MAIRAN.

IN VENEZIA, MDCCXLIII.
Presso GIAMBATISTA PASQUALI.
Con *Licenza de' Superiori, e Privilegio.*

FIGURE 12 Title page, *Instituzioni di fisica*, Venice, 1743.

4

The Enlightenment's Most Famous Woman

During the Enlightenment, most scientific, philosophical, and mathematical work was conducted in academies of science rather than in universities. Although a few notable figures held university positions—Isaac Newton at Trinity College, Cambridge, is a prominent example, followed by Immanuel Kant at the university in Königsberg—most of the leading philosophers and mathematicians were independent authors, tutors, travelers. Few were university professors, but nearly all of them enjoyed membership in one academy or another. After the Royal Society in London received a charter from King Charles II in 1662, it quickly became a model throughout Europe. Each scientific academy would elect members, sponsor presentations, produce new research, and publish a journal akin to the *Philosophical Transactions of the Royal Society* to disseminate knowledge. The Academy of Sciences in Paris opened just a few years later in 1666, and the Enlightenment soon saw a flurry of new institutional activity, with academies in Berlin, Bologna, and St. Petersburg hiring some of the leading mathematicians and scientists in Europe in the new century. These academies were the center of European science and philosophy at this time.[1] If one wished to discover the latest thinking about gravity, learn new differential equations, or find a novel experiment concerning air pressure, one read the *Philosophical Transactions* or the memoirs of an academy; one did not look to universities. This feature of modern life is nicely preserved in our word "academia," which refers to the universities that have taken over the function of the old academies.

The goal of every young thinker in Europe, from Prussia to Russia and Switzerland to England, was to become a member of an academy or perhaps to be hired by one to conduct research. For those, like Kant, who remained in university life, the prize essay competitions sponsored by the academies of Paris or Berlin remained of paramount importance for testing their ideas and sharing them with leading thinkers. These competitions concerned myriad topics, from the nature of fire to the calculation of a center of gravity to the existence of non-spatial substances ("monads"). They spanned philosophy, science, and mathematics. So, for most Enlightenment thinkers, intellectual life centered on the academies, their journals, and the prize competitions they sponsored.

But for women with intellectual interests, the distinction between the academies, where cutting edge research was common, and the universities, where old-fashioned curricula reigned, meant little. They were almost completely excluded from all of these institutions. Just as women were prevented from enrolling in colleges or universities, they were prohibited from joining an academy, or often from even attending one of their presentations. In this era, the exceptions prove the rule.[2] Although universities in Italy and in England were founded already in the twelfth century, and the institutions flourished throughout Europe in the early modern period, only a handful of women were allowed to participate.

For instance, after the great Dutch polymath and philosopher Anna Maria van Schurman read a Latin ode on the opening of a new university in Utrecht in 1636, she became one of the first women to attend university lectures. She was known at the time as one of the most erudite people in Europe and soon published a work arguing that women must be given access to education.[3] However, when attending lectures, she was required to stand behind a screen, lest her presence "disturb" the men in attendance. Her screen became famous, and she was quickly made the butt of jokes by many observers, including Descartes. In that case, she had the last laugh. Descartes once tried to debate theological questions with van Schurman in Holland on his way to visit Queen Christina in Sweden. It did not go well for the Frenchman: she ridiculed him for being unable to read the Bible in the original Hebrew. In her view, reading it in translation just wasn't the same.[4]

In Bologna during the Enlightenment, several women, most prominently the experimental physicist Laura Bassi, were able not only to attend lectures but to obtain degrees. Bassi later became professor of experimental physics in Bologna and conducted numerous famous experiments on a wide range of topics. Indeed, Bologna was an especially enlightened city at the time, for Bassi and other women—such as the great mathematician Maria Gaetana Agnesi, who published a major work on the integral and differential calculus in 1748—helped to enliven the Bolognese Academy of Sciences, which broke the gender barrier several times, including in 1746 when it elected Du Châtelet to membership.[5] But Du Châtelet and other women were barred from participation in the Royal Academy of Sciences in Paris. That was the norm throughout most of Europe. Although Margaret Cavendish made a famous visit to the Royal Society in London in 1667, no woman repeated the maneuver until the twentieth century. Similarly, the Paris Academy's ban on women held well into the twentieth century, preventing even the Noble Prize winner Marie Curie from joining. (Indeed, she won the prize twice!) Incredibly, women were excluded from the influential Académie Française until 1980.[6]

Despite these institutional barriers, women found other means of participating in intellectual life. Women in France especially, but also in Italy and England, ran salons, important centers for intellectual conversation and the dissemination of knowledge from the academies through less formal, but no less significant, means.

The salons became prominent enough in Enlightenment France that men hoping to make an intellectual mark on modern culture scrambled to be invited to some aristocrat's home, where they could test their mettle against leading thinkers. Their importance was also signaled by the opposition they felt from other men.[7] Salons have long been considered a key aspect of the development of a public sphere during the Enlightenment, along with coffee houses, gathering places for discussions of the pressing issues of the day.[8]

As important as the salons were to Enlightenment culture, some women found them unsatisfying. They sought to bypass institutional culture altogether, appealing to their fellow intellectuals directly by publishing scientific, philosophical, or mathematical works. Salons helped to shape intellectual culture, and gossip about the latest dispute between proponents of different philosophical sects would travel from their conversations in person to correspondence that circulated far and wide, but they could not match the reach of a major publication with a press in Amsterdam, London, Paris or Venice. The barriers to participation in intellectual life meant that many talented women did not learn Latin, so such publications were often written in the vernacular. For women in England like Cavendish, this meant that at least their initial publication would be in what was then a rather obscure language. The same was true for Agnesi: it is remarkable that her *Instituzione analitiche* (1748) was praised extensively at the time because few European intellectuals outside of Italy were able to read Italian. Again, the exception proves the rule: with her knowledge of Greek, Latin, Dutch, French, etc., Anna Maria van Schurman was able to communicate directly with the whole European scholarly world in any relevant language. She would even write letters in Hebrew for fun. But such cases were rare.

It was therefore especially fortuitous that as enlightenment spread in the early eighteenth century, French overtook Latin as the scholarly language of choice. It was indeed the *lingua Franca* of the new era. This meant that a Parisian aristocrat like Émilie Du Châtelet, who was able to read English and Latin so well that she undertook

major translation projects involving each language, could also communicate directly with the intellectual world in her native tongue.
Since France was the principal center of Enlightenment culture in
Europe, this gave Du Châtelet a means of connecting directly with
the growing Republic of Letters. She recognized that the standard
paths for intellectual women to participate in European culture
were through salons, or through the translation of works written by
men. She did not reject these avenues. For instance, she participated
in salon culture when she was in Paris, just as she had in her youth
at home. She also undertook several major translations, including a
controversial English text by Bernard Mandeville called the *Fable
of the Bees* and later a massive Latin one by Newton (the *Principia*).
Yet neither path fully satisfied her intellectual ambition. She in fact
chose the path of most resistance: she published the *Institutions*,
a major work of philosophy in French, under her own name. This
would enable her ideas to circulate far beyond the culture of the
salonièrres, and the ideas would assuredly be her own, rather than
mere translations. Like van Schurman before her and Agnesi after,
this move put Du Châtelet into an elite group of intellectual women
who contributed directly to Enlightenment intellectual life through
a vehicle used almost exclusively by men.

But for any woman during the Enlightenment, another barrier
would first have to be broken. That barrier had been erected years
earlier in the seventeenth century. Coincidentally, 1686 saw the
completion of works representing both the apotheosis of technical physics, Newton's *Principia*, and a famous popularization of
science, Fontenelle's *Conversations on the Plurality of Worlds*. Newton's audience was limited not only to Latinate readers but also to
sophisticated mathematicians, a tiny elite. In contrast, Fontenelle's
vernacular work helped to spawn a new era in which male philosophers would explain the latest developments in science to broad
audiences, including female readers. His *Conversations* addressed
a "naïve but intellectually receptive marquise," a fictional aristocratic woman interested in science, thereby creating a "template of

the scientific woman."[9] Fontenelle's later status as the long-serving secretary of the Parisian Academy of Sciences helped to ensure the influence of his approach well into the eighteenth century. Indeed, reaching an intellectual audience of women became a major theme of Enlightenment science.[10] Although Fontenelle himself was a lifelong Cartesian, even Newtonians and Leibnizians followed in his footsteps. From Francesco Algarotti's *Newtonianism for the Ladies* (1737) to Samuel Formey's *La belle Wolffienne* (1741), both of which reflected personal knowledge of Du Châtelet's ideas, many writers sought to reach women curious about science and philosophy. The official exclusion of women from academic institutions of all kinds did little to dampen the curiosity of many readers; perhaps it only increased it.

This powerful trend in Enlightenment science posed a problem for thinkers like Du Châtelet. As she was formulating her ideas about science and philosophy in the late 1730s, two of the leading Newtonians in Europe, both of whom were part of her intellectual circle in Cirey, published popularizations of Newton's ideas. The Venetian writer Francesco Algarotii published a popularization of Newton's main discoveries, including the complex work of the *Principia* but especially the more accessible ideas in the *Opticks*, under the title *Newtonianism for the Ladies*. It became a smash hit throughout Europe at the time, seeing a number of translations from its original Italian.[11] In part due to Algarotti's inspiration, Voltaire added *Elements of the Philosophy of Newton* to his growing stable of works. Like the *Philosophical Letters,* it would import British ideas from Newton, Locke, and Clarke to France to foment a transition to a more modern culture.[12] Neither Algarotti nor Voltaire feared that in presenting Newton's ideas, their own would be seen as derivative. Indeed, each garnered substantial fame from their efforts.

Du Châtelet understood that she would be accorded no such freedom. Algarotti and Voltaire were already working at the heart of the Republic of Letters, but given her institutional exclusion from that realm, Du Châtelet saw that no serious reader would pay much attention to yet another popularization of Newton's ideas if it were *written* by a woman, even if women were considered an important *audience* for such works. We now know that she once contemplated writing a popularization à la Algarotti and Voltaire. And she in fact wrote an "Essay on Optics" that presented Newton's experiments, discussing his conception of the heterogeneity of sunlight and its constituent rays that can be separated with a prism. In the end, however, she chose not to publish her essay. More important, she excised any discussion of optics from her *Institutions*, a clear sign that she was not following in Algarotti's or Voltaire's footsteps. A popularization of Newton could not ignore his optical ideas, which were in many ways even more popular than his theory of gravity during the Enlightenment. She chose instead a far riskier path: rather than finding a textual genre that was considered gender appropriate at that time, or adjacent to the appropriate realm of translating or popularizing the ideas of famous men, she would publish her own 500-page philosophical treatise.

Her gamble paid off. After years of studying the latest developments lying at the intersections of science, philosophy, and mathematics, Du Châtelet published a work with the imposing title, *Institutions of Physics*. Within a few short years of its publication in Paris in 1740, Du Châtelet's *Institutions* was read and discussed by Europe's leading intellectuals, including philosophers like Kant and Wolff, mathematicians like Bernoulli and Euler, scientists like Maupertuis and Clairaut, and the secretaries of the Berlin and Paris academies, Samuel Formey and Dortous de Mairan, respectively. After its initial press run in Paris, Du Châtelet rethought some of her ideas, revising the text for a second edition in French (1742). She did so partly to respond to Voltaire's reaction to her arguments in the new edition of his *Elements of the Philosophy of Newton*, published a year earlier. The revised version of her text was then translated the very next year into both German and Italian.[13] Hence, within a few short years, the work was published in Paris, Leipzig, and Venice. Through these four editions, Du Châtelet was able to reach the entire European intellectual world: any savant could read her original French, and intellectually curious men and women in German- or Italian-speaking lands could read her work in translation.[14] (Figures 7, 9, 10, 11, and 12)

The *Institutions* garnered the attention of a wide-ranging group of intellectual figures with disparate interests. It proclaimed the importance of the "revolutions" in the sciences, which soon became a major theme of Enlightenment thought. It also deftly tackled both philosophical issues of general import and also topics of concern mostly to academicians working in the sciences and in mathematics. Unlike Du Châtelet's translation of Newton's *Principia*, not to mention Agnesi's text on the integral and differential calculus, which were accessible only to sophisticated mathematical readers, her *Institutions* would appeal to a group of readers with disparate backgrounds and training. Unlike a narrow text in physics, Du Châtelet's *Institutions* opens with a general discussion of the principles of knowledge that would interest any philosophically minded reader. In tandem, unlike works in metaphysics, the *Institutions* would not merely appeal to readers with philosophical interests; it would also attract academicians interested in things like the theory of universal gravity and the laws of motion. Du Châtelet had cleverly found a way of discussing central issues in Enlightenment science and philosophy in a precise, yet broadly accessible, manner, thereby transcending the limits of salon culture and even of some aspects of publication-based intellectual life. She had not merely found her audience, but like any great author, she had helped to shape it.

Despite this great success, Du Châtelet was still excluded from participating in official academic life. So after publishing her magnum opus in 1740, which placed Du Châtelet into an intellectual elite, she made one more daring choice. She thought of a clever way to break one more barrier: the wall surrounding academia itself. She could not participate *directly* in academic life, but she found a way of using her published work to enter the academy through a clever route, one no woman had ever taken before.

Breaking into the Academy: A Debate about Force

A few years before Du Châtelet published the *Institutions*, she had written an anonymous essay on the nature of fire and heat, submitting it to the Academy of Sciences for one of its prize competitions. Her gender demanded her anonymity, but she did not stand out: many male authors wrote anonymously in that era to preserve their dignity if they failed to garner a prize. Her essay did not win the competition—the great mathematician Euler won—but it was later honored by publication in the Academy's *Memoires*, and in a way that allowed some readers to infer her identity. It was the very first text written by a woman ever published by the Academy of Sciences in France, an institution then in its seventy-third year. But Du Châtelet wanted to go further.

In her essay on the nature of fire and heat, Du Châtelet had praised the secretary of the Academy, Dortous de Mairan, for his views on the measurement of forces and of motion.[15] Although her submission was anonymous, many understood that she was the author. Her remarks obviously pleased Mairan. Although Du Châtelet had not yet published her major work, she was already famous in intellectual circles. Indeed, Mairan had enjoyed at least one supper with her and Fontenelle in Paris in late 1739 during one of her visits from the countryside.[16] Her move ensured that Mairan would regard her as an ally in his dispute with the heir to the Leibnizian tradition, the great Swiss mathematician Johann Bernoulli. Little did Mairan know, she had set her trap.

Two years later, in one of the very last sections of the first edition of the *Institutions*, Du Châtelet made her fateful move. This time around, she criticized Mairan.[17] She defended Bernoulli's position, which his own student Maupertuis had been reluctant to do, perhaps for fear of angering the powerful secretary of the Academy.[18] Mairan was clearly annoyed. He proclaimed that women change their minds easily and that Du Châtelet must have been converted by Leibnizian influences at her chateau in Cirey.[19] Clearly, Du Châtelet had used her newfound insider status to her advantage. The *Institutions* had quickly risen in prominence, so Mairan was forced to respond to her criticisms; to remain silent would have been interpreted as agreement. But she had also used her outsider status: since she was barred from joining the Academy of Sciences, Mairan had little power over her. She felt free to criticize his views publicly. The challenge was serious enough that Mairan published his response to Du Châtelet as a stand-alone volume in 1741. She then made two further moves: she published her retort to Mairan's reply as its own short text, also in 1741 (Figure 8), and then reprinted both his reply and her response in the *Institutions'* second edition just one year later.[20] These assorted publications ensured that their debate remained in the public eye.

Through this wily maneuver, Du Châtelet accomplished several goals. She successfully reanimated an old physics dispute in France,[21] ensnared the secretary of a powerful institution into a decidedly public debate with a woman who was barred from entering that institution's halls, and had shown the courage to defend the views of famous thinkers like Bernoulli when prominent French intellectuals such as Maupertuis—who would soon become the president of the Berlin Academy of Sciences—had not been willing to intervene. A triple twist! She knew that the public debate with Mairan would have another benefit. It would help her ideas to circulate even more widely, as would a similar debate she held with the secretary of the Royal Society in London a few years later.[22] Du Châtelet could not join the Royal Society or attend its meetings, but she could hold a debate with its leader. These maneuvers placed Du Châtelet into a position that was so elite, she was probably the only woman in the Enlightenment to hold it.

Which debate did she choose for her academic intervention? She chose the "living forces" dispute, which was usually called "vis viva" after its original Latin title. The dispute beautifully represented the mélange of physical and metaphysical, scientific and philosophical issues that captured Du Chatelet's imagination and shaped her *Institutions*. The original dispute began in 1686—that fateful year once again—when Leibniz published an essay in the scholarly journal *Acta Eruditorum* proclaiming an "error" of the Cartesian philosophy of nature. What was the error?

In his main contribution to physics, the *Principles of Philosophy* of 1644, Descartes had argued that there was a certain amount of motion in the world, that all physical interactions in nature involve the transfer of this motion, and that motion is conserved overall. No new motion could be created or lost. Descartes defended an austere version of the mechanical philosophy: nature consisted only of material particles characterized by size, shape, and motion. He argued that the quantity of motion in the world is measured by "volume x speed." Something like a billiard ball will have a certain volume, and as it moves across the pool table, its quantity of motion is measured by that volume multiplied by its speed. Since Descartes was a mechanist, he thought that all natural phenomena involve the impacts of material particles on one another. Countless tiny little particles, like little billiard balls, all with certain volumes and speeds, collide and create the incredible variety found throughout nature.

In his short paper of March 1686, Leibniz's criticism of the Cartesians is reasonably straightforward.[23] He argues that Cartesian physics had not absorbed the implications of Galileo's important experimental work from decades earlier. If one considers Galileo's free fall experiments, they show that the Cartesian quantity "volume x speed" is not what is conserved in nature. Consider two bodies: a one-pound body that must be raised four feet, and a four-pound body that must be raised one foot. The bodies are considered otherwise identical. Leibniz argued that the same force is required to raise these two bodies off the ground; he thought that force should be estimated by the effect it causes, in this case, raising a body off the ground. But do they have the same quantity of motion when they are dropped? They do not: one body's volume is larger than the other's even if their speeds are the same. So the quantity of motion is one thing, the quantity of force another. Finally, Leibniz argued that the quantity of force, measured by volume x speed^2, and not the quantity of motion, is conserved in nature. The idea was that speed^2 reflected Galileo's experiments on the acceleration of falling bodies. In this first essay, which Leibniz titled a "Brief Demonstration," he does not yet mention *vis viva* or the various metaphysical aspects of force that he would introduce into the discussion later. But he expressed what he took to be Descartes's basic error.

For a contemporary reader, Descartes's views and Leibniz's criticisms of them are bound to be confusing. Why did Descartes focus on *volume* as matter's important feature? Why focus on speed, rather than velocity (a scalar rather than a vector quantity)? And what did Leibniz mean by "force" if he wasn't using "f = ma" or the like? What kind of force was he talking about? He speaks of bodies as having weight, which is different from volume, but how did he understand that idea without using mass? The whole thing is a mess.

Coincidentally, at this very same moment, the other great mathematician of this era in European history was hoping to clear up that mess. Right when Leibniz published his article in March of 1686, Isaac Newton was furiously finishing his magnum opus. Just months after Leibniz published his criticism of Descartes, Newton's *Principia* challenged the dominance of Cartesian physics in an even more profound way. Like his German counterpart, Newton thought that Descartes had presented an overly austere mechanistic conception of nature, failing to recognize the importance of forces in his physics. But unlike Leibniz, Newton argued that entirely new concepts were required; one could not settle for discovering errors within Cartesian physics. Whereas Leibniz had put new wine into old Cartesian bottles, Newton threw out the bottles and began anew.

In the period 1684–86, as Newton wrote successive drafts of what would become the *Principia* after Haley's fateful visit to his rooms in Cambridge, he struggled to overcome what he saw as the limitations of conceiving of bodies as bearing volume or bulk (*moles* in Latin). The former was useless for physics, he thought, and the latter pretty obscure. There was no settled way of measuring the bulk of a body: one could weigh things, but mechanists insisted that weight and free fall were due to mechanisms pushing things downward, so what precisely *was* bulk? Newton decided a novel concept was needed. The idea of *mass* was born. Newton presented mass as a dynamical quality—a measure of a body's resistance to acceleration—to replace the old mechanical qualities of volume and bulk. He also noted that mass is always proportional to weight, but distinct from it, so one could measure an object's mass by weighing it. Since acceleration can involve a change in speed or a change in direction, Newton also replaced the scalar quantity *speed* with the vectorial quantity *velocity*. Whereas Leibniz had settled for fixing an error within Descartes's thought, Newton's work overthrew it. A revolution indeed.

After Newton sent Leibniz a presentation copy of his *Principia*, the great German mathematician read the text with interest while traveling in Italy in 1688, taking notes and pondering its implications. We would expect that Leibniz would respond to Newton in the form of a long treatise in physics of his own—he would surely have named such a treatise *Dynamics*, a word he himself coined. But he never did, he was too busy with numerous other tasks. The lack of a treatise in physics by the co-discoverer of the calculus is one of the greatest lacunae of the Scientific Revolution. As a result, scholars must piece together Leibniz's complex views in physics from manuscripts, fragments, correspondence, and the occasional article.

In 1695, Leibniz published another such article in his favored journal, the *Acta Eruditorum*, calling it the "Specimen Dynamicum." The title was apt: he was developing a dynamics, but for now would provide merely a sample of it. The essay revived and extended his criticism of the Cartesians from 1686, but now Leibniz presented his ideas in a post-*Principia* environment. Unsurprisingly, he emphasizes his continuing rejection of the Cartesian idea of the quantity of motion. Intriguingly, he *also* notes some agreements with Newton. In particular, he writes of the law of inertia: "Since this law does not derive from the notion of bulk [*moles*], it is necessary that it follow from something else inherent in bodies, indeed from force itself, which always maintains its same quantity even if realized in different bodies." The implication seems to be that Newton had made an advance over Descartes by speaking of the force of inertia, something "inherent in bodies" in virtue of which they follow the laws of motion. Leibniz then emphasizes the importance of explaining the motions of bodies "through the notion of forces," a task he began in 1686, and one heartily endorsed by Newton as well.[24] Leibniz may not have endorsed all of the implications of Newton's new concept of mass, but he appreciated the notion of the force of inertia and sought common ground when he could.[25] This episode occurred years before his vociferous dispute with Newton and his supporters.

Leibniz then recast his debate with the Cartesians by expanding his discussion of the forces of nature. He proposed that we call the preserved quantity *volume x speed*^{2} a measurement of living force, or "vis viva." He distinguished between "living force," which is exhibited by bodies in motion, and "dead force," which bodies exhibit when not moving. The metaphysics of forces in Leibniz is extraordinarily complex and the province of scholars. The key point here is that even after reading the *Principia*, Leibniz was perfectly clear that his notion of *vis viva* was not intended as a disagreement with Newton. Moreover, despite their numerous other disagreements—concerning space and time, gravity, vortices, the mechanical philosophy—Newton himself concurred with that point of view. Although the *Principia* went through two more editions after Leibniz published his thoughts on dynamics, Newton remained silent on the *vis viva* debate in all editions of the *Principia*. He never addressed the "quantity of force" in Leibniz's sense or the *vis viva* dispute.[26] (Unlike many of her peers, including most prominently Voltaire, Du Châtelet herself appreciated that point.)[27] That fact may reflect Newton's broader views: he was not especially interested in conservation principles, and he attached little significance to the fact that in his system what we now call momentum, which he defined as the "quantity of motion," is conserved.[28] He did not use this notion to enter the long-standing *vis viva* debate.[29] Throughout his long life, Newton simply ignored *vis viva*.

History is full of ironies. Although Newton himself showed no interest in the *vis viva* debate, his physics muddied the waters for many later discussions of *vis viva*. Indeed, nearly every article written on *vis viva* today views the debate through a post-*Principia* lens. Scholars typically declare that the dispute was between Descartes's view that the quantity of motion can be measured by *mv* and Leibniz's view that it is measured instead by *mv²*. *But in fact, both ideas are confusions.* Descartes analyzed matter in terms of speed and volume, not mass and velocity, and Leibniz explicitly employed Cartesian terminology, noting only the importance of using speed^2. In 1686, Newton was still finishing the *Principia* when Leibniz published his essay on Cartesian errors. The concept of mass had literally not been invented yet.

Alas, anachronism begets anachronism. Since Leibniz is said (anachronistically) to have argued that *mv²* is conserved, some contemporary scholars ask: why not go further and note that he came close to finding the formula for kinetic energy? After all, "K = ½ mv²" is *pretty close* to Leibniz's formulation, we are told.[30] This is a serious mistake. In the seventeenth century, the concept of energy had not been formulated yet; energy conservation was not discovered until the nineteenth century. Indeed, no Enlightenment figure even had the concept of energy. Reading historical figures through the lens of *where scientific research eventually ended up*, long after they had died, dooms us to confusion.[31] These anachronisms prevent scholars from grasping the debate: they sometimes note that Descartes's "*mv*" is akin to the modern law of the conservation of momentum, and Leibniz's "*mv²*" to a modern expression of the conservation of energy, so why didn't they realize that both sides were right?[32] A question expressing confusion, one better left unanswered.

The twist in the story is that these anachronistic understandings of the history of science actually began during the Enlightenment itself. They were not merely envisioned by later scholarship. And once again, discipleship, that leading bogeyman of Du Châtelet's thought, played a key role.

For Leibniz and Newton, it was perfectly clear that they were not disagreeing about *vis viva*. However, Newton's disciple Samuel Clarke had other ideas. At first, Clarke tried to entice Leibniz into a dispute over *vis viva* in their celebrated correspondence from 1715–16. But Leibniz ignored the bait. Writing just before he died in November of 1716, Leibniz sought peace on *vis viva* with the Newtonians. In §99 of his fifth and last letter, he notes that this is not the place to discuss "my dynamics (ma Dynamique)," then adds that he *agrees* with Newton's remarks in Query 31 to the *Opticks*, and finally concludes by saying that he has shown elsewhere that there is "a difference between the quantity of motion and the quantity of force," a reference to his old dispute with the Cartesians.[33]

But Clarke would not drop the issue. In a note appended to §99 of his last letter to Leibniz, he interprets the *Specimen* as indicating that Leibniz ignores the fact that the quantity of motion is measured by mv rather than mv^2.[34] So Clarke inserts the Newtonian idea of the quantity of motion into the debate between the Cartesians and the Leibnizians concerning *vis viva*. This involves a confusion. It should have been clear to Clarke that Leibniz was presenting an argument against the Cartesian view, which involves a body's volume or bulk, and not against the Newtonian view, which involves a body's mass.[35]

The confusion worsened after Leibniz's death in November 1716. At that time, he still had many supporters in Continental Europe, including the famous Swiss mathematician Johann Bernoulli, who Mairan later criticized and Du Châtelet defended. And in 1728, after both Newton and Leibniz had passed on, Clarke published an article in the *Philosophical Transactions of the Royal Society*, trying to bring Leibniz into a dispute with Newton, *après la lettre*. Clarke argued that Leibniz's arguments for *vis viva* were false because Newton's measurement of the quantity of motion was actually the correct value.[36] Clarke confused his readers into thinking that Leibniz's beef with Descartes was somehow really a beef with Newton. This may be the reason that subsequent interpreters nearly always said that the dispute involves "*mv vs. mv²*." The reason is that "mv" is the correct Newtonian measurement of the quantity of motion (what we call momentum). But that idea was never dreamed of in Descartes's philosophy. Indeed, Descartes died while visiting Queen Christina in Sweden in 1650 when Newton was just a little boy.

However, Clarke was not alone. And once again, Voltaire played an outsized role in developing a dominant narrative of what happened during the Scientific Revolution. Although Clarke's own publication in the *Philosophical Transactions* was obscure, not least because it was in English, his new friend Voltaire, who was visiting England when Clarke wrote his piece, adopted his perspective. In the chapter on "active force" in his *Elements of the Philosophy of Newton*, published ten years after Clarke's article, Voltaire presents Clarke's view that the *vis viva* dispute somehow divides Leibniz's ideas about force from Newton's. He presents Clarke's understanding in detail, recasting the entire *vis viva* debate so thoroughly that he ends up listing Newton along with Descartes and the Cartesians as thinking that "mass x velocity (masse x vitesse)" is the right measure.[37] In part through Voltaire's extremely influential work, Clarke's mischaracterization of the dispute spread far and wide.

These twists and turns of history help to highlight the distinctiveness of Du Châtelet's approach in the *Institutions*. Despite Voltaire's attempt to enlist her in the Newtonian cause, going so far as to address her directly by saying that the choice between Leibniz and Newton is "up to you,"[38] Du Châtelet rejects his approach. As with so many other important philosophical issues, she does not endorse Voltaire's perspective, which involves a creative blending of Clarke and Newton. She recognizes instead that Voltaire and Clarke have mischaracterized the *vis viva* dispute. But more important, she also recognizes the implications of a proper characterization of that dispute: since Leibniz's debate with Descartes involved Cartesian terminology that Newton eschewed, might it be possible to endorse both *vis viva* and some of Newton's views? Clearly, Clarke and Voltaire did not think so. But other philosophers—most prominently the Dutch thinker Willem s'Gravesande and Du Châtelet herself—thought it was.[39] As always, Du Châtelet's overarching approach is to reduce potential conflicts whenever possible.

If we read Du Châtelet's *Institutions* with this point in mind, we find a clear indication at the beginning of the very first chapter that one could in fact endorse both one of Newton's most important ideas of force, and also one of Leibniz's.[40] She first describes Descartes's mistake in thinking that the essence of body lies in extension alone, and then adds this pithy remark about her French predecessor. He[41]

> believed that in extension he had a clear and distinct idea of body, without bothering to prove the possibility of this idea that we will soon see to be very incomplete, since to it must be added the force of inertia and the active force (*force vive*).

Right at the outset, then, Du Châtelet emphasizes that both Newton's idea of mass (called here the force of inertia) *and* Leibniz's active force represent responses to the inadequacy of Cartesian physics. For her, bodies resist changes in their states of motion (the force of inertia), but they also exhibit active force when they are in motion. Both notions are required to explain the various phenomena found in nature. Although Leibniz's views conflict with Descartes's, they do not conflict with Newton's. In placing this comment at the beginning of her text, she signals that her dispute with Mairan concerns the inadequacy of Cartesian ideas and should not be read as involving Newton's views at all. Clarke and Voltaire were wrong.

Du Châtelet returns to the question of *vis viva* at the end of her *Institutions*, where she warns that we should avoid becoming swept away on speculative winds. In one of the last sections of her long book (1742, §570), she writes that the forces of nature cannot be handled solely through metaphysical notions without a practical dimension. She advises us that to understand any force, we must propose a means of measuring it through its effects, say through what resists it, or perhaps through what it displaces. This idea obviously applies to "living force," where bodies fall to the ground or collide, but it also holds of "dead force," where we consider, e.g., the pressure that a candlestick exerts while resting on a table. We know there is such a pressure because if the table were removed, the candlestick would fall to the ground. This overarching approach coheres with Newton's own emphasis on measuring forces.[42]

Narrow interpretations of the *Institutions* present Du Châtelet as a "Leibnizian" because she defended *vis viva*. But this misses the point. At a deeper level, she shows how Voltaire's zeal to follow in Clarke's footsteps as a disciple of Newton led him to mischaracterize the *vis viva* dispute in the first place. Once again, discipleship distorts philosophy.

When we jettison narrow readings of the *Institutions*, insisting that we read the text on its own terms without the distorting lenses of "Newtonianism" and "Leibnizianism," something else emerges from all of Du Chatelet's comments about forces. Not only has she found commonalities underlying various debates about force, she has said something new about the relation between science and philosophy. In the discussion of the forces of nature, we encounter her argument that metaphysics must accommodate itself to physics. We may be inspired by one of the greatest metaphysicians of the seventeenth century to embrace living forces, but she warns us that any notion of force must be useable by the physicist. And that requires, in turn, that we consider how such forces might be measured. At the

end of her text, then, Du Châtelet suggests an intriguing collabora-
tion between these two disciplines. Ending her text with a revival of
the *vis viva* dispute is especially apt because she had viewed matter
through the lens of forces earlier in her text. She understood that
underlying their many disagreements, both Newton and Leibniz
had reacted to Cartesian physics by proclaiming that the mechanical philosophy was too restricted, that forces must be added to our
conception of nature. So even when agreeing with Leibniz's famous
idea of *vis viva*, Du Châtelet avoided becoming his disciple by finding common ground between him and his great rival Newton. She
stayed true to her philosophical perspective and pushed her readers
to adopt a pluralistic attitude themselves.

The *vis viva* debate may now be irrelevant to science, but Du
Châtelet's lesson is not: one must avoid using a partisan lens through
which to view a dispute. Even today, anachronistic castings of *vis
viva* try to make it relevant by saying that they were really talking
about something a lot like kinetic energy, which distorts the historical facts. That idea involves reading history backwards through
concepts from *our* science. The right way to make this old debate
relevant is to follow Du Châtelet's lead. What was really interesting about the dispute is not its precise details—which involved
considerable repetition and lots of talking past one another, as
D'Alembert later emphasized—but rather the fact that partisanship
had distorted a debate in science. And that distortion, it turns out,
lasted for generations.

The *vis viva* dispute beautifully encapsulated everything Du
Châtelet needed. It was a heated topic that enabled her to break
through one last institutional barrier, ensnaring the secretary of the
Academy of Sciences in a debate; a dispute whose broad appeal to
philosophes would ensure the wide circulation of her ideas; and, an
argument that reflected her deep and abiding interest in the relation between science and philosophy. Perhaps one more chance to
disagree with Voltaire publicly on a key philosophical issue of the
day was just icing on the cake.

Du Châtelet in the "Supreme Text of the Enlightenment"

Du Châtelet's masterwork, including her dispute with Dortous de Mairan, ensured that her ideas would circulate in Enlightenment academic life for years. But incredibly enough, that was just the beginning. After holding her well-publicized debate with the secretary of the Paris Academy, she also caught the attention of the soon-to-be-appointed secretary of the Berlin Academy of Sciences. Indeed, he would quickly become one of her biggest fans. That secretary was a French-speaking member of a Huguenot refugee family living in Prussia named Jean-Henri Samuel Formey. Born in Berlin in 1711, Formey lived a very long life there, dying in 1797. Formey was not merely an extraordinarily prolific author; he was also an avid and prolific correspondent. It is sometimes claimed that his correspondence was like a Republic of Letters unto itself. And he lived for so long that Voltaire called him the "eternal" secretary of the Academy.[43]

First envisioned by Leibniz at the end of the seventeenth century, who surely had his eye on London and Paris, the Berlin Academy was restructured and revived in 1744 after Frederick II had become the Prussian leader following his father's death a few years earlier. Although Frederick and Formey were never close, unlike Voltaire and others in Du Châtelet's immediate circle, the new leader ensured that Formey would enjoy a long reign as a key academic figure in Berlin. And he was perfectly suited to the role: rather than developing his own philosophical positions, Formey was content to use his publications, and his role as secretary of the Academy, to promote some of the latest ideas circulating in Europe at the time. He was especially enamored of the ideas of Christian Wolff, the most prominent follower of Leibniz during the German Enlightenment.[44] Indeed, one of Formey's more important publications was his six-volume philosophical work *La belle Wolfienne*—the title signaled that Wolff's philosophy was for women as well as men.

In this text, he hoped to popularize Wolff's thought in the way that Algarotti and Voltaire had popularized Newton's.[45] And like those other savants, Formey was also a keen follower of Du Châtelet's philosophy.

Formey is a bit of a paradoxical figure. As the secretary of the Berlin Academy, and as one of the most prolific correspondents of the entire eighteenth century,[46] he was at the center of academic life in the Enlightenment. Indeed, his academic work and correspondence were part of the lifeblood of the movement. Yet he was no *philosophe*. Indeed, he opposed many of the Enlightenment's household names: he thought Voltaire was a blowhard, he regarded Rousseau's ideas as dangerous, and he looked askance at Diderot's flirtation with atheism. Indeed, Formey wrote a tract against Rousseau entitled "Anti-Émile" and a refutation of Diderot entitled *Rational Thoughts Opposed to "Philosophical Thoughts,"* using the title of one of Diderot's controversial texts. He was fighting something of a rearguard action, and his book titles were not particularly imaginative.[47] Formey took many of the *philosophes* to be impious, even heretical, in their criticisms of traditional religion and morals, regarding deism as especially dangerous.[48] Perhaps this is not surprising: Formey was the pastor of a famous French reformed church in Berlin.[49] So he was a conservative thinker, in the literal and original sense of the word. But for all that, he was not a reactionary. He still promoted the Enlightenment and sought enlightened women for readers. So his was a conservative Enlightenment: he wished to spread the gospel of the new science and philosophy, but not at the expense of the original gospel.

Once again, history is replete with ironies. Formey's intellectual conservatism is especially surprising because he was in fact the figure who helped to begin what would later become Diderot's most famous project. That project, an encyclopedic presentation of Enlightenment knowledge, would end up promoting the ideas of Voltaire and Rousseau and many of the other *philosophes* Formey disdained. The great "Encyclopedia" of Diderot and D'Alembert, known to every student of the Enlightenment, was actually begun by Formey several years before Diderot adopted the project as general editor in the summer of 1747.[50]

In 1742, Formey decided to transcend the bounds of academic life by embarking on a major publication project. He admired the Scottish author Ephraim Chambers's famous *Cyclopeadia, or Universal Dictionary of the Arts and Sciences* (1728), but it was in English, an obscure language at the time. So with Chambers's work as a model, Formey envisioned an encyclopedia in the scholarly language of French, one that would promote the wide range of new ideas spreading through Europe.[51] Formey drafted more than 100 entries for the new encyclopedia,[52] borrowing heavily from the work of leading philosophers of the day, including his beloved Wolff. That was perhaps to be expected: he did not regard these establishment figures as impious or radical; they could eventually serve as the common nodes of his moderate version of the Enlightenment and of Diderot's more controversial, not to say scandalous, version.

Formey's work has long since been overshadowed by the more famous efforts of Diderot and D'Alembert in creating the *Encyclopedia*, but he helped to shape it in one key respect. Nothing about Formey's profile could prepare us for his most consequential decision in drafting entries for the projected encyclopedia. Indeed, his own earlier writings make the choice all the more striking. Despite the fact that he himself had authored a multi-volume work on Wolff's philosophy, when Formey wrote about topics that are bread and butter within philosophy, such as the principle of contradiction, or the principle of sufficient reason, he ignored Wolff and chose instead to borrow heavily from the work of a French author. Indeed, he did not merely borrow, he copied verbatim, from Du Châtelet's *Institutions of Physics*. Several other philosophers also did so for their own texts.[53] In more than a dozen entries, Formey copied directly from her text, totaling thousands of words.

Formey's choice to copy from Du Châtelet was consequential, but also perplexing. Why did he copy from *her* work? Not only had

Formey himself written on many Wolffian topics at considerable length, but he also read German, a rarity for scholars in that time, which meant that he could read all of Wolff's massive corpus in the original.[54] Wolff was famous for having produced a series of German works early in his career, including a physics text and a book on metaphysics, before switching to Latin to reach a wider scholarly audience. So why not copy directly from Wolff himself, translating his ideas into French, as Formey had done in *La belle Wolfienne*? Why use Du Châtelet's words over and over?[55] Did he think that her views were superior to Wolff's? Whatever the reason, his decision gave Du Châtelet's main work a striking prominence in the new encyclopedia, which grew to become a groundbreaking compendium of Enlightenment knowledge. Indeed, it has a claim to being the most important text of the era.

Formey appreciated the wide range of topics in Du Châtelet's *Institutions*. As is appropriate for a wide-ranging text, Formey used the *Institutions* both for his general discussions of metaphysics and for his discussions in physics. In the philosophical areas, he employed Du Châtelet's ideas, and often her exact words, when writing the entries on the law of continuity, space, time, the principle of sufficient reason, the principle of contradiction, hypotheses, and God. The last entry is especially significant because Formey was not merely an academic but also a religious figure.[56] He followed the same pattern in physics when treating velocity, the pendulum, divisibility, motion, rest, and gravity.[57] These were central topics from the revolution in physics fomented by figures like Galileo, Huygens, and Newton. Roughly half the time, Formey acknowledged Du Chatelet's work, citing or mentioning the *Institutions*; roughly half the time, the extensive copying remained secret.[58] So, readers of Formey's entries would sometimes know that he was employing the work of a woman who had just published a treatise on the foundations of physics, but often they would not. This gave Du Châtelet a paradoxical status in the *Encyclopedia*: she was its most prominent woman, but was denied full recognition at the very same time.

Formey began the *Encyclopedia*, but he certainly did not finish it. His overarching philosophical and theological orientation would soon be eclipsed by Diderot's. Just as Formey was no fan of the *philosophes*, Diderot thought Formey was too conservative and insufficiently ambitious.[59] Although he and D'Alembert originally conceived of the text much as Formey had—as a kind of French version of Chambers—they soon transcended that notion.[60] In the end, the project expanded to include seventeen volumes in the first Paris edition, with more than 130 contributors and an incredible 74,000 entries. Diderot filled the *Encyclopedia* with the ideas of the very *philosophes* who Formey thought were too strident in their criticisms of the established social order. He had also explicitly dethroned theology from its perch as the "queen of the sciences," which was anathema for a pastor like Formey.[61] This should not surprise us: although it certainly became Diderot's project, with D'Alembert playing a leading role early on, the *Encyclopedia* was not a symphony; it included a cacophony of voices. It represented both the "radical" Enlightenment of figures like Voltaire, Diderot, and Rousseau, but also the "moderate" Enlightenment of figures like Formey and Wolff. And it prominently included the thought of Émilie Du Châtelet.

It is remarkable that despite their sharply divergent intellectual perspectives, Formey, Diderot, and D'Alembert all agreed that the more than a dozen entries containing extensive passages from Du Chatelet's *Institutions* would remain untouched in the published version of the *Encyclopedia*. They agreed on little else, but all of these figures concurred that her work was authoritative in these areas and therefore ought to be represented in the discussions of a wide range of topics in physics and metaphysics. Indeed, Du Châtelet's work was one of the main sources for D'Alembert's many scientific and philosophical entries in the *Encyclopedia*. However, like Formey, he acknowledged her work only intermittently.[62] This decision had profound consequences. The *Encyclopedia* was famously presented as the work of a "society of men of letters." With more than 130 contributors, only one was a woman, the Marquise de Jaucourt, and her essay concerned fashion.[63] Moreover, the entire *Encyclopedia* contained only one entry on a "women's" profession, namely, midwifery. Ironically enough, Diderot simply wrote that article himself.[64] Readers would encounter Du Chatelet's ideas and arguments more than a dozen times in reading the *Encyclopedia*, but she often received no acknowledgment. What recognition she did receive was clearly not enough to change the title to a "society of women and men of letters." And yet at the same time, she was surely the most prominent woman in the entire *Encyclopedia*, itself the most prominent text of the whole Enlightenment. A paradoxical status indeed.

Once again, anachronism can hamper understanding. Undoubtedly, today's readers will be outraged at Formey's plagiarism. How could he have stolen her ideas, using them for his own entries without acknowledging her work? How could Diderot and D'Alembert have gone along with it? Today, charges of plagiarism can end a career. Without reflexively defending Formey, Diderot, and D'Alembert, we must also avoid interpreting their decision to copy Du Châtelet's ideas through an anachronistic lens. The eighteenth century did not have our notions of copyright and intellectual property. So we can be outraged at the plagiarism of Du Châtelet's thought, but we should do so in a historically accurate way.

Now, this is not to say that the notion of plagiarism had not been formulated in the Enlightenment. Far from it. Diderot himself was accused of plagiarizing Bacon's ideas for the famous Prospectus to the *Encyclopedia*; he and D'Alembert were accused of stealing Chambers's ideas from his *Cyclopaedia*; and Diderot, in turn, accused his friend Condorcet of stealing his ideas about perception.[65] Indeed, numerous charges of intellectual theft were made among academicians at this time.[66] It is more accurate to say that our present-day intellectual norms had not yet been fully codified, legally or academically. This fact is evident in the wide range of texts involving a mélange of ideas from disparate figures, a practice that was well established before the *Encyclopedia* made it a central aspect of the Enlightenment's dissemination of knowledge.

Today, we have anthologies in which each chapter has been carefully checked for copyright infringement, or permission has been secured from the relevant copyright holder. Similarly, our translations carefully respect the original text. But during the Enlightenment, numerous kinds of text were published that would be unethical or even illegal today. For instance, Samuel Clarke appended a series of "Newtonian" notes to Jacques Rohault's avowedly Cartesian physics text when it was translated into Latin and published early in the Enlightenment. The French translation of Algarotti's *Newtonianism for the Ladies* contained anti-Newton remarks added by the translator, which amused Du Châtelet and Voltaire. Algarotti even challenged his translator to a duel! But he was not alone. Many eighteenth-century translators, including Du Châtelet herself, would modify their source texts, excising entire chapters and inventing others whole-cloth.[67] The famous Jesuits Le Seur and Jacquier appended Leibnizian-inspired ideas to their edition of Newton's *Principia*.[68] Finally, and most importantly, the encyclopedists borrowed and even copied from numerous sources, sometimes with acknowledgment, often without. Montesquieu was copied liberally in many articles of the *Encyclopedia*, as was Locke, often anonymously.[69] So Du Châtelet was in excellent company.

But she also lacked company. In her case alone, acknowledgment of her contributions could have altered the Enlightenment's notion of the "men of letters" who promoted the latest science and philosophy. Montesquieu was unquestionably a member of the Republic of Letters, so borrowing from his work without acknowledgment merely circulated his ideas further, it did not threaten to undermine his status as a thinker. The same is true of Voltaire's *Philosophical Letters*, which was apparently copied without acknowledgment because of its controversial nature. His status as a leading *philosophe* had already been established. The same cannot be said of Du Châtelet and her *Institutions*. Neither Formey, nor Diderot, nor D'Alembert seemed alive to this point. At the same time, there is no doubt that publishing long sections from Du Châtelet's *Institutions* in the most famous text of the Enlightenment enabled her ideas to circulate in a way that no other woman's ideas did at that time. Her ideas traveled in that text just as those of the leading *philosophes* did, including Voltaire, Montesquieu, and Rousseau, not to mention Diderot and D'Alembert themselves. Yet we must also acknowledge that full recognition of her ideas could have greatly expanded her reputation.

Just as we should not impose our legal or ethical notions of copyright on these figures, we should not be too hasty in thinking that each signed or attributed article in the *Encyclopedia* reflected solely the ideas of its author. It was not just that the *Encyclopedia* represented a huge range of voices,[70] even its constituent articles included cacophonies. To have one's ideas copied verbatim in the *Encyclopedia* is undoubtedly to have received a high level of recognition, to have one's ideas certified as authoritative on a given subject. But that does not mean that the author of the entry in which they appeared actually *endorsed* all of them. Diderot and D'Alembert adopted many of Formey's entries, but Diderot for his part lamented Formey's philosophy.[71] So, in using Du Chatelet's words and ideas, Formey, Diderot, and D'Alembert placed her into the center of major discussions in Enlightenment Europe in exactly the same way that they did with the ideas of men in their milieu. She was part of the conversation that made the Enlightenment thrive.

For his part, Diderot disagreed quite profoundly with Du Châtelet on basic philosophical issues. For instance, the anonymously written *Encyclopedia* article on sufficient reason contains passages from her *Institutions* that comprise an incredible 87% of the total article. In a surprising twist, however, the published article ends with a paragraph that questions the use of sufficient reason on the grounds that it can lead to Spinozism. That last sentiment certainly did not reflect Du Châtelet's view, for she had made extensive use of the principle of sufficient reason throughout her *Institutions*. Most likely, this final paragraph was written by Diderot himself, who was known to be skeptical of the principle.[72] Here we find a debate within an entry in the *Encyclopedia* between the editor-in-chief and Du Châtelet on a central topic of philosophy at the time. Far from undermining Du Châtelet, this kind of dispute is the lifeblood of the whole philosophical movement of the Enlightenment. To be part of the Republic of Letters is not to participate in widespread agreement; it is to be included in its often lively debates. Indeed, Diderot and D'Alembert conceived of the *Encyclopedia* project in differing ways, and D'Alembert eventually left the project in Diderot's hands.[73] This disagreement about a fundamental philosophical principle, then, served to include Du Châtelet in the Republic. And yet at the same time, the anonymity of the entry may have ensured that the *Encyclopedia's* readers were unaware of her membership. These twists and turns in Du Châtelet's reception can be dizzying at times.

As it turns out, Diderot's dispute with Du Châtelet was not an isolated case. In fact, her ideas were often subject to substantive debate within the *Encyclopedia's* complex structure. In one important case, a subtle, three-way debate emerges between Du Châtelet, D'Alembert, and Formey. D'Alembert was typically less confrontational about his disagreements with other authors than his colleague Diderot, but he was not averse to inserting his own remarks into an article.[74] This debate begins with Du Châtelet's *Institutions*. In her chapter on space, she expresses her characteristic view that many topics, including essences and the nature of space and time, concern the intersection of physics and metaphysics. She opens her chapter on space as follows (Du Châtelet, *Institutions*, 1742, §72):

> The question of the nature of space is one of the most famous that has divided ancient and modern philosophers; it is also one of the most essential because of its influence on the most important truths of physics and metaphysics.

Formey adopted this opening paragraph, modifying it ever so slightly for his entry on space (*Encyclopédie*, vol. 5: 949):

> The question of the nature of space is one of the most famous that has divided ancient and modern philosophers; it is also one of the most essential because of its influence on the most important truths of metaphysics.

By removing the word "physics," Formey does not merely tell readers of the *Encyclopedia* that the nature of space is an issue in metaphysics alone; he excises the characteristic view in the *Institutions* concerning the relations between the two fields.

In the next move in the dialectic, D'Alembert expresses dissatisfaction with Formey's removal of physics from the debate, but he also wishes to denigrate metaphysics. So at the end of the entry "Space," D'Alembert added this remark, employing the royal "we" as editor:

> This article is taken from the papers of Mr. Formey, who composed it in part from the *Collection of Letters* of Clarke, Leibniz and Newton (Amsterdam, 1740) and the *Inst. De Physique* of Madame du Châtelet. We will not take sides on the question of space; we can see by everything that has been said in the entry "Elements of Sciences" how this obscure question is useless in geometry and in physics. See also Time, Extension, Motion, Place, Vacuum, Body, etc.[75]

From Du Châtelet's view that questions about the nature of space are relevant in both physics and metaphysics we proceed to Formey's view that only metaphysics is relevant, concluding with D'Alembert's rebuke of such questions altogether. We know that it was D'Alembert who added this final comment in the article because it explicitly refers to the discussion in the "Elements of Science" article, perhaps his most famous contribution to the whole *Encyclopedia*.[76]

D'Alembert and especially Diderot intended their readers to follow these threads from entry to entry, cutting across the alphabetization, but also the intellectual domains, that comprise the overall text of the massive *Encyclopedia*. At times, these cross-references are sarcastic, subversive, even heretical. Famously, Diderot tells readers of the "Eucharist" entry to read "Cannibalism."[77] (Formey would have been aghast.) But in other instances, they form an argumentative thread. D'Alembert informs readers of the "Space" entry that his "Elements" article establishes that the questions about space addressed by these various philosophers are useless to geometry and physics. So of course, we must then investigate the "Elements of Science" entry. There, D'Alembert writes (*Encyclopédie*, vol. 5: 493):

> In the sciences there are other contested questions, less frivolous in themselves perhaps, but just as useless, that should be absolutely banned from a book on the *elements*. One can judge with certainty the absolute uselessness of a question on whose propositions philosophers agree, but which at first glance would seem to derive necessarily from that question. For example, the *elements* of Geometry and of calculus are the same for all the schools of philosophy; it follows from this agreement that geometrical truths do not depend upon contested principles on the nature of extension, and that on this matter there is a common point where all the sects unite.

Alas, here the industrious reader comes up short. We had previously read that debates about "the nature of space" involving figures like Leibniz, Clarke, Newton, and Du Châtelet are useless in geometry and physics, but here only geometry and calculus are mentioned; physics has dropped out. It is indeed reasonable to think that when analyzing a geometric figure, proving a theorem, or finding the equation for a curve, one can ignore the question of whether space is independent of matter. Du Châtelet might even agree with that point. But as D'Alembert knew full well, various philosophers, like

Euler, had argued that physics requires us to conceive of space as independent of matter (as "absolute," in Newton's terminology). So, we are left wondering why D'Alembert thinks that within *physics* one can ignore questions about the "nature of space" that are raised, e.g., by the application of the laws of motion.

Although the remainder of D'Alembert's most famous entry does not answer this specific question about physics, it does exhibit how he engages in a dialogue with Du Châtelet's *Institutions*. This is understandable if we remember that the French term *institutions* in this day could mean either *foundations* or *elements*—indeed, at times Du Châtelet called her text "elements of physics"—and if we also recall that physics was often taken just to mean science in general.[78] Hence, to speak of the *institutions of physics* was close to speaking of the *elements of science*. At first, D'Alembert presents the following conception (*Encyclopédie*, vol. 5: 492):

> If we limit ourselves here to some general rules, which are those principles in each science that provide the point of departure? Those simple facts, clearly observed and generally accepted: in physics the observation of the universe, in geometry the principal properties of extension, in mechanics the impenetrability of bodies, in metaphysics and ethics the study of our soul and its affections, and so on for the others. I take metaphysics here in the most rigorous sense it can have, since it is the science of purely spiritual beings.

D'Alembert thinks that physics and mechanics need not consider the "principal properties of extension," nor need they intersect in any way with metaphysics. The contrast with Du Châtelet's view was clear. Whereas she had presented a conception of the harmony between physics and metaphysics, D'Alembert presented them as distinct sciences that operate with distinct principles. Metaphysics here is no more connected with physics than ethics is.

But the dialogue continues. Next, D'Alembert considers the consequence of construing "metaphysics" differently than in the "rigorous" sense noted above:

> What I say here will be even more true when one regards metaphysics in a wider sense, as the universal science which contains the principles of all the others, for if each science has, and can only have, observation for its true principles, the metaphysics of each science can consist only of general consequences that result from observation, presented from the widest point of view possible. Thus even though, against my intention, I might shock some people whose zeal for metaphysics is more ardent than enlightened, I shall take care not to define it according to their wishes as *the science of ideas,* for what would such a science be? Philosophy, whatever its object, is either the science of facts or that of chimeras. Indeed it would be a vague and quite inaccurate idea about Philosophy to believe it is destined to lose itself in abstractions, in the general properties of being and in those of mode and substance.

For D'Alembert, we may take metaphysics to concern the study of the soul, and therefore to be entirely distinct from the sciences, or we may regard it as a more general investigation of the consequences of various sciences. Either way, he believes, the metaphysics of substances, modes, and accidents will be irrelevant to the development of science. With this argument, he directly disputes Du Châtelet's conception of science in the *Institutions*, for she had argued precisely that an analysis of essences is important for physics because it is necessary to clarify the science of gravity. Her insight is to show that the metaphysics of essences is not concerned with mere "abstractions" but in fact enables the philosopher to analyze a key problem from physics, namely, whether gravity is essential to matter. That was one of her distinctive contributions.

For D'Alembert, when we analyze the "elements of science" we must confront the question of which principles will guide science. In a nod to one of Euler's concerns, D'Alembert says that mechanics will have the "impenetrability of bodies" as its principle. But as Euler understood, we must also consider the question of how metaphysics is related to the sciences; this is true not least because previous thinkers like Descartes had argued that metaphysics provides some of the key principles of physics. D'Alembert then argues that whether we take metaphysics in a strict sense—as the science of the soul—or in a more general sense, we must realize that it is irrelevant to the various sciences, such as mechanics or physics. He is thereby tackling Du Châtelet's contention that when we construe metaphysics in a general way, considering basic concepts like substance and essence, we aid physics.

Here we see D'Alembert insisting that regardless of what we might mean by metaphysics, as *philosophes* we can now eschew this old discipline altogether because it is irrelevant for the sciences. Just as old metaphysical debates about the nature of space are irrelevant to geometry, old metaphysical concepts such as substance and essence are irrelevant to physics. This Newtonian view is placed in dialogue with Du Châtelet's own nuanced position. We can read D'Alembert as bemoaning the fact that she has strayed from the Newtonian path, precisely as Voltaire warned years earlier in his *Elements of the Philosophy of Newton*.[79] Intriguingly, Diderot, who was certainly no Newtonian, seems to take issue with D'Alembert's conception of the role of metaphysics. In his own most important entry, "Encyclopedia," which refers to "Elements of Science" early on, Diderot endorses a more positive role for metaphysics.[80] And that more positive role, of course, would have been endorsed heartily by Formey for his own reasons. The intertextual dialogue continues through these various entries in a seemingly endless process.

As is always the case with Du Châtelet's presence in the *Encyclopedia*, there are several distinct aspects of D'Alembert's dialogue with her work, and they are not always consistent with one another. Indeed, she can be acknowledged prominently in one episode, subtly disputed in another, ignored in a third. For instance, D'Alembert's representation of the sources of Formey's entry on "Space" is a bit peculiar. He was perfectly correct in stating that Formey sought (appropriately) to represent the debate about space by using some of the ideas in the Leibniz-Clarke correspondence. But it was misleading to say in the same breath that Formey also *used* some of the ideas in the *Institutions,* for in fact Formey had *copied* from that text. D'Alembert's remark left Du Châtelet in good company but obscured her actual, more profound role in shaping this entry on a major topic in science and philosophy at the time. Other entries are more forthright. For instance, the entry on "Motion" (mechanics) ends as follows, "You can read chapters 11 and 12 of *Institutions physiques* of madame du Châtelet, from which we have extracted part of this article," and then goes on to mention Muschenbroeek and Crousaz's works.[81] Here Formey—and D'Alembert, who helped to write the finished version of this entry—gives her work its due. The same is true with the articles on gravity (*pésanteur*), rest, and time.[82] In many of these entries, which are categorized by Diderot and D'Alembert as involving mechanics, physics, and metaphysics, her work receives substantial recognition, perhaps more than any other woman at the time.

The *Encyclopedia* is not the product of a single mind, a single sentiment, a unified perspective. So we should not be surprised when elsewhere in the text, D'Alembert adopts a distinct perspective. For instance, in another important entry, he trumpets Madame Du Châtelet's Newtonian credentials. In his "Newtonianism" entry, one of the most prominent discussions of Du Châtelet in the entire *Encyclopedia*, we find the following (*Encyclopedia*, vol. 11: 123):

> Several authors have tried to make the Newtonian philosophy easier to understand by leaving out many of its more sublime mathematical results, substituting either simpler reasonings or

experiments. That is what was primarily done by Whiston in his *Praelectiones physico-mathem.* and by Gravesande in his *Elemens* and *Institutions*. Mr. Pemberton, a fellow of the Royal Society of London, and editor of the 3rd edition of the *Principia*, also published a work entitled *View of the newtonian philosophy*. This work is a kind of commentary by which the author attempts to place this philosophy within reach of the greatest number of geometers and physicists. Fathers Le Seur and Jacquier, of the order of Minims, have also published, in three quarto volumes, the *Principia* of Newton along with a very extensive commentary, which can be most useful to those who wish to read this excellent work of the English philosopher. To these works should be joined Mr. MacLaurin's *Account of Sir Isaac Newton's Philosophical Discoveries*, translated into French a few years ago, and the commentary on Newton's *Principia* that Madame la Marquise du Chatelet left us along with a translation of the same work. Notwithstanding the great merit of this philosophy and the universal authority that it now has in England, it was at first only very slowly that it became established here; *Newtonianism* had at first scarcely two or three followers in the whole country, while Cartesianism and Leibnizianism were ruling in full force.

At first glance, one notices that D'Alembert has placed Du Châtelet in outstanding company, mentioning her work alongside that of major figures like the Dutch s'Gravesande, the English Pemberton, the Scottish MacLaurin, etc. Indeed, she is the only French figure mentioned, a clear snub to Voltaire, whose lack of scientific sophistication may have bothered D'Alembert. Needless to say, she is also the only woman. And yet Du Châtelet's treatment is different: whereas D'Alembert carefully cites some of the major works of these figures, in her case he mentions only her translation of and commentary on Newton's *Principia*, never citing her *Institutions*, the very text that he himself disputes in other entries. Why the difference?

Read on its own, this entry on Newtonianism could be interpreted as helping to foment what would become a tradition of construing Du Chatelet's work in derivative terms. Then again, read on its own, the entry could also be read as a reflection of the reasonable view that one can ignore Du Châtelet's *Institutions* in this context because it was not a commentary on Newton and therefore did not belong in this entry. But no entry can be read on its own. When we read the *Encyclopedia* as a reasoned dictionary, as D'Alembert proposes in the *Preliminary Discourse*, we must read the entries on "Space" and the "Elements of Science" together with this entry on "Newtonianism." When we do so, a new interpretive vista opens before us. D'Alembert is not merely engaging in a dialogue with all of Du Châtelet's texts in these entries. He is more specifically suggesting that although she contributed substantially to the Newtonian philosophical school, her *Institutions* is not a Newtonian text. On the contrary, in the "Elements" article, when supporting the brief criticisms contained in the "Space" entry, D'Alembert argues that figures like Du Châtelet, who see a continuing role for metaphysics in the development of physics, have strayed from the straight and narrow path. That is, Newton's path. He is saying that she has gone wrong because she has not stayed true to the Newtonian principles that he continues to endorse. He knew that she was no disciple of Newton. That, too, might be construed as a quiet rebuke of Voltaire's attitude.

There is an echo of this reasoning at the very end of the quotation from the entry on "Newtonianism" above. One can miss it unless one listens closely to D'Alembert's words. He does not conclude this passage as we would expect, noting, as everyone in the learned world knew, that Newtonianism arose slowly in France because *Cartesianism* had continued to "reign" for some time, especially in the academies. That sentiment is found in many texts. Instead, D'Alembert says that Newton's rise in France was slow because not only Cartesianism but also "Leibnizianism" was still in force. This is a curious remark. It is certainly not true of the early Enlightenment: indeed, when Du Châtelet wrote in 1740, she bemoaned the fact that Leibniz's ideas were still "little known in France." When his entry was published sixteen years later, however, D'Alembert endorses the opposite sentiment: Leibniz's ideas were so widespread that Newton's were blocked from adoption. Could it be that we should attribute this difference to the *Institutions* itself, which after all had often been associated with Leibniz's ideas, even by Leibniz's most famous followers, Wolff and Formey? Precisely that view had already been endorsed by other authors.[83] Was D'Alembert subtly giving her credit here for a shift in the intellectual landscape of France?

Perhaps the subtlety in D'Alembert's approach to the *Institutions* should not surprise us, because there is strong evidence that long before he wrote for the *Encyclopedia*, he understood that Du Châtelet herself was no Newtonian, even if her translation of Newton, and commentary on the *Principia*, would eventually contribute substantially to the Newtonian movement in France. Years before he wrote the "Newtonianism" entry, he had already cited Du Châtelet's work on a decidedly non-Newtonian subject, the *vis viva* dispute, once again diverging from Voltaire's Clarke-inspired attitude. In the preface to his famous *Treatise on Dynamics* (1743), he mentions Du Châtelet—calling her "une Dame illustre"—along with Leibniz and Bernoulli as the most significant contributors to the debate.[84] In this regard, he had good company: one of France's most important physicists, the Abbé Nollet, also referred his readers to Du Chatelet's discussion of *vis viva* after introducing the subject by describing the arguments Leibniz had published in 1686.[85] Unlike Nollet, who was reporting the state of the art, D'Alembert's goal in effect was to end the *vis viva* dispute, not by inventing a clever argument or by proposing a new experiment, but rather by convincing his readers that the debate had run its course and was probably nothing more than semantics. This idea, in turn, reflected D'Alembert's deeper view of physics: despite the fact that he wrote a treatise in what he called "dynamics," using the term from Leibniz, he in fact sought to promote the notion that physics ought to dispense with the notion of force altogether. That is, it was not merely "living forces" that he wished to jettison but the very notion of force itself.[86] He regarded the concept of force as too obscure to be of any use in physics. In that sense, his view of physics was diametrically opposed to Du Châtelet's, for she had recently emphasized the importance of forces in physics. She regarded the notion not only as perfectly clear, but as central to the understanding of the natural world. Nonetheless, D'Alembert respectfully and accurately described her philosophy.

In citing her along with the illustrious mathematicians Leibniz and Bernoulli, D'Alembert made his respect for Du Châtelet manifest, even as he fundamentally disagreed with her philosophy. There is no better sign that she had been ushered into the Republic of Letters. It was nominally a society of *men* of letters, but nevertheless included Du Châtelet at its core. Her fascinating, acknowledged, but also hidden, role in the dissemination of the philosophical and scientific knowledge of her day ought to be a component of every future discussion of the *Encyclopedia*, and therefore of every discussion of the Enlightenment.

A Twist of Fate

During the summer of 1749, Du Châtelet was working furiously to complete her translation of Newton's *Principia*, along with her commentary on the text, both of which would figure prominently in D'Alembert's description of Newtonianism in the Enlightenment. That same summer, Diderot was busily working on what would soon become his greatest project, the *Encyclopedia*. But Diderot's work was interrupted in late July when he was placed under arrest as part of a city-wide crackdown on dissent in Paris. The authorities rounded up a wide range of characters, including propagandists, atheists, and pornographers.[87] Diderot's arrest was partly due to

controversial remarks in his *Letter on the Blind* which were interpreted to promote atheism, a charge that had plagued him since the
publication of his *Philosophical Thoughts* a few years earlier.

At that time, the Bastille was full, so Diderot was sent to Vincennes, a prison fortress a few miles away from Paris. Originally
placed in solitary confinement, Diderot was later treated reasonably well after issuing a sincere apology. He was then given meat
and even wine on some days, and of course fish on Fridays. With
D'Alembert's help, he continued to work on the *Encyclopedia* project
from his cell.[88] But his friends, especially Voltaire and Rousseau,
were distraught. In his *Confessions*, Rousseau famously records his
meetings with Diderot in prison, movingly describing his condi-
tion.[89] Rousseau reports that he was so full of emotion when he
first saw Diderot in Vincennes that he could not speak; he could
only cry.[90]

Perhaps Diderot was lucky that the Bastille was full in those
summer days, for as it turns out, the governor of Vincennes was
a member of the Du Châtelet family and therefore a relative of
Émilie's. So Voltaire, who understood well what it was like to be
trapped by the French state, appealed to Du Châtelet to intercede
on his friend's behalf. She agreed to do so, writing a letter to Governor François-Bernard Du Châtelet encouraging an early release
for Diderot. Her intervention, along with Diderot's written apology, eventually worked: he was finally released on 3 November
1749 after three and a half months in prison.[91] The greatest project
of his life was announced the very next year. He never forgot her
assistance or her intellectual legacy. In his article "Epicureanism"
in the *Encyclopedia*, Diderot called her "the illustrious Marquise
du Châtelet."[92] However, before Diderot was released from prison,
tragedy would strike the Du Châtelet family.

During this period, Du Châtelet had grown bored with Voltaire
as an intimate partner, even though they remained good friends.
She eventually found romance with a dashing young officer serving

in the royal army. The officer, who was also an aspiring poet, was named Jean François de Saint-Lambert, and he was everything Voltaire was not: young, beautiful, and full of youthful admiration for Du Châtelet's work. She encouraged his poetry and they developed a passionate love for one another. Yet she remained close with Voltaire, and in a sign of the flexible social arrangements for a member of the high aristocracy, Saint-Lambert joined Du Châtelet and Voltaire in Cirey to celebrate Christmas in 1748.[93]

Du Châtelet certainly understood the dangers of a pregnancy for a woman in her forties, but she pursued her relationship with Saint-Lambert with fervor. And it eventually left her pregnant.[94] In one tender letter to him, she said that if he stayed at her bedside, it would help ease the pain of childbirth. All summer, Du Châtelet worked on her translation of Newton as the fateful day approached. The last letter she ever wrote was to an official at the Royal Library in Paris asking him to register and safeguard some of her manuscripts.[95] She knew that she had to secure her legacy. That was in early September, just a few days before she went into labor. Right after finishing her work on Newton, Émilie gave birth to a daughter. She named her Stanislas-Adelaide in honor of Stanislas, the duc de Lorraine, the father of the Queen of France, and Du Châtelet's generous host during the end of her pregnancy.

After the birth, everything seemed fine. But then Du Châtelet's fears were realized as her health deteriorated. She died from what was probably a pulmonary embolism a few days after giving birth. She was forty-two years old. There was simply nothing that a doctor in those days could do to help. When Voltaire heard the news, he threw himself down the stairs. Her husband, the Marquis, was devastated, as was the third man in her life, Saint-Lambert, whose love for her had only just begun. The baby survived, and the Marquis claimed her as his own to protect Émilie's honor.

This tragic turn of events meant that Émilie never knew that her efforts would help to secure Diderot's release from prison just two months after her death. It meant that she did not live to see the *Encyclopedia*, the central text in which her ideas played such a prominent role. Most tragically, it meant that although she was the most famous woman in science and philosophy during the entire Enlightenment, she died just as it was approaching its peak.

5

The Enlightenment's Most Dangerous Woman

Or the Making of Modern Philosophy

Philosophy is ancient. The very word says so: it comes from the Greek terms *Philo* and *Sophos*, meaning love of wisdom. The origin is preserved in many European languages, from German to French to Spanish. The spellings vary, but the idea remains the same. You could be forgiven for assuming that philosophy was invented by the Greeks. In fact, it may even seem obvious that what we now know as philosophy was invented by people like Socrates, who then instructed Plato, who ran an academy attended by Aristotle. Since so many of our university courses simply begin with Plato, or perhaps with pre-Socratics like Heraclitus or Parmenides, it may be difficult to envision any other conception of philosophy's origin. Although philosophy encourages questions that people ordinarily ignore, or regard as silly, or perhaps as serious but unanswerable, it has not encouraged much reflection about its own origins. Nowadays, people rarely question the idea that Philosophy began with Socrates and Plato.

What if you do question it? Were the Greeks really the first people in history to pose basic questions about truth, justice, or the origin of the world? Just formulating that question makes it sound odd. Haven't people been asking about such things for as long as they have been able to ask anything? The Greeks themselves acknowledged that theirs was not the first civilization, nor the first literate culture. The Jews wrote intricate texts generations before Socrates or Homer were born. So did the Egyptians. Indeed, as the Mexican writer Octavio Paz pithily puts it, "For the Greco-Roman world, Egypt *was* antiquity."[1] The Greeks were well aware of these earlier civilizations, and we can add ancient Hindu texts, generations of Chinese civilization, and much else besides. So where did we get the idea that philosophy began in Greece? Even assumptions have histories.

The assumption is certainly not new. Throughout the twentieth century, textbooks in the history of philosophy nearly always took ancient Greece as the starting point of philosophy and simply proceeded from there.[2] Many prominent texts from the nineteenth century adopted the same attitude. But if we go back even further to consider the history of philosophy as the figures of the Enlightenment presented it, we find a different story.

One of the most prominent texts in the history of philosophy written during the Enlightenment was Johann Jacob Brucker's monumental work, the five-volume *Critical History of Philosophy*, published in the middle of the eighteenth century. Although he is little known today, Brucker was read by every major Enlightenment thinker. Indeed, his work became the main source of ideas about the history of philosophy for Diderot and D'Alembert's *Encyclopedia*,[3] and his views circulated widely both in translation and via numerous other works. Of course, plenty of authors had discussed philosophical ideas from the past. But Brucker wrote what is often regarded as the first systematic and genuinely scholarly history of philosophy during the modern period.[4] He has even been called the "father" of the modern *history* of philosophy, just as Descartes was called the "father" of modern *philosophy*.[5]

Brucker's immense *History* does not begin with the Greeks. Instead, he starts (incredibly) with the beginning of the world, considering philosophy in both the prediluvian and postdiluvian periods. He considers biblical figures like Adam and also the so-called barbarians, the later Greek name for those who were not Greek. Only after discussing these various pre-Greek figures does he discuss ancient Greece, in considerable depth. After this first part of his *Critical History*, he acknowledges other pre-Greek sources, such as "de philosophia Judaeorum," noting that eventually Jewish philosophy became Aristotelian, but not until the work of Moses Maimonides in the Middle Ages. To be sure, Brucker portrayed pre-Greek philosophy as less systematic and less scientific than what we find in Plato and Aristotle, but he did not write them out of history on those grounds, any more than he excised the medieval Scholastics who devotedly followed Aristotle. He was self-consciously anti-Scholastic in his approach, taking his historical discussion "ad nostra tempora" (to our time) by praising the moderns for rejecting Aristotelianism, thinking for themselves and using reason once again as a guide.[6] To his credit, he did not simply assume that philosophy began in Greece.

Brucker's conception of philosophy's historical evolution was the Enlightenment's most prominent. He was read by leading *philosophes* with little else in common, like Diderot and Kant.[7] His views shaped numerous other Enlightenment histories of philosophy in English, French, and German.[8] The main problem with Brucker is that his work ran to five volumes; it was far too immense to be read cover to cover by the public. To solve this problem, many writers following in his footsteps presented the essential history more concisely. A prominent example is Samuel Formey, who published a *Short History of Philosophy* in French in 1760. Formey follows Brucker's basic periodization. Before tackling ancient Greece, he discusses a wide range of Western Asian and African views, including ideas from Egypt, the ancient Hebrews, and the Ethiopians. The encyclopedia format enabled Diderot and D'Alembert to be even more concise: they echoed Brucker's approach in countless entries on the history of philosophy.[9] Diderot, D'Alembert, and Formey did not accept Brucker's interpretations of philosophical history without qualifications, but his overall conception of the shape of that history strongly influenced their own.[10]

Due in large part to Brucker's influence, it was common for Enlightenment savants to ask whether Moses or Noah had been a philosopher, and whether the Egyptians thought philosophically about nature before the Greeks.[11] Such an approach is almost unknown today. Thus, a shift in our conception of philosophy's history occurred sometime between the end of the Enlightenment and the beginning of the twentieth century. Writers regressed from thinking that many non-western peoples contributed to philosophy to *assuming* that the story could begin in Greece without explanation. This largely nineteenth-century alteration happened especially in the hands of German scholars. Perhaps this should not be surprising: nineteenth-century German culture was fixated on all things Greek.[12] Although Johann Winckelmann first published his *Reflections on the Imitation of Greek Works* in 1755,[13] helping to create a cultural movement in which German scholars sought to trace western civilization back to Greek antiquity, it seems that his influence was not yet felt in the high Enlightenment. But it was certainly evident in the nineteenth century when famous German historians of philosophy, such as Kuno Fischer and Wilhelm Windelband, conceived of Greece as the birthplace of philosophy.

If we look for parallel developments in nineteenth-century French scholarship, we witness an intellectual shift happening. The most famous French historian of philosophy of that era, Victor Cousin, praises Brucker effusively, calling him the first modern historian of philosophy and one of the most erudite men of his age. But he chides Brucker for spending so much time looking for philosophical ideas in pre-Greek antiquity; these other ancient figures weren't really philosophers, says Cousin, but rather promoting religion.[14] The shift is not complete—Cousin does not *assume* that the Greeks invented philosophy—but it is well under way. The revision of Brucker's origin story helpfully serves as the clue we need in order to trace the precise origins of our *assumption* that philosophy begins with the Greeks. That idea is assuredly an invention of nineteenth-century scholars.[15]

The origin story tracing our conception of philosophy's history to the nineteenth century is well known, but it can be overinterpreted in one significant way. It is often thought that in addition to giving us our assumption that philosophy originated in ancient Greece, an assumption so deeply embedded that scholars today rarely teach their students even to ask the question of whether pre-Greek peoples created anything philosophical,[16] nineteenth-century scholars *also* gave us our conception of *modern* philosophy. It is often thought that it was nineteenth-century German scholars like Kuno Fischer and French authors like Victor Cousin who gave us the "modern" philosophy canon, with the idea, e.g., that Descartes is the "father" of modern philosophy (meaning the European philosophy of the seventeenth century). This idea was reinforced by major figures like Hegel.[17] One might even imagine it *had* to be that way: how could anyone chronicle modern philosophy *before* the modern era was over?[18] The idea of chronicling one's own era seems problematic—isn't that journalism, the so-called first draft of history? The most famous of all the modern philosophers, Immanuel Kant, died in 1804, so presumably it took until at least the beginning of the nineteenth century before scholars could view the modern era as a whole, as when we look back on the mountain we have just climbed, something we could not see while climbing it. It's common sense.

Common sense is important, but it's not a guide to history. And as a matter of historical fact, the era of "modern" philosophy was already proclaimed while the Enlightenment was happening. It was not a retrospective conception, nor a reconceptualization of a previous era whose end was now in view. It was a living conception of the age of Enlightenment itself. For as it turns out, Brucker not only conceived of the periodization of philosophy we still use today—ancient, medieval, modern—but he also produced a strikingly familiar conception of the *modern*. He already has a list of familiar characters from the modern era, including Bacon, Hobbes, Descartes, Leibniz, Newton, and Wolff. To be sure, Brucker's conception of "modern philosophy" is not *precisely* our conception. For instance, he regards Bacon rather than Descartes as the originator of modern philosophy, much as Voltaire had done in his *Philosophical Letters* years earlier. But even then, the reasoning is familiar: after all, it was Bacon who first rejected Scholasticism, refusing to follow the doctrines of some pre-established school of thought. In the *Critique of Pure Reason*, one of the most influential philosophical texts of the Enlightenment, Kant follows Brucker in that regard.[19] In other respects, where Brucker's vision diverges from ours, his is more accurate. For instance, his inclusion of Newton reflects the Enlightenment's conception of connections between science and philosophy rather than our anachronistic separation of them. That separation, too, arose in the nineteenth century. For instance, Fischer discusses Newton briefly when appropriate, such as in characterizing his debates with the Leibnizians, but otherwise he ignores him in favor of much lesser figures.[20] In contrast, Brucker discusses Newton extensively.

The Enlightenment's most influential text, D'Alembert's *Preliminary Discourse* to the *Encyclopedia*, refines Brucker's approach. D'Alembert distills Brucker's immense historical discussion into a pithy and recognizable modern canon. He focuses primarily on Bacon, Descartes, Newton, Locke, and Leibniz.[21] Indeed, the *Preliminary Discourse* aims to show that the *philosophes* were living in a *philosophical* age and also to characterize the modern science and philosophy that brought them to it. Hence it was not merely an historical task that D'Alembert inherited from Brucker, it was also his task as a *philosophe* to characterize modern philosophy. And crucially, society had made intellectual progress precisely through the work of these specific, heroic figures.[22]

Any student of modern philosophy will quickly recognize what D'Alembert's conception is missing: the two great Enlightenment philosophers David Hume and Immanuel Kant. D'Alembert wrote the *Preliminary Discourse* in 1750, so he can hardly be blamed for missing Kant, who at that time was an obscure young Prussian philosopher, the author of a single German essay on the estimation of living forces. Published in 1747, that essay expressed Kant's ideas about a subject that D'Alembert thought he had put to rest in 1743 in his *Treatise on Dynamics*.

Hume presents a more complex case. He had published *A Treatise of Human Nature* in 1739, and by the time he arrived in Paris in 1763, he was embraced by leading *philosophes* like Voltaire, Diderot, and D'Alembert himself.[23] However, English was an obscure language at that time, and none of Hume's work had been translated into French by 1750. The first French edition of a work that could help him join a canon focused on science, epistemology, and metaphysics was his *Essais Philosophiques sur l'Entendement Humain* (*Philosophical Essays on Human Understanding*), which did not appear until 1758.[24] So it was too late for him to make it into D'Alembert's canon in 1750.[25] In contrast, both Locke's and Newton's works were available in French or Latin by 1706.[26] The lesson remains: the key contours of the modern philosophy canon were already available in the middle of the eighteenth century, at the height of the Enlightenment.

We must not overinterpret this revision of our origin story for modern philosophy. After all, the modern philosophy canon is not merely a list, as if we're shopping at the grocery store and can just add a few more items as we walk through the aisles. Adding Hume or Kant to the end of the list will alter our conception of what came before. This is especially true in Kant's case. It was Kant more than any other thinker who proclaimed that his philosophy involved a "revolution"—apt for a revolutionary age—that would not only alter our conception of knowledge but also our conception of the philosophical history that brought us to the point of revolution in the first place. It was Kant's followers who helped to reorganize modern philosophy into its two great camps, the "rationalists" and the "empiricists," noting that it was Hume, the great empiricist who followed in Locke's footsteps, who awoke him from his own "dogmatic slumber" as a rationalist, one following Leibniz and Wolff. (Indeed, Kant regarded Wolff as the greatest of the "dogmatic" philosophers.) Thus, adding Kant to the list shifts our conception of everything that came before, pressing us into conceiving of Descartes and Leibniz as sitting on the opposite philosophical fence from Bacon, Locke, and Newton. That is certainly foreign to D'Alembert's conception. Of course, D'Alembert understood that Locke's analysis of knowledge differed fundamentally from Descartes's, a theme of his fellow French *philosophe* Condillac's thought, but he did not thematize this division.

The difference between D'Alembert's conception of modern philosophy and our post-Kantian conception is important, with a clear historical explanation. German scholars in the nineteenth century grew up in a fundamentally post-Kantian intellectual environment. Indeed, all of nineteenth-century Germany might be conceived intellectually as a post-Kantian environment, whether we focus on philosophy (think Hegel) or science (think Helmholtz). So German scholars used a Kantian lens when viewing the history of modern philosophy. That lens is foreign to Brucker, Formey, and D'Alembert. But we must not overreach. Although our *specific* conception of "modern philosophy" is indeed a post-Kantian idea originating in the nineteenth century, the earlier version formulated during the Enlightenment is closely akin to ours. Indeed, the modern philosophy canon articulated in the Enlightenment is *so* close to our own idea, its list of figures so familiar, it can be hard to think of it as having been invented in the first place. The same is true of the idea that philosophy began with the Greeks. In each case, we must strive to be philosophical about the history of philosophy, bringing an attitude of critical scrutiny to our own assumptions. The idea that "modern philosophy" was promulgated by a few famous men like Descartes, Locke, Leibniz, and Newton did not fall from the sky. It has not always been with us. Instead, it is a constituent of the Enlightenment's notion of the *modern* that was bequeathed to us.

But why did the Enlightenment give us a modern *canon*, a list of great thinkers with their major works? Why did D'Alembert distill Brucker's extensive discussion of modern thinkers into a short canon of heroes? Of course, philosophers have always considered their predecessors. Aristotle studied Plato, Aquinas Maimonides, Newton Descartes, sometimes to praise, often to criticize. So how were the moderns taught philosophy before the modern age was proclaimed? Not by listing a few famous men whose texts must be studied, but in a way the very opposite. When Descartes attended the Jesuit college La Flèche, or Newton Trinity College, they and their fellow students were taught the Scholastic curriculum that had lasted for generations; they were not given a canon. Of course, Aristotle was the most important figure in the philosophy curriculum, but his original works were rarely read. And there was no emphasis on a few key Scholastic authors: they were not told specifically to read Eustatius and Suarez, or some small list of Scholastic writers, as it were the Bacons and Lockes of the day. Instead, they were taught to read textbooks expressing the Scholastic consensus—it was the ideas of the schools, and the ability to dispute basic ideas with an Aristotelian pedigree, that mattered. It's not just that there was no "modern" philosophy as such; there was no idea that to learn the philosophy of the present, one must read a small set of famous texts by leading figures.

It was precisely the Scholastic conception of philosophy that Brucker sought to challenge. He was not merely an opponent of Scholasticism, as all the self-proclaimed *novatores* or moderns were.[27] He specifically presented a modern history of modern philosophy by beginning to present a list of canonical thinkers; D'Alembert then completed the task, producing a list that is completely familiar to us hundreds of years later. So again one wonders, why promulgate a canon? Why not simply teach modern philosophy by discussing its themes: skepticism, perhaps, or the new science, or maybe the theory of ideas? One could certainly learn about skepticism without Descartes, the new science without Newton, the theory of ideas without Locke. Alternatively, why not present philosophy in the traditional way of characterizing various schools of thought, such as Platonism or Cartesianism?[28] Why think of philosophy in terms of a canon of specific figures?

For Brucker and the more famous thinkers who followed his lead, philosophy became modern through the work of those figures who were "eclectic," i.e., those who thought for themselves rather than "slavishly" following the doctrines and dogmas of some School. This became a major theme of the era. The repetition of the notion that only the moderns avoided a "slavish" devotion to a philosophical school reflects an increasingly dominant metaphorical use of slavery during the Enlightenment, one that Achille Mbembe brilliantly shows was a means of forgetting real slavery.[29] The same is true of the frequent use of the word "master." We find a dramatic repetition of these themes in Diderot and others. Brucker considered the work of these eclectic thinkers inherent to the project of modernity within philosophy, inherent to its notion of intellectual progress. The idea that modern philosophy involves a canon of a few crucial thinkers is precisely what D'Alembert presents. Indeed, he not only makes it the centerpiece of his discussion of modern philosophy, but he also makes it the centerpiece of his conception of the Enlightenment and of the intellectual progress it represents, as did Voltaire before him and Diderot after. This eventually became our contemporary idea: modern philosophy concerns a canon of a few famous thinkers who overthrew Scholasticism and progressed intellectually by engaging in fundamental disputes in epistemology and metaphysics. That idea did not originate in German scholarship in the nineteenth century, it came from the Enlightenment itself.

The canon was a list of a few "great men." Why men? Surely, that reflects *another* assumption. As with philosophy's pre-Greek pedigree, if we critically assess the historical record, it speaks against the assumption. Looking quickly at history, we find the Dutch philosopher Anna Maria van Schurman, the British author Margaret Cavendish, Madame Du Châtelet, the famous Princess Elisabeth, and too many others to name. What happened to them?

It has often been said, reasonably enough, that if women were written out of the modern philosophy canon, if they were excised from the history of philosophy in modern Europe, it must have been by the pens of French and German scholars in the nineteenth century, like Fischer or Cousin. For it was those scholars who bequeathed to us our specific canon of modern philosophy. And it was that canon, in turn, that was taught to generations of students and budding scholars throughout the twentieth century.[30] But we are missing something here. If the fundamental idea of the modern philosophy canon was articulated during the Enlightenment, then we must ask the question: were women *already* written out of the modern canon then? Madame Du Châtelet and her philosophical ideas were well known to Diderot, Formey, and D'Alembert, the very people who articulated the modern philosophy canon for the first time. (One wonders: what about Brucker?) Were they the ones who blocked Du Châtelet from the canon at its very inception?

Inclusion and Exclusion in Modern Philosophy

Patriarchal intellectual structures in modern European history can take various forms. For much of modern history, we often encounter a rigid kind of patriarchy in Europe: women are *completely* excluded from participating in intellectual institutions, from colleges and universities to the all-important academies. Many institutions simply made no exceptions, leaving women little choice but to search elsewhere for an education, a chance to conduct research, an opportunity to participate in intellectual life. But when occasional exceptions were made, a second patriarchal structure emerges. When Anna Maria van Schurman attended university lectures in Utrecht because of her extraordinary intellect in the 1630s, or when Laura Bassi joined the Bologna Academy of Sciences a century later, becoming one of its most prominent members, then patriarchal structures and attitudes adapt. The old canard, *the exception proves the rule*, is a prominent reaction. The Bologna Academy admitted a few women and then stopped, and women were not able to follow in van Schurman's footsteps for many years—indeed, women were not formally admitted to any European university until 1866.[31] These institutions adapted by emphasizing how extraordinary a certain woman was, helping to prove some supposed general rule concerning male intellectual superiority, leaving the basic structures intact.[32]

But the shaping and reshaping of Madame Du Châtelet's work and reputation during the Enlightenment involves a third form of patriarchy. The men who led the Enlightenment's most important institutions, who controlled access to its most important text (the *Encyclopedia*), who wrote its official histories of philosophy, never allowed her to be the exception that proves the rule. To them, she promised to be a kind of unruly force within the history of philosophy, one with the potential, even as a singular exception, to upset the dominant narrative. So they sought to control her influence, to shape her reputation, by writing her out of the official history of philosophy. That is, the very figures who cited, copied, discussed, and debated her ideas sought simultaneously through other means to ensure that she would never enter the nascent official canon.

Samuel Formey is certainly the leading representative of this approach. From his perch at the Berlin Academy of Sciences, he promoted Du Châtelet's ideas as the best representatives of concepts in physics and metaphysics. He ensured that those ideas would circulate via the *Encyclopedia*'s entries throughout the Enlightenment alongside the ideas of other leading figures like Rousseau and Montesquieu.[33] Yet when it came time to write his own official history of philosophy based on Brucker's example, his *Short History of Philosophy* in 1760, *he never mentioned Du Châtelet*. He could not allow her to stand even as a single exception to the all-male canon he presented his readers. Following Brucker, he makes the profound choice to write of the "modern" era while it was still happening around him, bringing his analysis right up the present by discussing his beloved Wolff, who had died a few years before. And he includes the usual suspects before that, from Bacon to Descartes to Newton to Leibniz. But Du Châtelet never appears. Formey continued to respect her ideas long after her death,[34] yet the man who decisively ensured that her ideas would circulate more widely than those of any other woman in Enlightenment philosophy could not allow her to serve even as a unique exception to the rule that officially speaking, philosophy must be an all-male enterprise. Formey's all-male modern canon is evident as a normative structure—it expresses a norm concerning philosophy rather than a historical description of how modern philosophy actually evolved.

Formey's substantive conservativism did not guide his conception of philosophy's history in the way that we might expect. Indeed, he transcended Brucker's treatment, spending considerable time discussing pre-Greek thought, tackling everything from biblical figures like Abraham and Moses to Egyptian intellectuals to much else besides. He subjected much of recorded history to a serious analysis, searching for signs of philosophical thought in a huge range of pre-Greek texts and figures. But the critical scrutiny that he brought to his task had a clear limit: he asks whether Adam was a philosopher, but not Eve; he discusses Abraham, but not Sarah. He writes of Newton, Leibniz, and Wolff, bringing modern philosophy right up to his own door, shaping a notion of the modern canon even as modernity was still evolving, and yet never even *asks* the question, what about Madame Du Châtelet? As with Eve and Sarah before her, he does not even *reject* the idea that she was a philosopher. Just raising the possibility of including her in the modern canon would have allowed her to inhabit a distinct patriarchal form; it would have prompted readers to learn more about her ideas. Instead, Formey looked back to the beginning of humanity, going so far as to wonder whether there was any philosophy in the Garden of Eden, but he never asked whether any woman in all that time had ever officially contributed to philosophy.

Like most Enlightenment authors who penned a history of philosophy, Formey was heavily influenced by Brucker's *Critical History of Philosophy*. So, what about Brucker himself? Well as it turns out, Brucker was just like every Enlightenment figure writing in the mid-eighteenth century: he knew all about Madame Du Châtelet. We know this not from private correspondence or some manuscript that he left behind, perhaps a scribble in his notes, but rather from his own published work.

Collaborating with the artist Johann Haid, Brucker wrote an extensive popular work that ran into many volumes—it was called *Bilder-Sal*, or *Portrait Gallery of Today's Famous Authors*. Its first volume was published in 1741 and its last in 1755, presenting portraits and descriptions of 100 famous authors. They discuss the life and work of academicians like Formey and many others.[35] Brucker and Haid wished to include Du Châtelet in their work, so with the famous Swiss mathematician Johann Bernoulli II acting as an intermediary in 1743, Brucker and Haid included a portrait of Du Châtelet, along with a description of her ideas, in their compendium. They also included Laura Bassi, the great experimental physicist working in Bologna.[36] Like Du Châtelet and Bassi, Brucker was a member of the Bologna Academy of Sciences, a status proudly displayed on the title page of his *Portrait Gallery*.

When one reads Brucker's *Critical History*, however, his official history of philosophy, he never mentions Bassi or Du Châtelet. He discusses everyone in Du Châtelet's milieu, including even the works that Voltaire and Algarotti wrote during their days at Du Châtelet's chateau in Cirey! He was right at Du Châtelet's doorstep, but she never appears in his seemingly exhaustive history. Once again, the norm is clear and reinforced. A woman writing during the modern age can be acknowledged and cited and even promoted, but she could not be included in the official history, even as a singular exception.[37]

This same combination of intellectual recognition coupled with excision from the official history characterizes the most influential text of the whole Enlightenment. When Formey sent Diderot his articles for the *Encyclopedia* in the 1740s, and then Diderot and D'Alembert published them years later, Du Châtelet not only received substantial acknowledgment, her ideas also circulated in profoundly important ways. Yet when D'Alembert penned his conception of the official history of modern philosophy in his *Preliminary Discourse*, giving us the canon of Bacon, Descartes, Newton, Locke, and Leibniz, he ignored Du Châtelet. Indeed, although she appears in numerous places, hidden and revealed, throughout the physics and metaphysics entries of the *Encyclopedia*, and although he himself disputes her philosophical views within those entries, he never mentioned her in the "preliminary discourse" to that very text. When he characterizes the "modern" era as a philosophical age, listing the canonical philosophers who brought him to the moment of his writing in 1750, there was no exception to the group of men who achieved the intellectual progress of the Enlightenment.

This patriarchal intellectual formation characterized other reactions to Du Châtelet's philosophical work throughout the Enlightenment. Perhaps the most prominent example is found in the most famous of all Enlightenment philosophers. In his early days as a philosopher, Kant followed the path trodden earlier by influential figures like Brucker and Formey, spending considerable time discussing Du Châtelet's debate with Dortous de Mairan concerning living forces. In his very first publication, the *Thoughts on the True Estimation of Living Forces* of 1747, he treats her views respectfully, placing her in the august company not only of Mairan but also of the Swiss mathematician Johann Bernoulli II, whose arguments in favor of *vis viva* had provoked Mairan. Kant cannot quite pull off this feat without remarking explicitly that he is discussing the philosophical views of a woman, whom he refers to as "Frau von Chastelet." Near the end of this section, he adds:

> The note that I am adding here would appear impolite and pedantic to any other member of her sex, but the distinction of

understanding and scientific training of the person I am talking about not only makes her superior to all others of her gender, and to a large portion of the other sex as well, but this distinction also deprives her of the actual privilege of the fairer portion of humanity: flattery, and praise based on flattery.[38]

He clearly felt compelled to add this remark because of how unusual it was to be discussing the philosophical views of a woman. Kant chose a simple patriarchal form: the exception proves the rule. He is saying, in effect, "Yes, dear reader, I am spending several pages talking about the philosophical views of a woman, but she's superior to all other women, so my discussion need not upset any apple carts." Kant is polite and reasonably respectful, if somewhat patronizing. After this remark, he immediately resumes his discussion, noting that Mairan handled well the problem of measuring the force of a body by analyzing how much it was able to compress a spring. The juxtaposition is a bit jarring.

As Kant grew more famous, publishing numerous important pieces throughout the 1750s and early 1760s on a wide range of topics in science and philosophy, he was obviously not satisfied with his youthful maneuver. Something about it bothered him. The year was 1764, when Kant published his soon-to-be famous work *Observations on the Beautiful and the Sublime*. By this time, Du Châtelet had long since died, as had the old *vis viva* controversy. Yet in the *Observations*, he wrote:

A woman who has a head full of Greek, like Mrs. Dacier, or who engages in fundamental disputes about mechanics, like the Marquise du Chastelet, might as well also have a beard; for perhaps that might better express the appearance of depth for which they strive. The lovely understanding chooses for its objects everything that is closely related to finer feelings, leaving abstract speculation or knowledge, which is useful but dry, to the industrious, fundamental, and deep understanding. The woman will accordingly learn no geometry; she will know only so much about the principle of sufficient reason or monads as is necessary to find the salt in satirical poems which the insipid brooders of our sex have fabricated. The beauties can leave Descartes' vortices rotating forever without worrying about them, even if the courteous Fontenelle wanted to join them under the planetary system. The attraction of their charm loses none of its power even if they know nothing of what Algarotti has taken the trouble to explain for their benefit concerning the attractive forces of basic matter according to Newton. [Akademie Edition, vol. 2: 229–30]

Kant's decision to dispense with politesse, embracing instead the old trope of making an intellectual woman the butt of a joke,[39] even after her tragic death years earlier, puts him back in line with his Enlightenment brethren.

This passage from Kant's *Observations* is famous and can be found in numerous accounts of the Enlightenment. But it is often broken off when the offensive sexist joke ends, before we learn Kant's deeper aim.[40] He does not merely mock Mrs. Dacier and Madame Du Châtelet, both of whom had long since died.[41] He also promotes a return to a more gender appropriate intellectual form popular during the Enlightenment, the form in which male figures like Fontenelle and Algarotti explain the latest science to educated women. He cannot deny that Du Châtelet had engaged in "fundamental disputes concerning mechanics," for he himself had respectfully discussed them in print years earlier. But he now proclaims that this whole business is not appropriate for women. It's unseemly for women to discuss the principle of sufficient reason and the existence of monads—two major themes of Du Châtelet's *Institutions*, one cannot help but notice—except perhaps to study a bit of poetry. It must have annoyed Kant many years later when his critic Johann Eberhard cited the French edition of Du Châtelet's text as an authoritative source indicating that Kant was wrong on a point of philosophy.[42] He just could not avoid her ideas.

But why did Kant return to the scene of the crime, dispense with his youthful politesse, and mock Du Châtelet? Why did he insist that the supposedly gender-appropriate form in which the learned man, a Fontenelle or an Algarotti, explains science and philosophy to an intellectually curious woman, must be reinstated? His choice was poignant. Just a few years after Algarotti insulted Du Châtelet by presenting her as his supplicant student in *Newtonianism for the Ladies*, depicting her in the work's frontispiece in the Italian edition (Figure 5), she broke through a final gender barrier and published her own philosophical treatise, the very text Kant had read and discussed as a young man. Why was Algarotti still important to Kant's conception of women in philosophy so many years later? For that matter, why had Brucker praised Du Châtelet in a popular work, only to excise her from the official history? Why did D'Alembert and Formey also do so, after using so many of her words in their most influential and important work?

"Modern Men"

In the Greco-Roman world, numerous "schools" of philosophy arose. They were sometimes characterized by their doctrine or method, like the Sophists and Skeptics; sometimes by their leaders, like the Platonists and Pythagoreans. To write the history of ancient Greco-Roman philosophy was to write the history of these schools, describing their main debates among one another. Philosophy is nothing if not systematic, so the ancients also had a name for thinkers lacking allegiance to any school: they were the "eclectics," recognized already in the second century CE in Alexandria. The Scholasticism that pervaded early modern educational institutions, at least in the telling of the "moderns" who wished to overthrow it, was seen as continuing this emphasis on sectarian thought. Figures like Galileo, Descartes, and Newton reacted almost violently against Scholasticism. Brucker inherited and promoted this attitude, praising the moderns for their "eclectic" attitude toward philosophy, their refusal to continue the Scholastic tradition of devotion to some doctrine promoted by a school of thought. For Brucker, figures like Descartes and Newton were autonomous philosophers, analyzing the world without scholastic constraints.[43] That was why they were inspiring.

Brucker's emphasis on "eclecticism" provides an essential feature of the modern philosophical canon. The Enlightenment's conception of "modern philosophy" involves a small group of courageous, autonomous philosophers who refused to follow the doctrines of the schools. *That* is why Brucker starts to formulate a canon of single authors: to study philosophy in the modern way is not to study the thought of various schools, or the various problems like skepticism or idealism that occupied them. It is to study the independent individuals who made great intellectual progress when they philosophized anew. D'Alembert endorsed precisely this modern conception of modern philosophy. His *Preliminary Discourse* describes the Enlightenment by providing a now familiar list of canonical modern authors, those independent thinkers who refused to follow any pre-established doctrine or school, beginning with Scholasticism's greatest early critic, Chancellor Bacon.

Most important, Diderot then carries this notion from Brucker and D'Alembert into the *Encyclopedia* proper. Indeed, he borrowed heavily from Brucker for his entry on "Eclecticism." The result from Diderot reads like a manifesto:

> The eclectic is a philosopher who tramples on prejudice, tradition, seniority, universal consent, and authority, in a word, all that captivates the mind. He dares to think for himself and returns to general principles that are the clearest, most examined, most discussed. He admits nothing but what is based on the evidence of his experience and his reason. . . . The sectarian is a man who embraces the doctrine of a philosopher; the eclectic, on the contrary, is a man who recognizes no master.[44]

The melodrama of Diderot's expression is palpable. He embraces a philosophical notion of modern masculinity: to be a real philosopher is to be a real man, to have no "master." Once again, the metaphorical reference to masters and slaves, with all its brutality, is prominent. For Diderot, to write the *modern* history of modern philosophy is not to describe the achievements of schools and their various ideas; it is to trumpet the great men who dared to think for themselves.[45]

This conception of modern philosophy answers the question of why Kant returned decades later not merely to mock Du Châtelet but to emphasize Algarotti of all people. It is tempting at first to read Brucker, D'Alembert, Formey, and Kant as simply blocking a woman like Du Châtelet from *officially* becoming a philosopher. But when we reflect on the canon of "eclectic" thinkers, a more nuanced form of patriarchy is found. Recognizing this tactic helps us to grasp a basic paradox of Du Châtelet's intellectual life. She was considered a philosopher, and indeed, she became an exceedingly famous one. Yet no woman could become a *modern* philosopher. None could fit the conception of the "eclectic" thinker, the autonomous agent who thinks for herself without devotedly following the ideas of some established doctrine or school. The modern conception of the canon is itself the reason that so many critics, friends, and interlocutors all struggled mightily to place Du Châtelet's thought within some established school.

Attempts to enroll Du Chatelet within some male-focused school of thought abounded at this time. We find this attitude in her avid supporters, such as the mathematician Abraham Kästner, and in her most ardent critics, like Dortous de Mairan of the Paris Academy and James Jurin, secretary to the Royal Society.[46] Du Châtelet was a Newtonian; no, a Wolffian; no, a Leibnizian! Or maybe some combination? And by the way, could she be converted from the ideas of one man to those of another? She stretched the intellectual and gender boundaries of her age mightily, but to her male interpreters, *she could be a philosopher only in the old sense of being an adherent of some school, subordinated to a "master."* They simply could not accept the notion that she, too, was a fully autonomous thinker, even though that was a major theme of her work. *That* is the reason that Kant reminded his readers of Du Châtelet's supposedly subordinate status to Algarotti from so many years ago. Newtonianism for the ladies, indeed.[47]

This same conception is dramatically on display in Brucker's discussion of Du Châtelet in his popular work, the *Portrait Gallery of Famous Authors*. Before discussing her work in depth, he sets the stage by admonishing his readers not to reject an entry on a woman. After all, even in antiquity, women joined Plato's academy, and more recently, he reminds us, Princess Elisabeth of Bohemia and Queen Christina of Sweden were "pupils" of Descartes. Brucker then presents the main act, noting that Du Châtelet began where her royal predecessors left off, eventually following a more complex intellectual trajectory. He begins with the view of her old nemesis, the secretary of the Paris Academy, Dortous de Mairan:

> If Mr. de Mairan is to be trusted, in the beginning she was devoted to Descartes. The deeply penetrating understanding possessed by the Marquise Du Châtelet could not fail to spot the rare errors this great thinker made in his investigation of nature, and she was later in a position thoroughly to refute these errors. When Newton arrived and showed the insufficiency of the Cartesian doctrine of nature for discovering its secrets, this astute philosopher [Philosophin] saw clearly how fundamental the Newtonian proofs were. But even then, her deeply penetrating mind was not satisfied, she wanted to look more deeply into the essence of nature in order to derive from valid universal truths those principles that alone can satisfy an unbiased and truth-seeking mind. And this led her directly on the way to the principles of Mr. Baron von Leibniz, which the privy councilor Wolff perfected, erecting on them an extensive doctrine.[48]

And there she rested. Satisfied that she had found the true philosophical school, Brucker concludes, she defended Wolffianism in her *Institutions*. So officially speaking, she *was* a philosopher, and indeed a "famous author," but one of the *right type*. As a woman, she could be a philosopher following a leader, just as Elisabeth had followed Descartes, but not an independent thinker.

When Brucker wrote about Princess Elisabeth and Queen Christina as Descartes's "pupils," he had little to fear. Although Elisabeth corresponded extensively with Descartes, becoming the first person to formulate what we now know as the mind-body problem in 1643, she did not publish anything philosophical under her own name.[49] Neither did Queen Christina. There was no harm in calling them philosophers, since there was no risk that they would be understood as *modern* philosophers. They posed little threat. But Madame Du Châtelet was different from the start. Not only did she publish a major philosophical treatise in French, but she also did so at the height of the modern era, and her ideas circulated throughout Europe. Brucker handled this problem by reassuring his readers that her whole life was spent following one leader after another, from Descartes to Newton to Wolff. A recognized philosopher in the modern age, but not a true modern philosopher.

Yet Du Châtelet always threatened to break free from this interpretive schema, rendering her a dangerous intellectual figure in her milieu. Many *philosophes* instinctively recognized this threat: as soon as the *Institutions* was published, male readers scurried to affix some philosophical label to it. Some said it was another great "Newtonian" text, one to join the ranks of efforts by Algarotti and Voltaire, placing her in the role of the pupil or the handmaiden. This interpretation persisted, despite the fact that she had already published a critical review of Voltaire's *Elements of the Philosophy of Newton* in the famous *Journal des Sçavans* and said explicitly in the preface to her *Institutions* that she was not writing a work like his.[50] Some readers tried the opposite tack: maybe she was really an *anti*-Newtonian, a promoter of Leibniz's ideas. Indeed, having failed to convince her to remain a "disciple" of the great English-man, Voltaire himself eventually endorsed this last interpretation. In his "Historical Preface" to her posthumously published transla-tion of Newton's *Principia* in 1759, Voltaire writes that in addition to her superlative translation, she also published the *Institutions*, "an explication of the philosophy of Leibniz" (Newton 1759, v). Problem solved: either she was translating Newton's science or transmitting Leibniz's ideas. Readers can choose. The leader is not especially important, as long as she follows one.

For his part, the Prussian philosopher Christian Wolff actually endorsed *both* positions. At first, he told correspondents that she would be his new representative in France, helping to halt the ris-ing tide of Newtonianism in that all-important intellectual center.[51] This attitude ignored the fact that Du Châtelet's conceptions of physics and of philosophy differed radically from his. Du Châtelet clearly rejected Wolff's approach to physics, which involved the general science of body and speculative explanations of countless natural phenomena. Just as important, Du Châtelet never endorsed Wolff's controversial view that scientific knowledge involves the production of deductively valid syllogistic arguments or his rather outlandish idea that the Principle of Sufficient Reason can some-how be deduced from the Principle of Contradiction.[52] But Wolff simply failed to recognize her distinctive approach. In any event, his enthusiasm for her philosophical position in the *Institutions* soon faded: in a June 1743 letter, he lamented the fact that Maupertuis and Clairaut, who "understand nothing of philosophy, and there-fore accommodate themselves so easily to the so-called philosophia Newtoniana, have turned Mme Du Châtelet around."[53]

The various reactions to Du Châtelet's philosophy mirrored one another perfectly. Whereas Voltaire bemoaned her conversion to Leibniz, Wolff bemoaned her conversion to his rival, Newton.[54] For his part, the former secretary of the Royal Society in London, James Jurin, wrote to Voltaire encouraging him to "convert" Du Châte-let back to Newtonianism.[55] Finally, Brucker had a multi-layered conversion story to tell, with Du Châtelet shifting from the school of Descartes to that of Newton to Leibniz-Wolff. The assumptions underlying these disparate readings were fundamentally the same.

With respect to Du Châtelet's challenge to the patriarchy, the Enlightenment spoke with one voice. She could be a *philosopher in the old sense,* Diderot's sectarian or Brucker's "pupil," for then she would be subordinated to the doctrine of a "master." But she could not be like the men around her. Scholasticism was repugnant because it involved male philosophers subordinating themselves to a sect or doctrine or school. The Enlightenment is the movement in which philosophers become modern, read *real men,* by becoming their own "masters." They simply could not include her in that dynamic.

Du Châtelet rejected the attempts of the men in her milieu to contain her philosophy and its implications. They spoke with one voice, but so did she. Her powerful rejection of discipleship in her *Institutions,* her insistence that her readers think for themselves and reject intellectual authorities, was a direct challenge to the new consensus in her milieu. So was her insistence on her own intellectual autonomy. Her philosophy was therefore dangerous. Du Châtelet could not be acknowledged as a *modern philosopher,* an "eclectic," for then she would be a woman who rejected allegiance to any leader. And a woman who declared herself to be autonomous might fundamentally break the social order. After all, for a woman to be a modern philosopher would be for her to escape the intellectual patriarchy once and for all. And if her numerous readers endorsed her philosophy, they just might escape with her.

Modern Philosophy Today

The story of Du Châtelet's incredible rise, and her subsequent exclusion from the modern canon, is not of mere historical interest. It continues to be relevant today. Indeed, the many elements of Du Châtelet's fame and reception during the Enlightenment have surprising echoes in more recent scholarship. This is particularly clear if we trace scholarship in the twentieth century back to its source. Some of the most prominent works on the Enlightenment—especially Peter Gay's influential two-volume treatment from the 1960s, and Paul Hazard's monumental three-volume *European Thought in the Eighteenth Century*, published just after the Second World War—have a common root. They originate in the scholarship before the war published by the century's greatest historian of philosophy, Ernst Cassirer. As it happens, Cassirer not only influenced most of the subsequent accounts of the Enlightenment, he is still discussed regularly today.[56] A scholar of immense erudition, Cassirer knew Brucker's *Critical History of Philosophy* and also understood its impact on more famous figures such as Diderot and his *Encyclopedia*.[57] The twists and turns of Du Châtelet's fate are prominently displayed in Cassirer's work.

Born in 1874, Cassirer was from a prominent Jewish family and made his early career in Berlin before moving to Hamburg to work under Hermann Cohen, the leading neo-Kantian philosopher at the time.[58] Cassirer published *The Philosophy of the Enlightenment* on the eve of the Nazi rise to power, writing the preface from Hamburg in late 1932, just a few months before he would join the great exodus of Jews, artists, and intellectuals from Germany. Cassirer's choice to write about the Enlightenment and its ideals of freedom and equality just as fascism was rising in Europe was courageous and telling. Cassirer was strongly identified with the Weimar Republic, which he had publicly defended, and he was the first Jew to serve as a professor and later as the rector of any German university.[59] In 1929, he held a public debate about philosophy and modern culture with the other most prominent German philosopher of his day, the young Martin Heidegger, in Davos, Switzerland. The debate quickly became famous throughout Europe[60]—one of the founders of logical positivism, Rudolf Carnap, was in the audience. It was lost on no one in the ensuing years that Cassirer stood for Weimar's democracy and that Heidegger, who was a Nazi and who became a university rector in 1934 amid the purge of Jews from academia, stood for its abolition. Cassirer spent his final years living and writing in the United States. Having fled the Nazi regime, he died in New York just weeks before Hitler's defeat in Berlin.[61] If there is such a thing as the right side of history, Ernst Cassirer was on it.

Cassirer's *Philosophy of the Enlightenment* tackles all of eighteenth-century thought, including science, philosophy, politics, and aesthetics. In the chapter on how the *philosophes* treated history, Cassirer places substantial emphasis on Montesquieu's *Spirit of the Laws*, as one might expect, but also gives Voltaire's *Essay on Manners* a starring role. Unlike Montesquieu, who focuses on the basic principles that govern various kinds of state structure, from monarchy to democracy, Voltaire focuses more broadly on the diversity of customs throughout the world's many cultures. Like Montesquieu, however, Voltaire is not merely content to describe the fantastic variety of customs in human culture; he seeks to discover their underlying principles within human nature.

The notion of principles of human nature that underlie a plethora of customs, it turns out, hails from a more general Enlightenment idea concerning the relationship between the human and the natural sciences. Cassirer articulates the source of this idea as follows:

> The first draft of the *Essay on Manners*, as Voltaire reports, was intended for the Marquise du Châtelet, who had bemoaned the disconnected state of historical knowledge as compared with natural science. An analogue of Newton's science, a reduction of facts to laws, should also be possible here.[62]

Du Châtelet had argued that the state of historical knowledge was lacking in comparison with the state of knowledge within the natural sciences. Newton had succeeded in taking a great diversity of seemingly disconnected phenomena—the fall of a sparrow from its nest, the ocean's tides, the orbits of Jupiter's moons—and shown them to be connected through an underlying law of gravity. Surely, there must be some kind of analogue within history, she thought.

What was Voltaire's reaction to Du Châtelet's provocative suggestion? Four pages later, after the sudden introduction, and just as sudden disappearance, of Du Châtelet in this tale, we find our answer. Cassirer writes that in the end, Voltaire "views the work of the historian in the same light as that of the natural scientist. Both the natural scientist and the historian have the same task; they seek the hidden law amid the confusion and flux of phenomena."[63] So Voltaire *endorsed* Du Châtelet's idea that the scientist of the human could model his work on the scientist studying nature. This is a familiar theme: many philosophers at this time, from Hume to Rousseau to Kant, sought to become, or at least to find, the "Newton of the mind."[64] That is, they sought an understanding of human nature modeled on science.

In this episode, Du Châtelet plays the role of a philosopher—she isn't presented merely as Voltaire's "mistress."[65] However, one would never know from Cassirer's book that she had written a 500-page treatise on philosophy and science! Her request of Voltaire was not merely a suggestion from a fellow intellectual; it was a conception of history's potential that reflected a sophisticated understanding of the nature of modern science. She is briefly acknowledged as a philosopher, and then never mentioned again. If the reader is not already acquainted with her, she might wonder: wait, who was the Marquise Du Châtelet? Why did Voltaire write an entire essay based on her suggestion? Was he simply trying to impress some French aristocrat?

The Philosophy of the Enlightenment was not Cassirer's first exploration of the era. Like Brucker before him, Cassirer also wrote a major work in the history of modern philosophy. He gave his work the imposing title, *Das Erkenntnisproblem in der Philosophie und Wissenschaft der neuren Zeit*, that is, *The Problem of Knowledge in the Philosophy and Science of Modernity*.[66] First published in 1902, the *Problem of Knowledge* eventually spanned four volumes, running to well over 1,500 pages. Just like Brucker's work in the eighteenth century, Cassirer's history influenced every major subsequent discussion of modern science and philosophy.[67]

Unlike many Anglo-American historians of philosophy, who largely ignore the French context in favor of emphasizing British Empiricism in the early part of the century, culminating in David Hume's work, and Kant's revolutionary reply to Hume at century's end, Cassirer delves deeply into Enlightenment thought. He describes all of the major figures in the French milieu: Maupertuis, D'Alembert, Voltaire, Condillac, La Mettrie. All except one, that is. Madame Du Châtelet never appears in the *Problem of Knowledge*. The echo of Brucker is loud. In discussing Du Châtelet's contribution to a principal debate of the Enlightenment, but then ignoring her in his history, Cassirer echoes the Enlightenment's own conception of the philosopher. She was a philosopher, but not part of philosophy's official history. And no matter how comprehensive Cassirer's work might be, he never added her name to the modern philosophy canon.

In the twenty-first century, we are still living with this fundamental intellectual dynamic. Even today, major works designed to introduce students to the history of western philosophy echo the eighteenth-century's common view that a woman can be a philosopher only if she is seen as following some other thinker. For instance, a recent prominent anthology of works in early modern philosophy reflects this sentiment almost perfectly: when women are included in the nearly 900-page text, right in the table of contents they are placed *underneath* male philosophers. Princess Elisabeth falls under Descartes, Margaret Cavendish under Spinoza, Du Châtelet under Kant.[68] Is there any clearer graphic representation of how women's thought is supposedly derivative? As one might expect with a conception that is normative rather than descriptive, this one requires a peculiar historical maneuver. Although Du Châtelet published her magnum opus while Kant was still a student in the early 1740s, *he* responded to *her* work a few years later, and she had likely never heard of him, she is nonetheless placed under *his* name.

The tale of Du Châtelet's reception also indicates that if a woman's philosophical work cannot be characterized as derivative, there is always another tactic available, one used in the Enlightenment and in later scholarship: simply excise her from your official history. The editors of the recent *Norton Introduction to Philosophy* adopted that approach. Instead of seeing women as followers of some other thinker, the editors present more than 1,200 pages covering a span from Plato to the 1950s in which women contributed nothing at all to philosophy.[69] This editorial decision generated some criticism. So in the more recent second edition of the *Norton Introduction*, the editors added an excerpt written by a woman covering the period from Ancient Greece until 1956. They chose a single page from Princess Elisabeth's correspondence with Descartes.[70] This decision clearly reinforces the relevant norm: a woman did contribute something to the history of philosophy, one must admit, but only in reply to the thought of a canonical male figure. The message from these contemporary examples is essentially the same as it was in 1750: women can be philosophers, but not as their own thinkers. Their work can be presented as derivative, or it can simply be excised from the official history.

These aspects of contemporary scholarship enable us to recognize an important fact. To reinstate Émilie Du Châtelet's thought in the history of modern science and philosophy is not merely to correct the historical record. It is not merely to ensure that students learn what really happened during the Enlightenment. It is to challenge a dominant mode of presenting philosophy in the twenty-first century. Philosophy needs to hear her voice.

6

Du Châtelet's Enlightenment

Philosophy for Freethinkers

We write of *the* Enlightenment, but the definite article misleads. There were many Enlightenments. The new science and philosophy promoting enlightened thinking in St. Petersburg was different from that in Berlin, different in Edinburgh from that in Basel. It was different for colonial subjects scattered throughout the world than for those residing in prominent European capitals, different for religious minorities in those capitals than for Christians. These differences are crosscut by temporal ones: the "early" Enlightenment enjoyed by Locke or Newton differs from the "late" Enlightenment of Mary Wollstonecraft or Adam Smith. Women clearly experienced the Enlightenment differently from the men who excluded them from so many institutions.[1] Since geographical or historical coincidence never guarantees ideological agreement, these myriad divisions are bisected by ideology: the "radical Enlightenment" of *philosophes* like Diderot who challenged religious authority contrasts with the "conservative Enlightenment" of pastors like Brucker and Formey who defended it. Finally, the whole enterprise was opposed by the "counter-Enlightenment."[2] It would therefore be remarkable if we could discover some commonality underlying all of these divisions. Perhaps we wish to speak of *the* Enlightenment in at least one register, but can we do so?

The prospects seem dim. Not only is any commonality among the various "Enlightenments" difficult to discern, but our desire to write engaging historical narratives helps to hide whatever commonality there might have been. We have an understandable tendency to romanticize the *philosophes*, exaggerating how radical they were. After all, it's exciting to tell the story of a brilliant writer like Diderot or Voltaire placed under arrest and thrown in jail for publishing controversial views. The *ancien regime* obviously feared the radicals, and it makes for great history to write of their travails under the absolute state power wielded by Louis from Versailles. Diderot sits in Vincennes prison as Voltaire and Rousseau fret over his declining health—what could be better for telling a compelling story? In comparison, Formey's Enlightenment is admittedly rather boring: he was appalled at the ideas of Voltaire, denounced Rousseau, defended religion, preached on Sunday. He sat comfortably in Berlin while Diderot waited in prison. What could they possibly have had in common?

When we revivify our narrative of the Enlightenment with Du Châtelet's philosophy, our answer appears.[3] Whether we look to "radicals" like Diderot, "conservatives" like Brucker and Formey, or more neutral figures like D'Alembert; whether we look to one part of Europe or another, one historical moment or another, all the *philosophes* and savants adopted the same reaction to her work. They promoted its importance as a "school-based," sectarian approach to science and philosophy, picturing her as a mere disciple, but denied her the status of "modern" philosopher. This agreement is profound because these figures agreed on so little else. As Diderot and Voltaire were busy promoting challenges to authority, with Diderot accused of atheism, Formey denounced Diderot and chastised Voltaire. When Diderot incorporated ideas from Brucker's history of philosophy, he altered them to fit his deist and materialist agenda, moves that would have horrified a devout man like Brucker.[4]

Yet for all that, Diderot embraced Brucker's conceptual approach to Du Châtelet. So did D'Alembert and Formey, Kant and Voltaire. The commonality of their intellectual response to Du Châtelet highlights an element of the Enlightenment itself.

This surprising consensus among such a diverse group of thinkers is worth pondering. Conceptions of gender norms in Enlightenment philosophy were disassociated from other socio-political, philosophical, and religious commitments. One might expect that a radical thinker like Diderot who sought to challenge not only social and intellectual mores but also religious authority would be willing to challenge gender norms in a way that a conservative like Formey would not. One might imagine that Voltaire, who was imprisoned for his challenges to the social order of the ancièn regime early in his career and who was often on the run from the authorities afterward, would hold a more critical conception of gender norms than a figure like D'Alembert or Brucker. But in fact, across many years and many texts, from private correspondence to famous publications, their reactions to Du Châtelet mirrored one another perfectly. All were open-minded enough to discuss, debate and promote Du Châtelet's philosophy, perhaps even to consider her a derivative philosopher, but none were radical enough to dub her a *modern* philosopher.[5] None would place her in the emerging modern canon. As profound as their religious and ideological differences might have been, they all concurred that her thought must be construed as derivative from some "master's" original work. It made little difference *which* leader—Voltaire could trumpet Newton, Brucker Wolff, Kant Algarotti—as long as Du Châtelet did not disrupt the masculinity embedded in the notion of the modern philosopher. All would ensure that notion's integrity by leaving her out of any official history of modern philosophy. If we challenge this common conception among this wide array of thinkers, reconceiving of Du Châtelet as a modern philosopher, we therefore challenge a dominant narrative of *the* Enlightenment. We also challenge a dominant narrative of *scholarship* on the Enlightenment stretching back more than a hundred years.

Once again, we find echoes of eighteenth-century trends in contemporary scholarship. Despite her efforts to ensure that readers would acknowledge her intellectual independence, even sympathetic interpreters of the *Institutions* have tacitly continued to employ the labels affixed to Du Châtelet's work during her lifetime. To be sure, contemporary scholarship is far more sophisticated in its interpretations of her philosophy than earlier work was. But it often remains confined within the intellectual landscape expressed through the old labels of the eighteenth century. In recent years, scholars have tried to split the difference among the old approaches by proclaiming that the *Institutions* is actually *both* Newtonian and Leibnizian at the same time. They say that Du Châtelet provides *Leibnizian* metaphysical foundations for *Newtonian* physics.[6] One must admit that this interpretation has its merits. For instance, on the surface, it seems to make sense of the whole text: whereas the early chapters focus on the Principle of Sufficient Reason and other aspects of what one might call Leibnizian metaphysics, the later chapters focus on gravity and other aspects of what one might call Newtonian physics. One could then conceive of the former as a foundation for the latter.

This popular characterization is tempting, but it views the text through a distorting lens. Indeed, it ignores at least two aspects of the *Institutions*, one in its beginning, the other right at its end. It is as if Du Châtelet were bookending her text with warnings against this tempting interpretation. In the preface, she writes that metaphysics is the "summit" of the edifice of knowledge, not its foundation; she begins her text with metaphysics because it is obscured from our view by its high epistemic perch, not because it lies at the foundation of things.[7] And then Du Châtelet ends her text with a long discussion of *vis viva*. The physics of the treatise cannot plausibly be "Newtonian" when it ends with a prominent defense of that most Leibnizian of all ideas, living forces, a subject Newton himself simply ignored.[8] Moreover, Du Châtelet noted clearly at the beginning of her very first chapter that she embraced *both* Newton's "force of inertia" and Leibniz's "vis viva." So, her view of physics was ecumenical, not partisan. She signaled right up front that her text would fall into neither school.[9] But after two centuries of thought, even her sympathetic interpreters have insisted on enrolling her in one.

What is Du Chatelet's alternative to these dominant narratives? Great thinkers are often one step ahead of us, and Du Châtelet is no exception. Despite the fact that she died in the fall of 1749, just as the Enlightenment was gathering momentum as a pan-European intellectual and social movement, she had already recognized the threat that the categorizations used by the men in her milieu would pose to her intellectual legacy. But that is not all. She also understood her historical moment and its implications for philosophy. She understood that the new emphasis on the list of "great men" who produced modern science and philosophy reflected a deep hypocrisy within the movement. The lumières loudly proclaimed their intellectual independence. But Du Châtelet knew that many of them also promoted their ideas as "Cartesian" or "Newtonian," "Leibnizian" or "Wolffian." Formey would be an excellent example, as would Voltaire and Algarotti. Many authors were content to be "disciples" of great men; others sought disciples. By rejecting discipleship as a philosophical mistake, Du Châtelet could defend her independence and call out the men in her milieu for their hypocrisy all at once. And by urging her readers to remain free thinkers, she could undermine the attempt of some leading thinkers to convert disciples of their own. Hence the danger she posed was substantial.

To guide her readers, Du Châtelet used the preface of her *Institutions* to emphasize her overarching approach to the emerging categorizations of Enlightenment science and philosophy. She tackles what she calls the subject of "respect" for "great men," returning to the origins of Scholasticism (Aristotle) and then discussing the most prominent contributor to modern science (Newton). Having already warned her readers of nationalist partisanship in science, she writes (Du Châtelet, *Institutions*, 1742, preface, X):

> If I believed it incumbent upon me to caution you against the partisan spirit, I believe it even more necessary to advise you not to carry respect for the greatest men to the point of idolatry, as do the majority of their disciples. Each philosopher has seen something, and none has seen everything; there is no book so bad that nothing can be learned from it, and none so good that one may not improve it. When I read Aristotle, a philosopher who has suffered fortunes so diverse and so unjust, I am astonished sometimes to find sound ideas on various points of general physics next to the greatest absurdities. But when I read some of the questions that M. Newton put at the end of his *Opticks*, I am struck with a very different astonishment. This example of the two greatest men of their centuries makes you see that you who have reason must take no one at his word alone, but must always make your own examination, setting aside the consideration always given to a famous name.

So Du Châtelet declares, right at the opening of her magnum opus, that she would not be anyone's disciple, contrary to Voltaire's hopes.[10] She would not be beholden to another thinker. She was telling us that she was indeed a modern philosopher. A philosopher who belonged in the burgeoning modern canon.

Du Châtelet's philosophical orientation in the preface to her *Institutions* made her a great threat to her male interlocutors. For if her readers took her advice to heart, it would not only challenge an emerging theme of the Enlightenment; it would mean that young women would embrace intellectual freedom. They would threaten to break free of the male dominance of intellectual life in this era. Du Châtelet was not just undermining the hopes of many philosophers in her day to convert disciples of their own; she was threatening the social order. The men in her milieu took great pains to construe women as their intellectual subordinates, even in the pictures appended to their works. Du Châtelet's philosophy shatters this approach.

Even as we rewrite the canon through the inspiration of Du Châtelet, we must recognize that her remarks in the preface to the *Institutions* are also meant to inoculate her readers against *becoming* disciples themselves.[11] This helps us to recognize that the modern canon of philosophy inherently carries a danger with it. Modern writers like Diderot praised the overthrow of the Scholastics who followed the ideas of a school; they praised themselves for being "eclectic" thinkers, autonomous from any School. But paradoxically, the Enlightenment is also replete with thinkers who then proclaimed themselves to be "Newtonians," thinkers who willingly relinquished their autonomy by following the authority of a "famous name." That was certainly true of Voltaire, who converted to the Newtonian faith and then spread the gospel. And although he was not originally a Newtonian, Locke is also a prime example. After reading the *Principia* and re-thinking his *Essay*, Locke tells Bishop Stillingfleet in effect: I have no idea how matter gravitates, but Newton has convinced me that it does. Is there any better example of following an authority? Unable to follow the geometric proofs, Locke took Newton "at his word alone." No wonder Du Châtelet rejected his philosophical attitude in her *Institutions*.

In warning her readers not to become disciples of the great thinkers, Du Châtelet was at the same time implicitly criticizing those men for seeking disciples in the first place. For who seeks disciples? A man who thinks he has found *the truth*. Once the truth is discovered, the only task is to publicize it. Wolff finds the truth, Formey spreads the gospel; the same is true with Newton and Voltaire.[12] This approach expresses a conception of philosophy: the goal of the great philosopher penning a treatise is to *settle* the questions of philosophy. Once the old disputes are over, the task is merely to disseminate the new system. This is precisely the conception presented by Kant in one of the greatest works of Enlightenment philosophy,

the *Critique of Pure Reason*, first published in 1781. Looking back
on the "revolution in thinking" brought about by Bacon and other
moderns, Kant plans to revolutionize philosophy once and for all.
He wishes to do so in part by overthrowing the "dogmatic" system
of Wolff, but his conception of philosophy is similar: the goal is to
articulate the final system. One must then find acolytes who will
carry the system into the next generation. It worked: many thinkers
in this era became "Kantians," a central aspect of the intellectual
dynamics of the nineteenth century.

The task of finding followers for one's philosophical system is
also connected to the task of ensuring one's own canonical status.
Indeed, a prominent way of becoming and then remaining a canonical thinker is precisely to have disciples.[13] Kant certainly viewed
thinkers in his milieu in that way. Even if the consensus forming
around a "great thinker's" ideas is eventually broken, as happened
to Kant by the time Hegel arrived on the scene, that event can ironically ensure one's canonical status. After all, there is no better way
of remaining central to the philosophical conversation than to have
young upstarts challenging your dominant ideas.

Du Châtelet's conception of philosophy is starkly different.
For her, it would be folly to think that we can discover the final
philosophical system. We should dispense with this illusory goal,
for "no philosopher has seen everything," a remark that must be
self-referential. We can search for methods and principles that will
carry us forward—e.g., she calls the Principle of Sufficient Reason
our "compass"—but we must dispense with the notion of the final
philosophy penned by some great man who will convert the rest
of the learned world to his faith. The religious imagery constantly
employed by Voltaire, Wolff, and numerous others in her milieu
is inapt for her own view. Du Châtelet seeks no disciples because
she knows that she has not found the final truth. She is a modern
philosopher, one who seeks modern philosophers for readers. Cor-
respondingly, her conception of the Enlightenment is free from
the paradox found throughout her milieu, where her interlocutors

promoted freethinking on the one hand, even while seeking discipleship on the other.[14]

Du Châtelet promotes a philosophy in progress. In her view, no magnum opus, including her own, will settle philosophy's questions once and for all. She also explains, time and again, how science has been infected with the search for a final theory, one discovered by "great men." Their disciples are later led astray, producing bad science as a result. For instance, in discussing a potential mechanism for gravity, Newton cautiously observed that he does not know the reason that gravity follows his law, and he will "feign no hypothesis" about that. But then his disciples overreacted, seeking to banish hypothetical reasoning from science once and for all. In contrast, disciples of the great mechanical philosophers had such faith that there must always be some mechanism underlying natural phenomena that after promoting some hypothesis, they acted as if they had discovered the final truth. Later, Newton's disciples replaced mechanisms with principles of attraction, proclaiming that gravity, magnetism, cohesion, even fermentation, had now been explained. Throughout her *Institutions*, from the early chapter on hypotheses to the middle chapters on matter to the later chapters on gravity and forces, Du Châtelet warns against these approaches. They have led science and philosophy astray.

As Kant makes explicit in the preface to the *Critique of Pure Reason*, his notion of philosophy reflects a specific conception of science and mathematics. He promotes the idea that as history progresses, each discipline—geometry, logic, physics, and now philosophy—undergoes a transformation, embraces the "secure path of a science," and then never looks back. Certainly, future thinkers can refine an approach, expand the reach of some method, prove a new theorem. But the science itself is fundamentally stable. Geometry was set on the path of a science by Euclid, logic by Aristotle, physics by Bacon and Galileo. In the *Critique*, Kant's task is clear: using these achievements as an inspiration, he will set philosophy on the secure path of a science once and for all. Kant's conception of science undergirds his conception of philosophy's task, especially his view that sciences undergo revolutions that produce permanent intellectual structures.

Du Châtelet's alternative conception of science's history mirrors her rejection of the search for a final philosophy. There was indeed a profound transformation in physics, a "revolution" in the sciences, one that must be studied carefully by Enlightenment philosophers. Yet she argues that deep questions about physics remain, and therefore philosophy must continue to grapple with them. Newton did not settle the basic questions about the study of nature once and for all. Indeed, even the most profound and far-reaching conclusion of his new physics, that gravity is a universal force, was not yet fully understood. It would therefore be unwise to become Newton's disciple. It would be just as unwise to proclaim that with his inspiration, one had found the final philosophical system.

In the *Institutions*, Du Châtelet promotes harmony between science and philosophy not only for its own sake, but also to prevent one discipline from dominating the other. Just as she does not wish to follow some leader, she rejects the conception of science and philosophy in which one seeks to become the master of the other. She propounds a philosophy without masters.

The idea of a philosophy for freethinkers is just as salient today as it was in Du Châtelet's era. The Enlightenment is long over, but its interpretive tactics, its conception of the modern philosopher, its casting of the historical record remain stubbornly relevant. If we learn Du Châtelet's story and find inspiration in her alternative conception of philosophy, we help to undermine the still persistent conception of philosophy as a masculine discipline. We help to disassociate the notion that a philosopher answers only to reason, rejecting allegiance to any thinker, from a conception of masculinity.[15] Du Châtelet's conception of philosophy and her vision of the Enlightenment did not ultimately prevail. But now, we can give her the last word. "As for me, I confess that if I were king . . . I would reform an abuse that excludes, so to speak, half the human family. I would allow women to share in all the rights of humanity, and above all those of the mind."[16]

NOTES

Chapter 1

1. On the Gradot and the story of Du Châtelet, see Zinsser's influential biography, *La Dame d'Esprit*, 66–67; see also Terrall, *The Man Who Flattened the Earth*, 23–25.

2. For a lively and detailed account of Du Châtelet's life and intellectual work and influence, see especially the recent biography by Judith Zinsser, *La Dame d'Esprit*. For details of Parisian life, see Anthony Sutcliffe, *Paris: An Architectural History*, 22.

3. As Fontenelle famously said, this was an "age of academies"—see Roger Hahn, *Anatomy of a Scientific Institution*, 49. While in Paris, Du Châtelet sometimes attended one of the Academy's biannual meetings open to the general public: she mentions one such meeting in an April 1747 letter to Father Jacquier—see Zinsser and Bour's comment in Du Châtelet, *Selected Philosophical and Scientific Writings*, 254, note 8. But she could not join its ranks. The Parisian Academy of Sciences opened to women in 1962—see Michelle le Doeuff, *Hipparchia's Choice*, 251—having rejected the membership of Nobel Prize winner Marie Curie decades earlier.

4. The preface to her draft translation of Mandeville's *Fable of the Bees* is located today in the Voltaire Collection at the National Library of Russia, St. Petersburg. It was published by Ira Wade in his groundbreaking work *Studies on Voltaire, with Some Unpublished Papers of Mme du Châtelet*, Part II, 135. She writes about the "bon livre de physique" on that same page. For details of the Voltaire collection in Russia, see Gorbatov, "From Paris to St. Petersburg: Voltaire's Library in Russia" and more recently, Natalia

Speranskaya, "Émilie Du Châtelet's Manuscripts Preserved at the National Library of Russia."

5. See Zinsser, *La Dame d'esprit*, 33–34, along with the classic account in Ira Wade, *Voltaire and Madame du Châtelet: An Essay on the Intellectual Activity at Cirey*, and more recently, François de Gandt, editor, *Cirey dans la vie intellectual*.

6. See Zinsser and Hayes, "The Marquise as Philosophe," 27, and Zinsser, *La Dame d'Esprit*, 116. This description is indeed apt: during her time in the chateau Du Châtelet was at the center of a European-wide network of intellectuals and leaders. For instance, Prince Frederick sent her and Voltaire a translation of Wolff's German metaphysics for study at Cirey in 1736, and after visiting Cirey, Johann II Bernoulli later served as an intermediary for Brucker's *Bilder-Sal [Portrait Gallery]* entry on her, which promoted her intellectual status widely. Du Châtelet thanks Bernoulli for his support in this regard in a letter of June 1743: see Du Châtelet, *Correspondance*, vol. 2: 123. In the summer of 1739, Christian Wolff had told a correspondent that "Castle Cirey looks like an Academy of Sciences" (see Hans-Peter Neumann, "Émilie Du Châtelet within the Correspondence between Christian Wolff and Ernst Christoph of Manteuffel," 153).

7. Frederick made this remark in a letter from late July 1770, quoted in Besterman, *Voltaire*, 11.

8. In their outstanding edition of Du Châtelet's *Selected Philosophical and Scientific Writings* (5–6), Zinsser and Bour note that Voltaire could not return to Paris without explicit government approval.

9. Most scholars today follow the standard translation of Du Châtelet's text by Isabelle Bour and Judith Zinsser, rendering her title *Foundations of Physics*. In eighteenth-century French, the word "institutions" could certainly mean *foundations*, but it could also mean *elements* or *principles*. Indeed, Keiko Kawashima notes that Du Châtelet referred to her text as the "Élemens de physique" in a letter to Johann Bernoulli—see "Anonymity and Ambition: Émilie Du Châtelet's *Dissertation de feu* (1744)," 432. Because of these complications, I have decided not to translate the word, allowing readers to think of these various meanings as they become relevant at different moments.

10. In letter 14 of *Lettres Philosophiques* (101), Voltaire had mentioned that "the little book by Rohault was for a time a complete physics." But according to Du Châtelet, Voltaire's own *Elémens* had not presented a "complete book" of physics because it was really a commentary on Newton. Years later, she

decided to produce a complete French translation of Newton's *Principia* and append an extensive commentary to it—they were published posthumously together in a single two-volume edition in 1759. Her version of Newton, *Principes mathématiques de la philosophie naturelle*, remains the standard French translation today. The second volume contains the *Exposition abregée du systême du monde* (vol. 2: 1–116), her commentary on Newton, and is followed by *Solution analytique des principaux problems qui concernent le Systême du Monde*, which translates Newton's geometric reasoning into the new language of analysis (vol. 2: 117–286).

11. For details, see William Barber, *Leibniz in France*, 186–91 and the extensive introduction to the critical edition of Voltaire's *Elements* by Robert Walters and Barber, 102–10, which indicates that Voltaire's 1741 edition is clearly a reply to Du Châtelet (see Walters and Barber, 115, and note 1 on 245).

12. Since the second edition represents her considered views on important matters—she never published another revision—and since it represents her important retort to Voltaire's reply of 1741 to her earlier work, I cite it throughout. It is available in reprint as the 28th volume of Part III of Wolff's *Gesammelte Werke* (1988). Often, the changes made to the second edition clarify and extend views that are merely inchoate in the first; cf. Zinsser and Bour, *Selected Philosophical and Scientific Writings*, 108. The second edition also contains her full dispute with Dortous de Mairan, secretary of the Academy of Sciences in Paris: the first edition's discussion of Mairan in a single section (1740, §574) of a few pages is expanded into a sixty-six-page appendix in the second edition (1742, 476–542). Zinsser explains the importance of this exchange and its connection with the second edition in "Émilie du Châtelet and the Enlightenment's *Querelle des femmes*," 143.

13. For instance, just limiting the discussion to works on her ideas published in French, German and Italian, see Gilbert-Joseph Vallé, *Lettre sur la nature de matière et de la mouvement a l'auteur des institutions de physique*, which runs to ninety-six pages; Abraham Gotthelf Kästner's "Brief" (letter) on the German translation of Du Châtelet's "Naturlehre" (discussed in Baasner, *Abraham Gotthelf Kästner, Aufklärer*, 533–49); Julien La Mettrie, "Lettre Critique de M. de La Mettrie sur l'Histoire Naturelle de l'Âme à Mme. La Marquise du Châtelet," appended to his *L'Histoire Naturelle de l'Âme*; and the discussion of Du Châtelet's views in the Abbé Conti's *Dialoghi Filosofici*. For discussion, see Kathleen Wellman, *La Mettrie: Medicine, Philosophy, and Enlightenment*, 183*ff*; Le Ru, *Émilie du Châtelet philosophe*, 151–60; and, on Conti, see Romana Bassi, "Émilie Du Châtelet and Antonio Conti: The Italian Translation of the *Institutions physiques*," 339–41. Several years later,

Vallé anonymously published his *Réfutation du Système des Monades,* which discusses her views in depth.

14. For instance, reviews appeared in the *Journal des Sçavans* in France, the *Gottingische Zeitung der Gelehrten Sachen* in Prussia, and Italian journals in both Florence and Venice (on the latter, see Sarah Hutton, "Émilie Du Châtelet and Italy," 315).

15. See Diderot and D'Alembert, eds., *Encyclopédie,* vol. 5: 785.

16. Zinsser and Hayes, "The Marquise as Philosophe," 28. Du Châtelet has long been considered the most famous intellectual woman in the Enlightenment—see, e.g., Elisabeth Fox-Genovese, "Women and the Enlightenment," 255.

17. For instance, Andrea Reichenberger shows that Du Châtelet's views on space and time were discussed extensively in the 1740s by figures like Abraham Kästner, and were still being discussed in print twenty years later ("The Reception of Émilie Du Châtelet in the German Enlightenment," 133–34). Italian writers were still praising her discussion of *vis viva* years after her death (see Sarah Hutton, "Émilie Du Châtelet and Italy," 323).

18. Indeed, he sometimes seemed unconcerned with historical accuracy in the *Principia.* For instance, he attributed results to Galileo that everyone knew came from Descartes (see, e.g., the concluding remark in Diderot, *Penseés sur l'interpretation de la Nature,* 205–6). Indeed, the phrase above attributing the "laws of motion" to Descartes, rather than, say, to Galileo or to Newton himself, is not a slip. As Newton knew full well, although Galileo studied free fall and what was later called "inertia," he did not think in terms of the laws of nature. That was Descartes's contribution in 1644 in his *Principles of Philosophy,* a text Newton studied and criticized in great depth in his unpublished manuscript *De Gravitatione* before the *Principia* was published (see Newton, *Philosophical Writings,* 26–58).

19. See the helpful discussion in I. B. Cohen, *Revolution in Science,* 4–6, 85; Cohen contrasts the attitudes of the great thinkers of the seventeenth and early eighteenth centuries in this respect with the self-proclaimed revolutionary work in chemistry by Priestley and Lavoisier in the late eighteenth century (Cohen, *Revolution,* 225).

20. In fact, in September of 1738, Du Châtelet had already mentioned "une entière révolution dans la Physique" in her "Lettre sur *Les Elemens de la Philosophie de Newton,*" 535; see Ursula Winter, "From Translation to Philosophical Discourse," 179. The great Newton scholar I. B. Cohen credits the

French mathematician Clairaut with being the first to proclaim a "revolution" in physics involving Newton's work at a meeting of the Academy of Sciences in Paris in November of 1747—see Cohen, *Revolution in Science*, 216; and, Cohen credits Fontenelle with describing a revolution in mathematics in the 1720s, but not one in physics or science, at Cohen, *Revolution*, 213–15. Clairaut knew Du Châtelet's work from earlier in the decade; indeed, he collaborated on her translation of, and commentary to, Newton's *Principia*, informing Father Jacquier in March of 1746 that she was working on the translation night and day—see the excellent discussion of the details concerning the translation and commentary in Véronique Le Ru, *Émilie du Châtelet philosophe*, 93–103 and also Michel Toulmonde, "Émilie Du Châtelet and Newton's *Principia*," 242–49. The translation was published posthumously in June of 1759 but was largely finished before she died in early September of 1749. On the notion of a revolution, see Hatfield, "Was the Scientific Revolution Really a Revolution in Science?," 505; and on the use of "revolution" in socio-political contexts, even before the French Revolution in 1789, see Keith Baker, "Revolution," especially 54.

21. See Du Châtelet, *Institutions*, preface, section V, page 5.

22. As Guicciardini shows, Enlightenment (especially Continental European) readers of Newton's *Principia* tended to focus, at least by the middle of the century, on the famous notes in the "Jesuit edition" by Le Seur and Jacquier, rather than trying to wade through Newton's geometric demonstrations themselves (*Reading the Principia*, 248–49). That is why, in her translation of Newton, Du Châtelet also included the *Solution analytique des principaux problems qui concernent le Système du Monde*, which translates Newton's geometric reasoning into the new language of analysis (*Principes mathématiques de la philosophie naturelle*, vol. 2: 117–286).

23. See the discussion in Genevieve Lloyd, *Enlightenment Shadows*, 118ff, one of the rare cases in which a contemporary philosopher in the Anglo-American tradition discusses the *Encyclopedia* of Diderot and D'Alembert. Another is Rom Harré's intriguing discussion in "Knowledge," 36–44.

24. Technically, the old saw that Kant proclaimed a "Copernican revolution" in philosophy is inaccurate; instead, he uses the word "revolution" only at *Critique of Pure Reason*, Bxii, attributing a "Revolution der Denkart" to Bacon and his followers. It is true that he cites Copernicus as an inspiration for having overturned the astronomical order by proclaiming that the sun, rather than the earth, lies at the center of our solar system. Kant would similarly reorient the study of knowledge by making the human subject its center,

declaring that the object of knowledge conforms to our cognition (rather than the other way around). But Kant did not call this maneuver a "revolution." See Kant, *Critique of Pure Reason*, Bxii–xiii, for the discussion of Bacon and Galileo, and Bxvi–xviii for the discussion of Copernicus, with the note to Bxxii explaining Newton's role. For intriguing details, see Cohen, *Revolution in Science*, 237–53, a text unjustly neglected by Kant scholars.

25. Brucker's influence was immense, and his focus on the present state of philosophy in his day is also found in other major works that followed his example. For instance, Samuel Formey, a great promoter of Madame Du Châtelet's ideas in the 1740s, also ended his discussion of the "electic"—i.e., the modern, non-school-based—philosophy of his day with Wolff. See *Abrégée de l'histoire de la philosophie*, book 3, chapter 2. Formey's text is indeed "*abrégée*": it is thousands of pages shorter than Brucker's, but follows his lead in this key regard. Similarly, although the famous English version of Brucker's text had only 670 pages to represent his thousands of pages of material, it preserved his discussion of modern philosophy, ending also with Wolff—see William Enfield, *The History of Philosophy*, vol. 2: 570–72. Brucker's influence continued to be felt later in the century: e.g., in his multi-volume *Histoire des philosophes modernes*, published in 1760, Alexandre Saverien singles out Brucker's *Historia Critica* among the many texts he consulted, writing in his preface that it is a learned text that contains "immense research" (preface, Part I: vi–vii). For discussion of Brucker, see Hatfield, "Was the Scientific Revolution Really a Revolution in Science?," 515–18; also, Leo Catana characterizes Brucker's methodology in considerable detail in his "The Concept 'System of Philosophy': The Case of Jacob Brucker's Historiography of Philosophy."

26. We may now anachronistically think of Newton, not to mention Galileo, as "scientists" rather than "philosophers," but Brucker and his milieu knew better. He devoted substantial attention to Newton and his many followers. The reason is that any distinction between science and philosophy in this era was blurry at best. Brucker has an extensive and detailed discussion of Newton at *Historia critica philosophiae*, vol. 4.2: 639–55 [part 2 of volume 4 is sometimes referred to as volume 5], including a detailed description of many commentaries on Newton (*Historia*, 642–46). See Hatfield, "Was the Scientific Revolution Really a Revolution in Science?," 517.

27. See *Encyclopedia Britannica*, accessed 17 August 2023.

28. Pagden, *The Enlightenment*, 103.

29. Jonathan Israel, *Radical Enlightenment*, 85. This is part of the "Women, Philosophy, Sexuality" chapter. In case the reader misses this paragraph, the

index lists Du Châtelet as "Voltaire's mistress"—see Israel, *Radical Enlighten-ment*, 784.

30. See Paul Hazard, *La Pensée Européenne au XVIIIème siècle*, vol. 1: 350, which devotes a decent paragraph to Du Châtelet and Voltaire. There are no citations here to the discussion of Voltaire and Du Châtelet—see vol. 3: 103. To his credit, however, Hazard does mention Du Châtelet's main work in passing at vol. 2: 43, although the sentence ends with a focus on Maupertuis, who is then discussed in more depth; and cf. vol. 2: 54, where Du Châtelet's *Institutions* is used to illustrate a point about Christian Wolff's ideas.

31. See especially the historically nuanced discussion in Judith Zinsser, *La Dame d'Esprit*, 105–6. Moreover, as Joan Kelly shows in several classic essays, there were various moments in European history, even in medieval times, when women could exercise sexual freedom by sleeping with or loving men who were not their husbands, as long as that specific social arrangement was part of a larger system that benefited men overall—see, e.g., *Women, History and Theory*, 27–30. For discussion of a similar historical dynamic, see Anne-Sophie Sørup Wandall, "Contested Identities," 50–53.

32. The narrative is surprisingly influential, reappearing in a wide range of works without any questions raised. A good example would be this descrip-tion from Joyce Chaplin's book on Benjamin Franklin, *The First Scientific American*, 256: "In the 1730s, Voltaire had allied himself with the French Newtonians, including Maupertuis and Gabrielle Émilie le Tonnelier de Breteuil, Marquise du Chatelet, the French translator of Newton's *Principia*. (Du Châtelet was mistress to both her fellow Newtonians.)" More recently, the sole mention of Du Châtelet in the *Encyclopedia of the Scientific Revolution*, 599, occurs under the "Sex and Gender" entry: her translation of Newton is noted, but not the *Institutions*.

33. Influential accounts from the 1970s and 1980s include Carolyn Iltis, "Madame du Châtelet's Metaphysics and Mechanics;" Linda Gardiner Janik, "Searching for the Metaphysics of Science: The Structure and Composition of Mme. Du Châtelet's *Institutions de physique*, 1737–1740"; Elisabeth Bad-inter, *Émilie, Émilie*; and, Esther Ehrman, *Mme du Châtelet: Scientist, Philoso-pher and Feminist of the Enlightenment*.

34. Zinsser's influential articles include "Translating Newton's *Principia*: The Marquise du Châtelet's revision and additions for a French audience," "Entrepreneur of the 'Republic of Letters': Emilie de Breteuil, Marquise du Châtelet, and Bernard Mandeville's *Fable of the Bees*," and "Émilie Du Châte-let and the Enlightenment's *Querelle des femmes*." With Julie Candles Hayes,

Zinsser also edited the important collection *Émilie du Châtelet: Rewriting Enlightenment Philosophy and Science*. Her biography, *La Dame d'Esprit*, was first published by Viking in 2006.

35. For classic discussions of this topic, see Londa Schiebinger, *The Mind Has No Sex?*, on modern science, and Eileen O'Neill, "Disappearing Ink," on modern philosophy. For a fascinating discussion of the early modern intellectual network involving Elisabeth, van Schurman, and others, see Carol Pal, *Republic of Women*. For recent insightful discussions of the development of the exclusionary canon in early modern philosophy, see Lisa Shapiro, "Revisiting the Early Modern Philosophical Canon" and Mary Ellen Waithe, "From Cannon Fodder to Canon Formation," both of whom propose remedies.

36. That conception, which I regard as normative rather than descriptive, is paired with an equally normative conception of the (supposed) gender neutrality of philosophy itself, with its self-conception as a discipline focused on the neutral application of rationality to pressing questions. Because these conceptions are normative, they are often immune to "mere empirical refutation," as Charlotte Witt insightfully notes in her "Feminist Interpretations of the Philosophical Canon," 542.

Chapter 2

1. For the comparison to great ancient thinkers, see *Lettres Philosophiques*, letter 12, 82.

2. See Vinson Cunningham, "Review of Jefferson's Bible," 78.

3. For Halley's quotation, see Mordechai Feingold, *The Newtonian Moment*, xiv; and 143–44 for Pope's famous lines.

4. Desaguliers, *A Course of Experimental Philosophy*, vii.

5. See the introduction to Voltaire, *Elements of the Philosophy of Newton*, 32–33.

6. See Voltaire, *Elements of the Philosophy of Newton*, 186 and 193, respectively. The poem was also included in the posthumous (1759) publication of Du Châtelet's translation of Newton's *Principia* [Du Châtelet 1759]. This continued to be a major theme of Voltaire's reception of Newton throughout his life: he told the Académie Française in 1776 that we are all Newton's "disciples" now (Peter Gay, *The Enlightenment: The Science of Freedom*, 128–29).

7. See Du Châtelet, *Institutions*, preface, §VI and VII, respectively. For discussion of Voltaire's letter—viz. D1630 of 19 October 1738—see the introduction to *Elements of the Philosophy of Newton*, 54. In his letter to Algarotti

in May of 1738, Voltaire wrote of "mon petit *essai* du cathechisme neutonien," continuing his use of religious imagery—see Algarotti, *Opere*, vol. 16: 72–73.

8. Besterman quotes and discusses the letter at *Voltaire*, 202. Besterman quotes the original, which was (impressively) written in English, but I have modernized Voltaire's spelling. Even toward the end of his long life, Voltaire was still using religious imagery, noting that in his work on Newton, he had been "the apostle and the martyr of the English"—see Feingold, *The Newtonian Moment*, 104, quoting a letter from 1768.

9. Indeed, an entire chapter of Feingold's important work, *The Newtonian Moment*, is devoted to "The Voltaire Effect."

10. For an outstanding and historically detailed description of that influence, see Mordechai Feingold, *The Newtonian Moment*.

11. On Franklin's Newtonianism, see the classic account in I. B. Cohen, *Franklin and Newton*, and more recently, Jessica Riskin, *Science in an Age of Sensibility*, 85ff; on Adam Smith's potential Newtonianism, see Eric Schliesser, *Adam Smith*, chapter 13.

12. For a fascinating discussion of the philosophical differences between Newton's conception of the "fluxional" method and Leibniz's approach to the calculus as one aspect of an overarching symbolic system undergirded by logic, see Ernst Cassirer, "Newton and Leibniz," 380–86.

13. In fact, Newton told Leibniz as much in an October 1693 letter: see Newton, *Philosophical Writings*, 143.

14. The *locus classicus* for all contemporary discussions of mechanism is Marie Boas, "The Establishment of the Mechanical Philosophy."

15. Huygens's famous objections from 1690 are in his *Discours sur la cause de la Pesanteur*; for a helpful discussion, see Rienk Vermij, "Newton and Huygens," 717–20.

16. See the discussion in Bertoloni Meli, *Equivalence and Priority*, chapter 6. In a letter to Leibniz in October of 1693, Newton brushes aside the criticism that he lacks a mechanism, proclaiming that the celestial and terrestrial phenomena follow from "nothing but gravity acting in accordance with the laws described by me"—see Newton, *Philosophical Writings*, 144. Neither Leibniz nor Huygens could embrace that idea.

17. For a wide-ranging discussion of Euler's life and his numerous technical accomplishments, see Calinger's monumental biography, *Euler*.

18. Newton had labored mightily, e.g., in Book II of his *Principia*, to undermine the rival Cartesian theory according to which gravity is reducible to

the motion of a swirling imperceptible fluid in the heavens, a vortex. Descartes had been a major proponent of the vortex theory of planetary motion; Leibniz presented a more mathematically sophisticated version of the vortex theory after reading Newton's *Principia* in 1688. But the theory did not die with Leibniz early in the new century. For instance, many years later, Euler defended vortices or at least a fluid subtle matter like an ether—see Aiton, *The Vortex Theory*, 251–52, and Euler's letter to Du Châtelet from the end of 1741 in which he discusses hypotheses concerning subtle matter (Du Châtelet, *Correspondance*, vol. 2: 93). For an excellent discussion, see Curtis Wilson, "Euler on Action at a Distance," 400.

19. For a discussion of the substantial distance between Newton's and Clarke's understanding, see Janiak, *Newton as Philosopher*, 58–74, and 143, for discussion of Newton's difference from Clarke on God's relation to space.

20. See Voltaire, *Lettres philosophiques*, 196; 204–7; and 246–47, respectively. On solidity, see letter 14, 97.

21. The initial phrase in Latin is "*Gravitatem in corpora universa fieri.*" Throughout, I use the standard English translation by I. B. Cohen and Anne Whitman, deviating from its familiar renderings only when necessary. The Latin original is taken from the 1972 critical edition by Cohen and Koyré. The quotation above is from Newton, *Mathematical Principles*, 810, and the Latin is at *Principia mathematica*, vol. 2: 576. For recent influential interpretations of Newton's argument for universal gravity, see the classic account in George E. Smith, "How Did Newton Discover Universal Gravity?," and more recently, William Harper, *Isaac Newton's Scientific Method*, esp. chapters 3, 4, 7–8.

22. In fact, this is a major topic of the famous correspondence between Newton and the editor of the *Principia*'s second edition, Roger Cotes. See Cotes to Newton, 18 March 1713, in Newton, *Philosophical Writings*, 156. Years later, in correspondence with Tobias Mayer in 1751 but also elsewhere, Euler indicates that he, too, is well aware of this problem in Newton's reasoning. Unlike Cotes, however, Euler was convinced that the two bodies were in fact interacting with something like an ether. For discussion of Cotes, see Zvi Biener and Chris Smeenk, "Cotes's Queries," and for discussion of Euler, see Arnold Koslow, "Changes in the Concept of Mass from Newton to Einstein," 124. Thanks to Qiu Lin for discussing this issue with me.

23. For classic accounts, see Alexandre Koyré, *Newtonian Studies* and Ernan McMullin, *Newton on Matter and Activity*.

24. See J. E. Edleston, editor, *Correspondence of Sir Isaac Newton and Professor Cotes*, lxxvii.

25. See Newton, *Mathematical Principles*, 796; I have slightly modified the translation. The original Latin is at Newton, *Principia mathematica*, vol. 2: 552–54.

26. Biener emphasizes this point in his recent interpretation of the *Regulae*, noting also that the claim of universality should not be understood to involve a claim about necessity or essentiality—see Zvi Biener, "Newton's *Regulae Philosophandi*," 10–11. There are many questions about the goals and success of the *Regulae* that I cannot discuss here—see the historically informed treatment in Steffen Ducheyne, *The Main Business of Natural Philosophy*, chapter 3.2.

27. See Newton, *Mathematical Principles*, 796 and *Philosophiae Naturalis Principia Mathematica*, vol. 2: 554.

28. Newton, *Mathematical Principles*, 391–92, and *Philosophiae Naturalis Principia Mathematica*, vol. 1: 26–27.

29. The idea's lineage is famous: first broached by Galileo in his *Assayer* in the 1620s, Descartes endorsed the distinction, followed by Boyle, who gave us the relevant words in English, with Locke making the distinction even more famous in his *Essay* in 1690.

30. Both mathematicians and philosophers took special note of the definitions. This is certainly true of Leibniz, who took significant notes on the definitions, as one might expect from a geometer: see Domenico Bertoloni Meli, *Equivalence and Priority*, 96–104, 306.

31. See Newton, *Mathematical Principles*, 405, and *Principia mathematica*, vol. 1: 41.

32. Although Clarke may not have been an Arian like Newton—or perhaps Locke—before him, due to his *Scripture Doctrine of the Trinity* (1712) and other works and remarks, he was thought to eschew the standard Anglican interpretation of the Trinity. As a result, he was prevented from rising further in the Church of England. The ever-witty Voltaire, a great ally of Clarke, reports that an influential bishop in the church once told Princess Caroline that although Clarke was the most learned and honest man in England, he had the defect of not really being a Christian. For discussion, see Vailati's edition of Clarke's *A Demonstration of the Being and Attributes of God*, xi–xii, and H. G. Alexander's famous edition of the Leibniz-Clarke correspondence, xii.

33. For a helpful discussion, see Bertoloni Meli, "Newton and the Leibniz-Clarke correspondence," 458–59, and Roger Ariew's introduction to his edition of the Leibniz-Clarke Correspondence, vii–viii.

34. See Clarke 5: 110–16 for the first quotation, before the ellipsis, and Clarke 5: 124–30 for the second one, after it (all good editions preserve the letter and section numbering for handy reference). There are related passages in Clarke 5: 118–13—see Samuel Clarke and G.W. Leibniz, *A Collection of Papers*; also available in Leibniz, *Die philosophischen Schriften von Gottfried Wilhelm Leibniz*, vol. 7: 352–440, and in English translation in Ariew, editor, *G. W. Leibniz and Samuel Clarke: Correspondence*. For a discussion of instrumentalist readings of universal gravity like that presented by Clarke, see Janiak, "Newton and the Reality of Force."

35. For a classic account, see Margaret Jacob, *The Newtonians and the English Revolution*, 145–46.

36. See Bentley, *The Correspondence of Richard Bentley*, and Bentley, *Eight Boyle Lectures on Atheism*. For a classic account of the widespread social, intellectual, and political significance of the Boyle lectures in early modern England, including their connection to the influence of the Latitudinarians, see Margaret Jacob, *The Newtonians and the English Revolution*, 144–76.

37. The question of action at a distance in Newton's physics has received substantial scholarly attention. The best general account of the topic is in Mary Hesse, *Forces and Fields: The Concept of Action at a Distance in the History of Physics*. In *Newton as Philosopher*, I argued that Newton dismissed the notion that material bodies could act on one another at a distance—for a sympathetic discussion, see Noam Chomsky, *What Kind of Creatures Are We?*, 34–35. My argument is questioned in Steffen Ducheyne, "Newton on Action at a Distance and the Cause of Gravity," 154–59; John Henry, "Gravity and De Gravitatione: The Development of Newton's Ideas on Action at a Distance," 11–27; and, Eric Schliesser, "Newton's Substance Monism, Distant Action, and the Nature of Newton's Empiricism," 160–66. I reply to Ducheyne, Henry, and Schliesser in "Three Concepts of Causation in Newton," 396–407. See also Hylarie Kochiras's two papers, "Gravity and Newton's Substance Counting Problem," and "Gravity's Cause and Substance Counting: Contextualizing the Problems."

38. Newton, *Philosophical Writings*, 136.

39. Ironically, we now know that Cotes himself had a strong conception of essences in mind when editing the second edition of Newton's magnum opus many years later, one rejected, in turn, by Clarke. As Cotes prepared the

second edition, Clarke sent him some (now lost) objections to his proposed preface, to which Cotes replied on 25 June 1713 as follows: "I received Your very kind Letter, I return You my thanks for Your corrections of the Preface, & particularly for Your advice in relation to that place where I seem'd to assert Gravity to be Essential to Bodies. . . . My design in that passage was not to assert Gravity to be essential to Matter, but rather to assert that we are ignorant of the Essential propertys of Matter & that in respect of our Knowledge Gravity might possibly lay as fair a claim to that Title as the other Propertys which I mention'd. For I understand by Essential propertys such propertys without which no others belonging to the same substance can exist: and I would not undertake to prove that it were impossible for any of the other Properties of Bodies to exist without even Extension." [Newton, *Correspondence*, vol. 5: 412–13.] It is doubtful that either Newton or Clarke agreed.

40. See the pithy essay by Jeremy Gray, "Non-Euclidean Geometry."

41. This aspect of Du Châtelet's treatment of gravity in the *Institutions* is a principal theme of Katherine Brading's *Émilie Du Châtelet and the Foundations of Physical Science*. Also, as George Smith has shown, even when Du Châtelet wrote her commentary on Newton's theory for her translation of his *Principia*, she did not adopt the role of the disciple, taking care to note various remaining empirical problems facing the theory—see "Du Châtelet's Commentary on Newton's *Principia*: An Assessment," 300–301. Keiko Kawashima makes a parallel point about Du Châtelet's "electic" attitude in the 1744 printing of her dissertation on fire (see "Anonymity and Ambition: Émilie Du Châtelet's *Dissertation de feu* (1744)," 434), where she defends *vis viva* even while beginning to work on the Newton translation and commentary.

42. Perhaps the most influential discussion of this historical point can be found in Clifford Truesdell, *Essays in the History of Mechanics*, 106–16. Truesdell also expends considerable energy identifying the locus of false narratives about "Newtonian mechanics" in the eighteenth century, singling out especially Ernst Mach for having had a pernicious historical influence. A more measured account can be found in the recent work by Katherine Brading and Marius Stan: *Philosophical Mechanics in the Age of Reason*.

43. Niccolò Guicciardini notes that it would be most accurate historically to say that the eighteenth century eventually used the "Eulerian" calculus rather than a Newtonian or Leibnizian one (*Reading the Principia*, 259). For an outstanding account of Euler's role in eighteenth-century mechanics, see Henk

Bos, "Mathematics and Rational Mechanics," 335–37, who also discusses the difficulty of achieving a historically accurate account of the calculus (342).

44. Newton, *Principia*, 404. In her commentary on Newton, Du Châtelet marks this distinction in his thinking by noting that definition 3 concerns "la force d'inertie," an exact translation, and that definition 4 concerns the "force active," which is her translation of *vis impressa*. Hence she implies that the force of inertia involves *passivity*, impressed force *activity*. See Du Châtelet, *Exposition abregée du Système du monde*, vol. 2: 8.

45. For a helpful discussion of Euler's evolving views on this subject, see Koslow, "Changes in the Concept of Mass from Newton to Einstein," 122–23. See also P. M. Harman, *Metaphysics and Natural Philosophy*, 15, and Thomas Ahnert, "Newton in the German Speaking Lands," 51–52. In his letter to Du Châtelet from the end of 1741, Euler ponders the question of whether one can consider the "property" of inertia to be given the name of a force, but then the letter breaks off (Du Châtelet, *Correspondance*, vol. 2: 93).

46. Euler, "Recherches sur l'origine des forces," part ix, 423.

47. Newton, *Opticks*, Query 31, 401.

48. For further details on the problems with assuming that the eighteenth century involved a development of something like the Newtonian paradigm, see Simon Schaffer, "Natural Philosophy," 55–56, 70–71, which also notes Euler's important role, and Margaret Jacob, "Newtonianism and the Origins of the Enlightenment," especially 24–25.

49. D'Alembert, *Traité de Dynamique*, 3. For discussion, see Alain Firode, *La dynamique de D'Alembert*, 11, although Firode calls it the "principe d'inertie" here, which does not reflect D'Alembert's view in the first edition of 1743; the text was reprinted in 1758.

50. He writes: "In the definition of the force of inertia, I used the term 'property,' rather than 'power,' because the second of these words seems to designate a metaphysical and obscure being, which resides in bodies, and of which we have no clear idea"—see "Force d'inertie," *Encyclopedie*, vol. 7: 110, which is attributed to D'Alembert.

51. See Clifford Truesdell, *Essays in the History of Mechanics*, 113. For discussion of a related disagreement between D'Alembert and Euler in the middle of the century, see René Dugas, *A History of Mechanics*, 245–46.

52. For discussion, see Curtis Wilson, "Euler on Action at a Distance and Fundamental Equations in Continuum Mechanics," 418.

53. For an excellent discussion of a host of related topics, see Brian Hepburn, "The Quiet Scientific Revolution," and J. B. Shank, *Before Voltaire*, 1–18, which is sharply critical of leading descriptions of the emergence of Newtonian mechanics. See also Roy Porter's introduction to the *Cambridge History of Eighteenth-Century Science*, especially 1–5. The most extensive discussion now available of these issues is Brading and Stan, *Philosophical Mechanics in the Age of Reason*, the first three chapters of which indicate in great detail how various disputes concerning collision theory, matter theory, and related topics often did not include the notion of mass, or perhaps even the notion of force, during the first decades of the eighteenth century. See also *Philosophical Mechanics in the Age of Reason*, chapter 7.3, on what Brading and Stan call the "elusive" notion of mass well into the eighteenth century (also chapter 9.3, on D'Alembert's vexed relationship with the notion of mass). There is no clearer indication that no Newtonian paradigm on these topics had yet been established.

54. See the illuminating fifth appendix, "Relativity and the Problem of Space," in Albert Einstein, *Relativity: The Special and the General Theory*, 135.

55. Technically, anything that might count as a reason to place the earth in (e.g.) region R_1 would also count as a reason to place it in R_2 because prior to matter's creation, R_1 and R_2 are qualitatively, although not numerically, identical.

56. As Cassirer indicates, the Newtonian Colin Maclaurin made a similar argument about the relation between the law of inertia and absolute space in 1748 (*Das Erkenntnisproblem, Werke*, vol. 3: 402), although Euler's version seems to have been more influential. This episode highlights the usual problem of characterizing an argument as "Newtonian"; in this case, Newton's own approach differed from his followers' in a deep way.

Chapter 3

1. As Heilbron puts it pithily, "Descartes then replaced Aristotle as the foil against which British physics would test its metal" (*Electricity in the Seventeenth and Eighteenth Centuries*, 38).

2. See especially the prominent and compelling interpretation advanced by Howard Stein in "Newton's Metaphysics," who emphasizes the link to the Aristotelian tradition.

3. See her discussion in the *Institutions* (1742, §299) and her translation of Newton's proposition seven of Book III in *Principes mathématiques*

(Du Châtelet 1759, vol. 2: 21). She explains later in the *Institutions* (1742, §388) that some Newtonians then argue that gravity is essential to matter.

4. So, on her view, for a property P to be essential to a bearer B is both for P to make B the kind of thing that it is, and also for P to be intrinsic to B.

5. Philosophers would appreciate this point: a property P of a body may be intrinsic to it without P being essential. For instance, I can have my legs crossed, which is a feature that is non-relational, but of course it's not essential to me. When I uncross my legs, I don't become a different person. I owe this example to Sally Haslanger.

6. The conclusion requires a reasonable supplement: if it turns out that the force of gravity depends on the ether in some way, then it seems reasonable to conclude that material bodies do not have gravity as part of their essence in the traditional sense, for they would lack it in the absence of the ether. This seems reasonable, in turn, because to deny this contention would be to deny that material bodies would still be material bodies in the absence of the ether, which seems ad hoc.

7. As Katherine Brading notes (*Émilie Du Châtelet and the Foundations of Physical Science*, 26–32), in an early draft of the *Institutions*, Du Châtelet followed the approach found in many texts in the early eighteenth century by presenting a version of Newton's Rules for Philosophizing (*Regulae philosophandi*). Many philosophers, like s'Gravesande and Musschenbroek and others, thought that the Rules would clarify Newton's controversial theory of universal gravity. Du Châtelet, however, came to realize that the Rules could not play that role effectively, so she substituted a discussion of the principle of sufficient reason and of essences in the published version of the *Institutions*. Perhaps Du Châtelet had a realization: Cotes's and Newton's differing attempts to use the Rules to undergird the empirical argument for gravity's universality without clarifying the notion indicates that the Rules are not up to the task.

8. Perhaps the most influential version of the classic narrative is in Ernst Cassirer, *Die Philosophie der Aufklärung*, who emphasized how the French *philosophes* rejected Cartesianism, embracing a combination of Newton's and Locke's ideas. In a recent study of Enlightenment historiography, Edelstein argues that the *philosophes* often embraced Descartes as much as Newton— see *The Enlightenment*, 26–28, 36–40, 48. However, he also shows that there is much to the classic account, noting (115) that Newton and Locke were key Enlightenment figures because the French *philosophes* succeeded in promoting their narrative.

9. D'Alembert, *Discours Préliminaire*, 131. Just before beginning his discussion of Locke, D'Alembert notes that Newton did not cause "any revolution" in metaphysics. On D'Alembert's status as a "Lockean" philosopher, see Peter Anstey, "D'Alembert, the 'Preliminary Discourse' and experimental philosophy," 501–2.

10. François de Gandt argues that in 1732, Maupertuis had already presented a Newtonian view colored by the Lockean idea that our knowledge of substances is fundamentally limited in a way that many of Newton's critics failed to recognize—see "Qu'est ce qu'être Newtonien en 1740?," 34–35.

11. Stillingfleet was open to hearing Locke's endorsement of Newtonian ideas: he himself was known for having compared Descartes's views unfavorably with Newton's (see John Gascoigne, *Cambridge in the Age of the Enlightenment*, 65) and eventually came to endorse aspects of Newtonian natural philosophy (see Margaret Jacob, *The Newtonians and the English Revolution*, 32). For a discussion of Stillingfleet's opinion that Locke's view of substance might undermine the Trinity, at least in its standard Anglican interpretation, see Gerard Reedy, *The Bible and Reason*, 12, 112–13, 136–39.

12. See *The Works of John Locke*, vol. 4: 467–68.

13. As quoted by Howard Stein, "On Locke, 'the Great Huygenius, and the Incomparable Mr. Newton,'" 32–33.

14. Newton, *Treatise of the System of the World*, 38. Importantly, Véronique Le Ru notes that Du Châtelet read and referred to the *Treatise*—see *Émilie du Châtelet philosophe*, 103.

15. Stein emphasizes the importance of this passage in the *Treatise*, since it involves a rare case in which Newton is forthcoming: "the almost obsessive iteration in this passage seems clear evidence of Newton's intention to bring emphatically forward a new notion of the *unity* of interaction as the form of a force of nature. In terms of the fields already referred to, this means that exactly those bodies that are susceptible to the action of a given interaction-field are also the *sources* of the field" (Stein, "Newton's Metaphysics," 288, italics in original). Whether Newton has an inchoate notion of the gravitational field here is subject to dispute.

16. See the excellent discussion in Brading, *Émilie Du Châtelet and the Foundations of Physical Science*, 93–94.

17. Du Châtelet makes this point by noting that a hypothesis must cohere with the principle of sufficient reason, that is, it must purport to explain something by presenting the reason for it, or its cause. See *Institutions*, 1742,

§61. For a subtle interpretation of Du Châtelet's conception of hypotheses, see Detlefsen, "Du Châtelet and Descartes on the Roles of Hypothesis and Metaphysics in Natural Philosophy."

18. The *locus classicus* for scholarly discussions is Eric Aiton, *The Vortex Theory of Planetary Motions*.

19. See Du Châtelet, *Exposition Abregée du Systême du Monde*, 1–8. Indeed, by the early Enlightenment, astronomy had transcended the dispute between Ptolemy and Copernicus, arriving at the Newtonian stage of development when one can, for the first time, appreciate the fact that the "center" of the system may now be understood as its center of mass. Since the Sun contains most of the mass in the solar system, this new center is very close to the Sun. This idea required new concepts in physics that were not yet available in Copernicus's day.

20. Paganini intriguingly notes that Du Châtelet's view in the *Institutions* shifts from attributing the attitude toward hypotheses to Newton himself (in the 1740 edition) to attributing it primarily to his disciples (in the second edition of 1742)—see "Rehabilitating hypotheses in the French Enlightenment: Émilie Du Châtelet and Condillac," 336. Once again, the second edition has a more precise view.

21. In her insightful discussion of the *Institutions*, Véronique Le Ru emphasizes that one's "sagacité" is risked if one follows an authority too closely—see *Émilie du Châtelet philosophe*, 58–59 and 108.

22. In a fascinating essay on the development of the canon of modern science, Simon Schaffer emphasizes the notion that canonized thinkers are treated like "saints" and their texts become sacred, a major theme of Du Châtelet's thinking. See "Contextualizing the anon," 215–16.

23. See the classic account in John Earman, *World Enough and Space-time*, and the more recent discussion in DiSalle, *Understanding Space-time*.

24. It is debatable whether Kant makes that assumption in his familiar arguments concerning the representation of space in the Metaphysical Exposition that appears near the opening of the *Critique of Pure Reason*. He certainly argues that the a priori character of our representation of space is important.

25. See especially her discussion in the *Institutions* (1742, §135).

26. In his discussion (§46) of space—"was der Raum ist"—in the *Deutsche Metaphysik* [*Vernünftige Gedancken*, 1720], Wolff assumes explicitly that the representation of space reflects what space really is. We represent space to be the order of things, he thinks, and it really is such an order ("die Ordnung der

Dinge")—see also §§132–134. In tandem, for Wolff, an order is an epistemic notion: the order of things is nothing but the similarity of the multiplicity in the series of things next to one another, and similarity, in turn, involves the notion that one recognizes ("erkennen") that things are distinct based on the same variable (such as location); see §18 and §133. For a discussion of the ways in which Du Châtelet may be said to adopt Wolff's metaphysics, see Stan, "Emilie Du Châtelet's Metaphysics of Substance."

27. Her seriousness regarding this point is reflected in the very structure of the chapter itself: after briefly rehearsing the well-known argument using the principle of sufficient reason against Newton's position (Du Châtelet, *Institutions*, 1742, §§72–74), she then spends considerably more time discussing our representation of space and its consequences (§§77–87). For a related discussion of her conception of time and of our representation of time, which depends on the succession of our ideas, see Clara Carus, "Du Châtelet's Contribution to the Concept of Time."

28. For the argument that Du Châtelet's conception does in fact work reasonably well, see Brading and Lin, "Du Châtelet on Absolute and Relative Motion."

29. In his magisterial biography of Kant, Manfred Kuehn dispels several myths and also greatly enriches our understanding of Kant's life—see *Kant, a Biography*.

30. This intellectual dynamic was already evident to the great theorist of the transition from the Enlightenment into the nineteenth century, Madame De Staël, who wrote pithily about Kant in a section of her work *On Germany*—see the translation in *Major Writings of Germaine de Staël*, 302–3.

31. One might think of the monad as akin to a mathematical point, something that could not be divided. For discussion, see Friedman, *Kant and the Exact Sciences*, 9ff, and see Friedman, *Kant's Construction of Nature*, 14–20, for connections between the project of the pre-critical "Physical Monadology" and the critical *Metaphysical Foundations of Natural Science* published in 1786.

32. Ironically, Maupertuis, the president of the Berlin Academy, could not read German, so Formey had to translate into French for him several German articles denouncing Euler's maneuver—see Calinger, *Euler*, 250–52. In tandem, when the mathematician and poet Abraham Gotthelf Kästner presented his German *Vermischte Schriften* to Maupertuis as the president of the Berlin Academy, he wrote to him personally in French (Kästner 1755, 1–4).

33. Perhaps even more surprising, despite his reputation as an anti-metaphysical philosopher, one often credited with promoting

"empiricist" ideas in Enlightenment France, Condillac submitted an anonymous essay—later published as *Les Monades*—that was somewhat sympathetic to the theory. See the interesting discussion of Condillac's early view of monads and later philosophical conception in Gianni Paganini, "Rehabilitating Hypotheses in the French Enlightenment: Émilie Du Châtelet and Condillac." He also charts the potential influence that Du Châtelet had on Condillac.

34. See Thomas Broman, "Metaphysics for an enlightened public."

35. See Broman, "Metaphysics for an Enlightened Public," 8–10, on Euler's arguments against monads in his *Gedancken* essay.

36. One of her arguments for simple beings is simple: if we cannot take extended things as a brute fact, if there must be some explanation for them, then it's no help to proclaim that extended things like tables exist because they are made of smaller extended things like particles or atoms. For that is no explanation. She proposes instead that we explain extended things through simple beings that are *not* extended.

37. Du Châtelet even notes that a parallel structure can exist within physics itself: for instance, if I'm studying the compression of the air, à la Boyle, it may be irrelevant whether atomism is true.

38. See *The Feynman Lectures on Physics*, chapter 6–11.

39. To put this interpretation into more contemporary philosophical terminology, we can read Du Châtelet as arguing that physics can be realist while philosophy is idealist. For the physicist, one can *treat* the world of matter as a brute fact, and also as real: one uses experimentation and observation to find the smallest bits of matter, while ignoring the question of whether matter itself, including its most basic constituents, is real in the sense of being mind-independent. Physics does not ask the latter question. The philosopher, of course, will ask precisely that question: just as she does not treat matter as a brute fact, demanding a deeper explanation through the principle of sufficient reason, she reaches the conclusion that matter is in fact mind-dependent. What is real, in the end, are the simple beings, and creatures like us perceive them to be material things.

40. This is much clearer in the second edition (Du Châtelet, *Institutions*, 1742) of the text, in the last section (viz. §183) of chapter 9, than in the first edition (1740).

41. But is this solution entirely fair to physics? After all, perhaps atomic theory is not the right place to look when we're talking about an esoteric

topic like the question of whether the existence of matter is a brute fact. For physics includes cosmology, a discipline which *does* ask the question of why there's a material world at all. In the Enlightenment, cosmology had not yet progressed enough to propose what we now know as the Big Bang, so one must discuss it with a historical caveat in place. Even then, we can characterize Du Chatelet's solution in a relevant way. It may *seem* that physics and metaphysics pose the same question when they ask, what is the origin of the world? But they do not. Physics asks a question that must admit of an empirical answer through some kind of observation—say, involving the red shift observed through long-range telescopic investigations. In contrast, metaphysics asks a question that can be answered through the principle of sufficient reason, proposing simple beings, or perhaps God, as the right kind of answer. They can avoid conflicts after all.

42. See the discussion in Gould, *Rocks of Ages*, 6, 52–59.

43. For a wonderful discussion, see Hatfield, "Was the Scientific Revolution Really a Revolution in Science?," especially 508–10; rarely among historians of philosophy, he discusses Diderot and D'Alembert's *Encyclopedia* in this context, noting that its characterization of the "science of nature" fits this broad conceptualization.

44. See Du Châtelet (*Institutions*, 1742, preface, 4). Rohault's *Traité de physique*, originally published in 1671, circulated widely in French and also in Latin and English translations, most famously with "Newtonian" notes by Samuel Clarke in the early eighteenth century, retitled *System of Natural Philosophy*. Du Châtelet was familiar with the Clarke edition—see Sarah Hutton, "Between Newton and Leibniz," 84–85. On Rohault, see Mihnea Dobre, "Rohault's Cartesian Physics," 206–7. Rohault did not present a metaphysical foundation for physics like Descartes, but he was certainly a Cartesian in other respects, and presented physics as a general science of body.

45. In his *Vernunftige Gedancken von den Würkungen der Natur*, Wolff begins with the properties of body in general, discusses the system of the world, tackles numerous topics concerning the Earth (including the weather), and finishes with a discussion of many aspects of plant and animal life. On Wolff's inclusion of meteorological phenomena in his physics, see Richard Yeo, "Classifying the Sciences," 259. Although Wolff's physics is not well known today, he had a substantial presence in Diderot and D'Alembert's *Encyclopedia*, with many articles reflecting his views in metaphysics but also in physics—see Sonia Carboncini Gavanelli, "Das paradox der Aufklärung," 84; and, Hankins, *Science and the Enlightenment*, 49. Moreover, although they

were rather skeptical of his metaphysics, important mathematicians like Euler and Daniel Bernoulli were more receptive to Wolff's physics, perhaps because he embraced vortices—see Heilbron, *Electricity in the Seventeenth and Eighteenth Centuries*, 121. For Heilbron's more general discussion of the huge range of topics covered by eighteenth-century physics textbooks, see "Experimental Natural Philosophy," 363–65, which surveys two dozen texts published between 1735 and 1790.

46. See s'Gravesande, *Mathematical Elements of Natural Philosophy*, lvii–lxiii. The text has the usual discussions of motion, forces, motion in liquids, centers of gravity, etc., and then moves on to air, fire, light, etc., in volume two.

47. Hartsoeker's posthumously published *Cours de physique*, for instance, explained everything from gravity to motion to fire and light to the nature of water and air, etc. For similar conceptions of physics, see, e.g., the discussion of Polinière in Robert Locqueneux, "Physique expérimentale vers 1740," 91–92. This conception of physics did not change substantially until the end of the century.

48. This is especially clear in the second (1742) version of the text, the basis for the Italian and German translations in 1743, which circulated widely in Europe. Note, however, that the Italian translation apparently contains "traces" of the 1740 edition on occasion—see Romana Bassi, "Émilie Du Châtelet and Antonio Conti: The Italian Translation of the *Institutions physiques*," 329–31.

49. Du Châtelet's discussion perfectly captures Robert Boyle's actual practice with his air pump experiments in using the notion of elasticity, or the "spring of the air," to great effect without providing any mechanical explanation of that feature. Indeed, Boyle presents what he calls his "doctrine" of elasticity on the basis of numerous such experiments, noting that it is a mere "hypothesis" to say that this feature is mechanical or mechanically explicable.

50. In the first edition of the text, she seems to take a somewhat different position on this issue by chastising the Newtonians but then concluding chapter 10 with the sentiment that a "mechanical reason" for the phenomena in question must be sought (*Institutions*, 1740, §210). That remark is removed in the second edition, which has a clearer meaning. For that reason, I agree with Katherine Brading's analysis that at least in the first edition, Du Châtelet can be read as endorsing a "methodological" mechanist outlook—see *Émilie Du Châtelet and the Foundations of Physical Science*, 87ff. In the second edition, she distances herself further from mechanist thinking.

51. Amazingly, the scholar Fritz Nagel found an intact copy of her "Essai sur l'optique" in the Bernoulli archive in Basel in 2006. See his " 'Sancti Bernoulli

orate pro nobis': Emilie du Châtelet's rediscovered *Essai sur l'optique* and her relation to the mathematicians from Basel." Until then, only one chapter of the essay was known: see Ira Wade, *Studies on Voltaire, with Some Unpublished Papers of Madame Du Châtelet,* Part II, section two. The "Essay" was published for the first time, and also translated by Bryce Gessell, on Project Vox—for discussion, see Gessell, " 'Mon petit essai.' "

52. For Voltaire, the principle of attraction unifies Newton's science of mechanics in the *Principia* with the science of the *Opticks*—see the beginning of Part III of the *Elements,* in *Oeuvres complètes,* vol. 15: 396; see also Voltaire's claim that attraction is involved in all the operations of nature (see Part III, numbered chapter 16, page 530). For a discussion of Voltaire's enthusiasm in this regard, see Shank, *The Newton Wars,* 383, 389.

53. As Fritz Nagel indicates ("Les Corps Agissent Sur La Lumière," 230), Goethe had noted that Du Châtelet did not provide a theory of colors in her *Institutions,* as Voltaire had done in his own *Elements,* a text Goethe opposed because of its Newtonian character. To his credit, Goethe does not merely see Du Châtelet as a Newtonian like Voltaire, or as his sidekick, but instead cites her magnum opus. For details, see Goethe, "Geschichte der Farbenlehre," in his *Sämmtliche Werke,* vol. 39: 322.

54. A major theme of the classic account in Becker, *The Heavenly City of the Eighteenth-Century Philosophers.*

55. Technically, since Leibniz and Clarke defended distinct conceptions of the principle of sufficient reason relative to their distinct conceptions of the divine will, it was also incumbent upon Du Châtelet to discuss the divine being in order to present her Leibnizian conception of the principle of sufficient reason. In brief, for her as for Leibniz, the principle of sufficient reason governs not only the workings of nature but the divine will as well, such that God always has a reason for choosing one state of affairs over another. The Clarkean version of the principle, in contrast, does not envision reason as governing the divine will, which enables Clarke to avoid the Leibnizian argument that the principle is incompatible with atomism and that it also entails the identity of indiscernibles. Therefore, for Du Châtelet to employ the principle of sufficient reason in her text she was required to discuss God's existence. This is significant not least because, as Brading shows (*Émilie Du Châtelet and the Foundations of Physical Science,* 57), Du Châtelet was originally sympathetic to Clarke's version of the principle.

56. Surveying the work of a single man, Euler, between 1730 and 1780, would indicate the enormous amount of research—in mechanics, optics, acoustics,

hydrodynamics, number theory, the differential calculus, etc.—that was produced during the Enlightenment. See Calinger's monumental biography, *Euler*, which does justice to this huge range of work, and also chapter 10 of Brading and Stan, *Philosophical Mechanics in the Age of Reason*.

Chapter 4

1. A key claim of Dan Edelstein's *Enlightenment*.

2. As Sabrina Ebbersmeyer reminded me, Descartes himself also publicly employed the trope of the exceptional woman (one whose genius proves the rule) in his dedicatory letter to Princess Elisabeth from his *Principles of Philosophy* (in the French edition of 1647). He writes that Elisabeth transcends the "customary upbringing of girls" that "condemns them to ignorance" in his praise of her intellect—see *Principles*, AT IX B: 22–23.

3. For a wide-ranging and illuminating discussion of van Schurman's fascinating life, see Anne Larsen, *Anna Maria van Schurman, "the Star of Utrecht,"* which analyzes her complex and varied relations with Descartes (e.g., 81–100) and many other figures.

4. Carol Pal discusses this famous episode in *Republic of Women*, 250.

5. For discussion of Bassi's career, see Paula Findlen, "Science as a Career in Enlightenment Italy: The Strategies of Laura Bassi"; on Agnesi, see Findlen, "Calculations of Faith." For her part, Du Châtelet explained how her membership in the Academy would be an encouragement to other women in a letter to Zanotti of June 1746 (Du Châtelet, *Correspondance*, vol. 2: 264).

6. Although she had won two Nobel Prizes, Marie Curie was not elected to the Academy of Sciences in Paris in 1910. The Académie Française elected its first woman, Marguerite Yourcenar, in 1980.

7. For a classic discussion of the role of salons in eighteenth-century intellectual culture, see Dena Goodman, "Enlightenment Salons: The Convergence of Female and Philosophic Ambitions," who notes that although some men opposed the influence of salons, others like Diderot would use that venue to test their ideas before publication (336–37, 334, respectively). On the influence of Madame Ferrand's salon—she has been called a French Newtonian—see Gelbart, *Minerva's French Sisters*, 17–19.

8. For an influential account that highlights the role of salons alongside coffee houses in England, France, and Germany, see Jürgen Habermas, *The Structural Transformation of the Public Sphere*, especially 27–33; Habermas also emphasizes the role of salons as intellectual testing grounds (34).

9. The first quotation is from Mary Terrall, "Gendered Spaces, Gendered Audiences: Inside and Outside the Paris Academy," 210; she also discusses how Algarotti followed in Fontenelle's footsteps: 225. The second quotation is from Paula Findlen, "Becoming a Scientist: Gender and Knowledge in 18th-Century Italy," 60. First published in 1686, Fontenelle's *Conversations* was wildly popular and was continually updated by the author until 1742—see Fontenelle, *Conversations*, xli. See also the chapter "Fontenelle and the Ladies" in Erica Harth, *Cartesian Women*; J. B. Shank, "Neither Natural Philosophy, nor Science, nor Literature—Gender, Writing, and the Pursuit of Nature in Fontenelle's *Entretiens sur la pluralité des mondes habités*," 88; and, Srinivas Aravamudan, *Enlightenment Orientalism*, which explores Fontenelle's extensive influence on figures like Aphra Behn, Jonathan Swift, and Voltaire (127, 141, 150–51).

10. See especially Geoffrey Sutton, *Science for a Polite Society*.

11. For discussion of Algarotti's text, which became an eighteenth-century bestseller and was translated into French, English, German, and Dutch, see Massimo Mazzotti, "Newton for Ladies," 119–46.

12. For the idea that Algarotti's endeavor served in part to inspire Voltaire, see the introduction to *Elements of the Philosophy of Newton*, 42–45.

13. In addition to the German translation of the second edition of the *Institutions*, completed by W. B. A. von Steinwehr in 1743, Du Châtelet's debate with Mairan was translated into German in 1741 by Louise Gottsched, an important intellectual in Prussia at the time. Gottsched was at the center of proto-feminist philosophical discussions in German-speaking Europe, translating many works that promoted free-thinking and equality between the sexes. For a wide-ranging discussion of Gottsched's ideas, see Katherine Goodman, "Louise Gottsched, Freethinker," 24–28 especially.

14. For an intriguing discussion of the circulation of her ideas, see Le Ru, *Émilie du Châtelet philosophe*, 115-50.

15. On the dissertation on fire, see Le Ru, *Émilie du Châtelet philosophe*, 37, 149. For a helpful discussion of Mairan, see Abby Kleinbaum, "Jean-Jacques Dortous de Mairan," 130.

16. See Philip Sloan, "Metaphysics and 'Vital' Materialism: Émilie Du Châtelet and the Origins of French Vitalism," 56–57, which details Du Châtelet's influence on Buffon, who also attended that dinner. Moreover, in a long letter to Mairan in September 1738, Voltaire assured him of Du Châtelet's friendship—see Voltaire to Mairan, D1611, in *Oeuvres complètes*, vol. 89: 291.

17. See the rather long discussion at *Institutions*, 1740, §574.

18. For discussion, see Mary Terrall's excellent biography of Maupertuis, *The Man Who Flattened the Earth*, 52–53.

19. See the discussion in Zinsser, *La Dame d'Esprit*, 191–93.

20. In her short 1741 essay, written in reply to Mairan, Du Châtelet continued to maintain the anonymity she had used for the first edition of her *Institutions*, calling her text the reply of "Madame ***." But just a year later, her name was proudly displayed on the second edition of her main text. As for the latter, in addition to the discussion in §574, which appears in the second edition of the *Institutions*, that edition also includes Mairan's letter in reply to the objections from the 1740 edition in §574, and Du Châtelet's response to that reply in an additional sixty-six pages of text—see Du Châtelet, *Institutions*, 1742, 476–542 (these are page numbers because the appendix lacks sections).

21. For discussion, see Mary Terrall, "Vis viva revisited."

22. After the dispute with Mairan, Du Châtelet debated *vis viva* with the former secretary of the Royal Society in London, James Jurin, in a letter to him from May of 1744 (Du Châtelet, *Correspondance*, vol. 2: 163–68; for an English translation, see *The Correspondence of James Jurin*, 463–67). Although his original letter to her has been lost, her reply to him was published in French in the Italian journal *Memorie sopra la fisica* (vol. 3, 1747), which she notes in a letter to Father Jacquier in April 1747 (Du Châtelet, *Correspondance*, vol. 2: 279–81). Jurin published an article in the *Philosophical Transactions of the Royal Society* in 1745 arguing against *vis viva* ("An Enquiry"), although he uses the misleading view that *vis viva* is measured by mass, or by weight, multiplied by velocity (Jurin 1745: 425–26). Jurin was already familiar with Du Châtelet because Algarotti brought him a copy of her dissertation on fire during his visit to England in 1739. Many thanks to Sarah Hutton for discussion of these important historical details.

23. I am indebted to the insightful and historically precise discussion in George Smith, "The vis viva dispute," an essay that dispels centuries of confusion in a few pages. Thanks also to George for many discussions about related topics. Anne-Lise Rey also provides a historically and philosophically precise discussion of the history of the *vis viva* dispute and of Émilie Du Châtelet's role in it ("The Vis Viva Controversy," 446–48).

24. Leibniz, "Specimen Dynamicum," in *Philosophical Essays*, 124–25. Here I use Ariew and Garber's translation because it nicely differentiates between *moles* (bulk) and *massa* (mass), which reflects the fact that Leibniz had read Newton's *Principia* before writing this essay.

25. Did Leibniz shift his thinking about matter and force after having read Newton's *Principia* in 1688? Sometimes, it seems reasonably clear that Leibniz includes mass as one of the features of a body that is relevant for understanding various phenomena, such as collisions; it also sometimes seems that he accepts the conservation of a quantity that we would now call *momentum* (Garber, "Leibniz: Physics and Philosophy," 329), which is obviously a function of mass and velocity. And yet at other times, he seems to forget about mass, even when he is explicitly discussing forces. For instance, in a famous passage, he says that he is willing to accept forces (such as the magnetic force) within nature as long as we think of them as "arising" from "motions and shapes" (Garber, "Leibniz: Physics and Philosophy," 334; cf. 327). Newton does not think that the force of gravity arises from motions and shapes alone—it is therefore not "mechanical" in that bare sense—because it depends in part on the masses of the interacting bodies. One possibility is as follows. Leibniz's rejection of Newton's understanding of gravity is famous (see below for some details), but his acceptance of the law of inertia and its implications for our understanding of matter are reasonably clear. So, it is possible that Leibniz was happy with inertial mass but not with gravitational mass (to speak somewhat anachronistically).

26. See Smith, "The Vis Viva Dispute," 35.

27. She notes in her reply to Dortous de Mairan in the *Institutions* (1742, 540 [there are no sections in this part of the text]) that Newton himself did not discuss *vis viva* and may even have been in a position to agree with at least part of Leibniz's overarching view. For a helpful discussion, see Sarah Hutton, "Emilie Du Châtelet," 772–73.

28. See Bertoloni Meli, *Thinking with Objects*, 297–98.

29. The measure of the quantity of motion is *mv*, and its conservation is stated in the third corollary to the laws of motion. One of Newton's *potential* contributions to the *vis viva* debate is his discussion, in the corollaries to the laws of motion (in the Scholium following corollary six), of collisions that are not perfectly inelastic (where the bodies are not perfectly "hard"); for such collisions, mv^2 is not conserved. But that is a relatively minor point, and he does not argue that mv^2 is not conserved in collisions involving perfectly hard or inelastic bodies.

30. See, e.g., Jonathan Israel, *Enlightenment Contested*, 762. The online translation of Diderot and D'Alembert's *Encyclopedia* goes so far as to translate the title of the article on vis viva (*forces vives*) as "kinetic energy!"

31. Some historians of science have long bemoaned this tendency—see, e.g., the excellent discussion in Charles Gillispie, "The *Encyclopédie* and the Jacobin Philosophy of Science," 260.

32. See Hankins, *Jean D'Alembert: Science and the Enlightenment*, 206.

33. See L 5: 99, which corresponds to Leibniz, *Die philosophischen Schriften*, 413–14.

34. See *Leibniz and Clarke: Correspondence*, note 158, 81.

35. Clarke cites page 156 of the original edition of the *Specimen* in the *Acta Eruditorum* (April 1695), but the discussion on that page is clearly presented as a move against the Cartesians. First, near the top of the page, concluding a long discussion, Leibniz states his view: in general, "the forces in bodies are jointly proportional to the size of the bodies and the squares of the speeds" [in universam esse in rationae composite ex corporum simplice, et celeritatum duplicate]. Second, lest there be any doubt that this is meant as a criticism of the Cartesians, Leibniz begins the next paragraph by noting that the "contrary view," which is held "particularly amongst the Cartesians," holds that force is measured by the size of a body and its speed. So Clarke should have known better.

36. See "A Letter from the Rev. Dr. Samuel Clarke," 381–88.

37. See Voltaire, *Elements of the Philosophy of Newton*, 246–51.

38. See Voltaire, *Elements of the Philosophy of Newton*, 252, which addresses the reader directly as "vous," a clear reference to Du Châtelet, whose sympathetic presentation of Leibnizian metaphysics in 1740 prompted Voltaire to add his "La métaphysique de Newton" to the beginning of the second edition of his *Elements* in 1741—see the introduction to the *Elements*, 102–3, 104, 115.

39. For an enlightening discussion of this issue, see Anne-Lise Rey, "La figure du Leibnizianisme dans les *Institutions de physique*," 237.

40. Here I strongly agree with Sarah Hutton's discussion, "Between Newton and Leibniz: Emilie du Châtelet and Samuel Clarke," 90–91. See also the excellent clarifications in Anne-Lise Rey, "Agonistic and Epistemic Pluralisms," 49–51.

41. See Du Châtelet, *Institutions*, 1742, §2. She also embraces the notion of the "force of inertia" later in the text: see, e.g., §304. In an insightful essay, Andrea Reichenberger notes that other thinkers, such as Musschenbroek, attempted to integrate *vis viva* with some version of Newtonian mechanics—see "Die Rolle der Familie Keyserlingk und des Gottsched-Kreises für Kants Du Châtelet-Rezeption," 252.

42. Moreover, she concludes by noting that *vis viva* can be supported both by experiments and by the use of the principle of sufficient reason, thus both by physics and metaphysics, so there is less danger of metaphysical speculation carrying the philosopher away. See especially Du Châtelet, *Institutions*, 1742, §588, and for an illuminating discussion, see Anne-Lise Rey, "The Vis Viva Controversy."

43. In *Early German Philosophy*, 573, Lewis White Beck writes that Formey was the most prolific correspondent in Germany since Leibniz. For Voltaire's remark that he was the "eternal" secretary of the Academy, see Calinger, *Euler*, 299.

44. The Formey Nachlass in the Staatsbibliothek zu Berlin is full of his discussions of Wolff. For instance, Formey corresponded frequently with Jean Des Champs, a promoter of Wolff's ideas, who apparently often agreed with Formey's rather negative attitude toward the *philosophes*, especially Voltaire and Rousseau. In a July 1761 letter to Formey, e.g., Des Champs mentions *Candide* and writes of the "caustic Voltaire," and in June of 1766, he complained about the libertine culture in France created by figures like Rousseau and Voltaire. So, the two correspondents clearly agreed that Wolff's version of the Enlightenment was superior to the more prominent French variety.

45. The six volumes of Formey's *La Belle Wolfienne* were published in the Hague beginning in 1741 and finishing with the last volume in 1753. All six volumes are reprinted in Christian Wolff, *Gesammelte Werke*, Third Abteilung, vol. 16.1–2.

46. The Formey Nachlass in the Staatsbibliothek zu Berlin and other sources, including Formey's own *Souvenirs d'un Citoyen*, indicate that he corresponded with just about every major Enlightenment figure between, say, 1740 and 1780, including Voltaire, Wolff, Maupertuis, several of the Bernoullis, Condorcet, Condillac, Réamur, Des Maizeaux, Euler (and his son Johann), Eberhard, Baumgarten, Father Jacquier, D'Alembert, etc. He also conducted a substantial correspondence with Frederick II of Prussia, which he reprints in the first volume of the 1789 edition of *Souvenirs*. There are several thousand letters in the Formey Nachlass now housed in the Jagiellonische Bibliothek in Krakow, Poland—the manuscripts were dispersed due to the war.

47. In Formey's book *The Logic of Probabilities*, he discusses the work of contemporary philosophers like Toland, Collins, and La Mettrie (he refers to *L'homme machine* disparagingly), criticizing anyone he takes to be skeptical of religion. Part of the overall argument of this short work is to suggest that

it is more probable that the world was created by a loving and intelligent agent, rather than being the result of mere chance. See Formey, *The Logic of Probabilities*, 11–12.

48. For details on these points, see Geissler, "Formey critique des philosophes français," 507–8; Marcu, "Formey and the Enlightenment," 31–32, 44.

49. This Berlin church was an important perch for many reasons, including the fact that Euler attended services there while he lived in Berlin, which meant that Formey was Euler's pastor for years. See Calinger, *Euler*, 218–19.

50. For a discussion, albeit an older one that does not recognize Formey's role, see Furbank, *Diderot*, 34–35.

51. See Margarete Smith, "In Defence of an Eighteenth-Century Academician," 85.

52. On Formey's role, see Glenn Roe, "A Sheep in Wolff's Clothing," 185, and Franz Kafker, *The Encyclopedists as a Group*, 37.

53. Scholars have long known that Julian La Mettrie, the author of the famous *Machine Man*, may have copied from chapters 7 and 8 of Du Châtelet's *Institutions* for his *L'histoire Naturelle de l'Âime*—see Ann Thomson, "Émilie Du Châtelet and La Mettrie," 382, 387; for more details on the similarities between Du Châtelet's and La Mettrie's views, see Theo Verbeek, *Le Traité de l'Ame de la Mettrie: edition critique du texte avec une introduction et un commentaire historiques*, vol. 1: 58–62, 63. More recently, Andrea Reichenberger has argued that Formey also copied from Du Châtelet for his reply to Euler on monads—apparently, five or six sentences from Formey's *Recherches sur les éléments de la matière* are identical to sentences in her *Institutions* (Reichenberger, "The Reception of Émilie Du Châtelet in the German Enlightenment," 133).

54. For instance, both Voltaire and Du Châtelet were master linguists, able to read not only Latin and French, but also English well enough to translate from it, a rarity in those days. Indeed, some of Voltaire's Nachlass in the National Library of Russia in St. Petersburg contains Voltaire's careful corrections of small typographical errors in English works. But neither could read German. Prince Frederick—a few years before he became Frederick II—had Wolff's German metaphysics translated into French for them in 1736; roughly half of the translation (§§771–1089) is extant in the archives of the Stiftung Preußicher Schlösser und Garten, Berlin-Brandenburg. At this time, Formey's translations of Wolff in *La Belle Wolfienne* were still several years off. See Hans-Peter Neumann, "Der preusissiche Kronprinz Frederich und die französische Übersetzung der 'Deutschen Metaphysik' Christian Wolffs im Jahr 1736."

55. For his part, Christian Wolff had told at least one interlocutor that Du Châtelet was better at explicating philosophy than Formey (see Hans-Peter Neumann, "Émilie Du Châtelet within the Correspondence between Christian Wolff and Ernst Christoph of Manteuffel," 160).

56. The first person to notice that Formey copied from the *Institutions* for the entry "Dieu" in the *Encyclopedia* was Eszter Kovács. She found that "Dieu" (at *Encyclopédie* 4: 980) copies 114 words in order from the *Institutions* (Kovács cites the first edition, 1740, 46), changing the punctuation. See her illuminating discussion in " 'La liberté est la santé de l'âme': du pouvoir soi-mouvant au culte de la liberté chez Émilie Du Châtelet" in *Émilie Du Châtelet: son monde, ses travaux*, 296.

57. See the outstanding article by Roe ("A Sheep in Wolff's Clothing," 189). This typology is not anachronistic: the published version of the *Encyclopedia* categorized the entries on space, hypotheses, time, contradiction, and sufficient reason as falling into "métaphysique," those on gravity and rest as falling into "physique," and those on motion, the pendulum and velocity as falling into "méchanique." These categorizations were added by Diderot and D'Alembert—in these cases, most likely just by D'Alembert.

58. See Roe, "A Sheep in Wolff's Clothing," 187, and also John Lough, *Essays on the Encyclopédie*, 505–55, which describes articles attributed to Formey in the published text.

59. See Grimsley, *Jean D'Alembert*, 164.

60. See Darnton, *The Business of Enlightenment*, 28–33. Marian Hobson discusses Chambers's influence on Diderot's approach to the encyclopedia project in "Diderot, the European Underground and English Radical Thought," 147–49, where she also notes that Diderot was known in Paris as a translator of works from the English.

61. See Darnton, *The Business of Enlightenment*, 7.

62. Alexandre Guilbaud lists Du Châtelet's *Institutions* as one of D'Alembert's principal sources, conceiving of it as a source separate from Formey's own articles, which themselves often copied her ideas—see "D'Alembert's Contribution to the *Encyclopédie*," 326.

63. See Lough, *Essays on the Encyclopédie*, 479. There is some debate about the details. Whereas Roe ("A Sheep in Wolff's Clothing") says that a single woman was an author, Elisabeth Fox-Genovese ("Women and the Enlightenment," 262) says that there were two: an anonymous woman and also Mme. Delusse. For further discussion, see Sara Ellen Procious Malueg, "Women and the *Encyclopédie*," especially 263–64.

64. As Lieselotte Steinbrügge notes in *The Moral Sex*, 29–30. More generally, she argues that the encyclopedists were nearly silent about learned women in their entries (334).

65. Diderot was accused of plagiarizing Bacon when the text of the *Prospectus* was first published in 1750—see Peter Anstey, "Bacon, Experimental Philosophy and French Enlightenment Natural History," 233, and Robert Darnton, *The Great Cat Massacre*, 198. As Wilda Anderson points out, there was also the (questionable) charge of plagiarizing Chambers—see *Diderot's Dream*, 104, 118. On Diderot's charge against Condorcet, see Gelbart, *Minerva's French Sisters*, 50–51.

66. In one of the great intellectual controversies of the century, Samuel König—who once accused Madame Du Châtelet of stealing his ideas—charged Maupertuis, president of the Berlin Academy of Sciences, with plagiarizing the "principle of least action" from none other than Leibniz himself. Perhaps there was a bit of historical irony, or poetic justice, to the charge: Maupertuis was a famous Newtonian, so this episode allowed the Leibnizian König to exact revenge for Newton's charge of plagiarism against Leibniz many years earlier during the calculus priority dispute. There wasn't much to König's charge in the end, but it helps to illustrate that Enlightenment intellectuals certainly had the concept of plagiarism and were prepared to employ that concept publicly.

67. See Zinsser, "Entrepreneur of the 'Republic of Letters'"; on that point, see also Ira Wade, *Studies on Voltaire*, 27–28, 76.

68. For details on the Geneva edition, see Guicciardini, "Editing Newton in Geneva and Rome," 337–80, and François de Gandt, "Qu'est ce qu'être Newtonien en 1740?," 143*ff*. George Smith has shown that Du Châtelet used the Geneva edition when translating Newton's *Principia* (see "Du Châtelet's commentary on Newton's Principia: an assessment," 259–60). On Du Châtelet's idea that Le Seur and Jacquier provided a kind of continual commentary on the *Principia* in their edition, see Heilbron, *Electricity in the Seventeenth and Eighteenth Centuries*, 363 note 76. On Algarotti, see Cheryl Smeall, "How to Become a Renowned Writer: Francesco Algarotti," 188–93, and Franco Arato, "Minerva and Venus: Algarotti's Newton's Philosophy for the Ladies," 117. Buffon added some rather anti-Newtonian comments on the infinite and the nature of space and time to his preface to Newton's posthumous *La méthode des fluxions* (Paris, 1740), as discussed in Marian Hobson, "Diderot, the European Underground and English Radical Thought," 152–53.

69. See Edelstein, *Enlightenment*, 95, and for more intriguing details, see Edelstein, Robert Morrissey and Glenn Roe, "To Quote or not to Quote."

70. As Edelstein notes, e.g., the *Encyclopedia* included a huge number of references to Newton, but also numerous references to Descartes—see *Enlightenment*, 48–49; and, as he also persuasively argues, the editors did not even systematically choose the "moderns" over the "ancients" in their famous quarrel (55–57).

71. For example, Roe ("A Sheep in Wolff's Clothing," 191) notes that Diderot would often undermine what Formey had written because he was skeptical of the Wolffian philosophy that Formey promoted: see the articles "Eternité" and "Conservation." Throughout, I cite the first Paris edition of the *Encyclopedia* unless otherwise noted. Volumes 1–7 were all published by June of 1757; the remaining ten volumes (i.e., 8–17) were published in January of 1766 (or at the very end of 1765).

72. Roe, "A Sheep in Wolff's Clothing," 190.

73. As Wilda Anderson shows in *Diderot's Dream*, 77–79, 93–95, there is good reason to question the idea that D'Alembert was speaking for Diderot in the conception of the *Encyclopédie* and its organization of knowledge expressed in the famous *Preliminary Discourse*. Indeed, she argues that Diderot himself expressed a rather different understanding of the whole project within the self-reflexive article "Encyclopedia" which was published in the midst of the project, a few years after the *Preliminary Discourse* appeared at its beginning. For further discussion of Diderot and D'Alembert's distinct conceptions of science, see Charles Gillispie, "The *Encyclopédie* and the Jacobin Philosophy of Science," 261, 269, 279–80, who especially emphasizes Diderot's distrust of Newtonian science.

74. See Roe, "A Sheep in Wolff's Clothing," 191–92.

75. See "Espace," *Encyclopédie*, vol. 5: 952; for excellent discussions, see Koffi Maglo, "Mme Du Châtelet, *l'Encyclopédie* et la philosophie des sciences," 260, and Le Ru, *Émilie Du Châtelet philosophe*, 134. D'Alembert refers here to the second edition of Des Maizeaux's famous collection of works including the Leibniz-Clarke correspondence but also other materials of Newton's, hence it is no mistake to refer to Newton as part of the correspondence here. For the original edition, see Pierre Des Maizeaux, *Recueil des diverses pieces*; volume 2 contains some of Newton's correspondence. In drafts intended for this first edition of Des Maizeaux's collection, Newton described the distance between his understanding of space's ontology and Clarke's characterization of it—see Draft E of Cambridge University Library manuscript Add. 3965

fol. 290, published in I. B. Cohen and Alexandre Koyré, "Newton and the Leibniz-Clarke Correspondence," 101–2. Des Maizeaux corresponded with Newton on June 4, 1720 (*Correspondence of Isaac Newton*, vol. 7: 92–93).

76. It is prominently mentioned at the beginning of the most important entry in the whole *Encyclopedia*, Diderot's clever, self-referential entry, "Encyclopedia." See vol. 5: 635.

77. See Curran, *Diderot and the Art of Thinking Freely*, 120–22. In *Between the Library and the Laboratory*, 47–52, Wilda Anderson persuasively argues that Diderot's system of cross-references, which he took to be essential to the *Encyclopédie*, was subversive and even revolutionary in some ways, undermining the dominant intellectual modes of the day.

78. As Keiko Kawashima points out, Du Châtelet referred to her magnum opus as the "Élemens de physique" in a letter to Johann Bernoulli (see "Anonymity and Ambition: Émilie Du Châtelet's *Dissertation de feu* (1744)," 432.

79. Unfortunately, D'Alembert's discussion of "Fire" is not much of an exception, for he merely mentions that Du Châtelet and Voltaire both sent "dissertations" in answer to the Academy of Sciences prize essay competition on the nature of fire, but does not describe any of her ideas or arguments in that text. See "Fire" (physics) in *Encyclopedia*, vol. 6: 603.

80. See Diderot's positive remarks about metaphysics in "Encyclopedia," vol. 5: 642.

81. See "Mouvement" (méchanique), *Encyclopedia*, vol. 10: 840.

82. See "Pésanteur" (physique), *Encyclopedia*, vol. 12: 446; "Tems" (métaphysique), *Encyclopedia*, vol. 16: 96; and, "Repos" (physique), *Encyclopedia*, vol. 14: 139. The article on rest by Formey cites §§220–229 of the *Institutions* at its end, and his entry on time directs readers to chapter 6 of the *Institutions*, along with the Leibniz-Clarke correspondence and Wolff's work on ontology.

83. The view is endorsed in Gilbert-Joseph Vallé's anonymously published work, *Réfutation du Systême des Monades*, 3, where he trumpets Du Châtelet's role explicitly.

84. See D'Alembert, *Traité de dynamique*, preface, xvi–xvii; for discussion, see Hankins, *Jean D'Alembert: Science and the Enlightenment*, 22, and Véronique le Ru, *D'Alembert philosophe*, 89.

85. Abbé Nollet, *Leçons de physique experimentale*, vol. 1: 201–2. His praise is rather effusive: before noting Mairan's contribution to the *vis viva* debate, Nollet says that Du Chatelet argued for her position with as much wisdom as possible.

86. For discussion, see Thomas Hankins, *Jean D'Alembert: Science and the Enlightenment*, 3, 152–58. For a discussion of the "paradox" generated by D'Alembert's idea of a dynamics without forces, see Alain Firode, *La dynamique de D'Alembert*, 22–26.

87. See Furbank, *Diderot*, 48.

88. See Paul Bonnefon, "Diderot prisonnier à Vincennes," 214–15, 220–22, 224, and Andrew Curran, *Diderot*, 84–86, 88, 93–95. Indeed, D'Alembert informed Formey that he was getting pulled into the *Encyclopedia* project in part because Diderot was in prison—see Richard Schwab's introduction to his edition of the *Preliminary Discourse*, xxiv.

89. See Rousseau, *Confessions*, 327–28. For his part, Diderot describes Rousseau as his "dear and worthy friend" in perhaps his most important article for the *Encyclopédie*, viz. "Encyclopedia," vol. 5: 646. Rousseau, Diderot, Condillac and D'Alembert dined together weekly in the 1740s (see Gelbart, *Minerva's French Sisters*, 26–27).

90. For discussion of this small social world and of Diderot's subsequent development of the *Encyclopedia*, see Shank, *The Newton Wars*, 493–95.

91. See P. N. Furbank, *Diderot*, 48–50. For details, see Du Châtelet, *Correspondance*, vol. 2: 468 in the long note appended to that letter; cf. J. B. Shank, *The Newton Wars*, 493. See also the notes to Diderot's letter to Voltaire of 11 June 1749 in Diderot, *Correspondance*, vol. 1: 81. On Diderot's release, see Furbank, *Diderot*, 72, and Bonnefon, "Diderot prisonnier à Vincennes," 223.

92. See *Encyclopédie*, vol. 5: 785. He also praised her understanding of mathematics in a letter to Voltaire in June of 1749, just before he was imprisoned—see Diderot, *Correspondance*, vol. 1: 79.

93. See especially the moving account of Du Châtelet's last days in Judith Zinsser's biography, *La Dame d'Esprit*, 2–4, 276–79; she discusses Saint-Lambert's role in her life at 270–71, noting also that the marquis could have rejected Du Châtelet, but instead bragged to others that her new pregnancy meant that he might potentially have another son and heir for his family. Although Saint-Lambert is often portrayed merely as a dashing young officer who caught Du Châtelet's eye, he turned out to be a minor poet and in fact became a member of Diderot's circle of encyclopedists, writing many entries himself (287–88). Many credit his literary career to her encouragement.

94. In a moving letter to Saint-Lambert in late May of 1749, she notes that her pregnancy is healthy so far, but also mentions the possibility that she might die in childbirth (Du Châtelet, *Correspondance*, vol. 2: 453).

95. The letter to Saint-Lambert is translated at Bour and Zinsser, editors, *Selected Philosophical and Scientific Writings*, 347; the last letter she wrote is at Du Châtelet, *Correspondance*, vol. 2: 478.

Chapter 5

1. See Paz's beautiful rendering of the life and philosophical thought of Sor Juana in *Sor Juana, or the Traps of Faith*, 349.

2. Indeed, perusing introductory anthologies published over the past century indicates that they nearly always begin with Plato, occasionally with one of the pre-Socratics. See, e.g., Feinberg's famous introductory text, *Reason and Responsibility*, which ran to thirteen editions over several decades, and most recently, the *Norton Introduction to Philosophy*, which has already seen a second edition and remains influential.

3. Daniel Roche notes that Brucker was "a constant model for Diderot" and that *Historica Critica Philosophiae* "must be regarded as one of the mainsprings of the whole *Encyclopédie*"—see "Encyclopedias and the Diffusion of Knowledge," 175, 192–94.

4. Rainer Jehl emphasizes that Brucker founded the modern scholarly study of the history of philosophy by insisting, e.g., not only that the scholar read each philosopher's works, but cite carefully which edition of the text was consulted, a practice taken for granted by subsequent scholarship. See Jehl, "Jacob Brucker und die 'Encyclopédie,'" 253. Brucker discusses some of his methods in the "dissertatio praeliminaris" in volume 1 of the *Historia Critica Philosophiae*.

5. Victor Cousin, *Cours de Philosophie, Introduction a l'histoire de la Philosophie*, 20. For a translation, see Cousin, *Course of the History of Modern Philosophy*, vol. 1, 236. This is noted by Longo, "A 'Critical' History of Philosophy and the Early Enlightenment: Johann Jacob Brucker," 565. Jacques Proust says that Brucker is justly known as the first historian of modern philosophy—*Diderot et l'Encyclopédie*, 244–45; see also Lucien Braun, *Histoire de l'histoire de la Philosophie*, 395.

6. See Longo, "A 'Critical' History of Philosophy and the Early Enlightenment: Johann Jacob Brucker," 518 and 533 for a helpful discussion.

7. Brucker's text is widely recognized as shaping Diderot's many entries on the history of philosophy in the *Encyclopedia*: see Mario Longo, "A 'Critical' History of Philosophy and the Early Enlightenment: Johann Jacob Brucker," 477–78; and Cassirer, *Philosophie der Aufklärung*, 301. Kant cited Brucker in

both editions of the *Critique of Pure Reason* (A316/B372), and Lewis White Beck writes that Brucker was "probably Kant's chief source of information and misinformation on the history of philosophy" (*Early German Philosophy*, 277 note 4).

8. Brucker's views circulated widely in English in the translation by Enfield, published in 1791 and again in 1819 and 1837. See Longo, "A 'Critical' History of Philosophy and the Early Enlightenment: Johann Jacob Brucker," 574–75. On Brucker's influence, see also Peter K. J. Park, *Africa, Asia and the History of Philosophy: Racism in the Formation of the Philosophical Canon*, 14–15 and 161 note 35.

9. The second volume's corrections list notes that the "Aristotelianism" entry in volume 1 of the Paris edition consists in part in an extract from Brucker, adding that the *Historia Critica* was used for a great number of entries on the history of philosophy in the *Encyclopedia*. See "Corrections et additions pour le premiere volume," *Encyclopédie*, vol. 2: iv. Indeed, as later scholars have discovered, at least forty-three entries were "drawn almost entirely from the *Historia Critica*"—see Longo, "A 'Critical' History of Philosophy and the Early Enlightenment: Johann Jacob Brucker," 557. See also Constance Blackwell, "Jacob Brucker's Theory of Knowledge and the History of Natural Philosophy," 217.

10. For instance, Diderot, who studied Brucker's text after borrowing a copy from the Bibliothèque de Roi in 1750, would sometimes simply translate his Latin into French, but at other times he would playfully use Brucker's ideas in a sarcastic way—see the helpful discussion in Rainer Jehl, "Brucker und die 'Encyclopédie,'" 245, 250. See also Proust, *Diderot et l'Encyclopédie*, 265 note 62.

11. Martin Bernal's famous account in *Black Athena*, vol. 1 (197–99), discusses Brucker's huge influence on the writing of the history of philosophy, carefully noting that whereas Brucker credited the Greeks with systematizing philosophy, Egyptian thought also required serious study in his eyes. See Brucker, *Historia Critica Philosophica*, vol. 4, Part 2, book 3: 804–923. Before Brucker, Voltaire credits the Egyptians with influencing early Greek thought in certain respects: see *Lettres philosophiques*, Letter 17, 121. On this theme in early modern literature more generally, see the illuminating account in Srinivas Aravamudan, *Enlightenment Orientalism*, 14.

12. See especially the account in Bernal, *Black Athena*, vol. 1, which discusses a huge range of sources.

13. See Johann Joachim Winckelmann, *Reflections on the Imitation of Greek Works in Painting and Sculpture*. One possibility is that Brucker's influence

was spread in the 1740s and 1750s before Winckelmann's was felt, at least as far as the history of philosophy is concerned. This periodization seems consistent with the notion that Goethe, who famously called the eighteenth-century "Winckelmann's century," was the figure who consummated Winckelmann's ideas, spreading them into the nineteenth century. That seems to be the view of the German classicist Rudolf Pfeiffer—see *History of Classical Scholarship*, 170.

14. See Victor Cousin, *Cours de la Philosophie, Introduction a l'histoire de la philosophie*, 16–17 and then 18–19, respectively.

15. This fact may surprise us. Why should nineteenth-century scholars, especially those in Germany, have exercised such a profound influence? Part of the reason might be this: although colleges and universities have existed for nearly a thousand years, the modern "research university" is essentially a nineteenth-century German invention, one often attributed in part to the work of Alexander von Humboldt in Berlin. During the Enlightenment, the academies throughout Europe, all the way to St. Petersburg, conducted most of the age's fundamental research in philosophy, science, and mathematics; it rarely occurred in educational institutions. It was only during the nineteenth century, most prominently in Germany, that universities began to take over that role from academies in numerous fundamental ways. It is no coincidence that in Prussia, unlike in much of the rest of Europe, the greatest thinkers held university positions during the Enlightenment, from Wolff in Halle to Kant in Königsberg to Fichte and Schelling in Jena. The German system then became a model for other universities around the world, most notably in England and the Americas. Johns Hopkins is often cited as the first American research university, and it copied the German model explicitly. Others quickly followed suit.

16. See Jay Garfield and Brian van Norden, "If Philosophy Won't Diversify, Let's Call It What It Really Is," which was published in the *New York Times*.

17. In his monumental, six-volume *Geschichte der neuren Philosophie* (Heidelberg, 1867), Kuno Fischer places great emphasis on Descartes and his school in the first, very long, volume. He presents a substantial discussion of the Scholastic background to Descartes, but the latter is the first modern figure to be discussed. Cousin calls Descartes the "father" of modern philosophy in *Cours de Philosophie, Introduction a l'histoire de la Philosophie*, 20. He edited an edition of Descartes's oeuvre in Paris in 1824. In his *Lectures on the History of Philosophy* from the 1820s, Hegel notes that modern philosophy begins with Descartes—that idea is cited and discussed by Christia

Mercer, "Empowering Philosophy," 73. In a recent article, Alberto Vanzo corrects certain misconceptions on this point, noting (e.g.) that what he calls the "standard narrative" of the development of modern philosophy became dominant only in the early twentieth century, having replaced an alternative "Hegelian" historical perspective. See "Empiricism and Rationalism in Nineteenth-Century Histories of Philosophy," 265–66, 274. Cf. also Jonathan Rée's intriguing and wide-ranging account, "Women Philosophers and the Canon," especially 650 on this issue.

18. It is true that (e.g.) Fischer ends his six-volume work with post-Kantian German idealism, discussing Schelling's ideas in the very early nineteenth century in great depth, but the modern canon is still present, and later scholars would carve out nineteenth-century philosophy as its own historical era. Fischer's last volume of the *Geschichte*, volume six, presents German idealism, especially the work of Schelling and his *Naturphilosophie*, in roughly 1,000 pages.

19. Voltaire says of Bacon (*Lettres philosophiques*, letter 12, 84): "Il est la père de la philosophie expérimentale." In the famous preface to the second edition of the *Critique of Pure Reason* (Bxii), Kant follows Brucker closely, describing the revolution in natural science as originating with Bacon, never mentioning Descartes as a revolutionary. As J. G. A. Pocock notes, Brucker's "heroes" in the *Historia critica* were "Bacon, Grotius and Locke"—see "Historiography and Enlightenment: a view of their history," 90. While he was a student at the University of Jena, Brucker studied and came to admire the thought of Boyle and Locke, with a special admiration for Locke's *Essay*, which he read in the French translation by Pierre Coste. See Constance Blackwell, "Jacob Brucker's Theory of Knowledge and the History of Natural Philosophy," 200, 205.

20. Indeed, Newton receives less attention than (e.g.) figures like Father Malebranche and amazingly enough, Solomon Maimon. Fischer discusses Newton in sections on his disputes with Leibniz and Wolff in *Geschichte*, vol. 3, book I, chapter 7, which concerns Kant's days "under the influence" of the Wolffian philosophy. There is even an argument to be made that Fischer's conception of the modern canon in the middle of the nineteenth century is not much closer to our own view than Brucker's was from a century earlier. For instance, Fischer substantially downplays the importance of British philosophy: there is no volume devoted to empiricism or to British thought in his six-volume work. The only substantive discussion of British philosophy occurs in volume 3 in an early section on Kant's influences. In contrast, the

rationalists—Descartes, Spinoza, Leibniz—comprise all of the first two volumes, Kant the third and fourth volumes, and post-Kantian idealism volumes five (focused on Fichte) and six (focused on Schelling). So the "empiricist-rationalist" dispute is not an organizing principle of Fischer's work. This is also in sharp contrast to famous French works from the nineteenth century: for instance, Victor Cousin grants Locke his own volume (*Cours de l'histoire de la philosophie*, vol. 2).

21. Perhaps the most significant disagreement among the various savants on the modern canon is the question of Wolff. Whereas Brucker and Formey promote his importance, Voltaire ignores him in the *Lettres philosophiques* and later, D'Alembert excises him from the canon, thereby disagreeing with Brucker on the endpoint of the modern conversation. This reflected a wider view: for instance, although Voltaire remained on friendly terms with Formey into the 1750s, he thought that Formey's beloved Wolff represented a new Scholasticism (see Barber, *Leibniz in France*, 194–95). Proust notes that D'Alembert's conception in the *Preliminary Discourse* closely matches Diderot's—see *Diderot et l'Encyclopédie*, 242.

22. As Sabrina Ebbersmeyer pointed out to me, Diogenes writes the history by writing about the lives of great philosophers, but he lacked the modern notion of the canon because the latter included the Enlightenment's idea of intellectual progress.

23. See Michel Malherbe, "Hume's Reception in France."

24. Hume's *Enquiry* is significant not only because it was published in 1758 as the first volume of the soon-to-be-popular *Oeuvres philosophiques de David Hume*, but also because the *Treatise of Human Nature* was unknown to the French Enlightenment. See Malherbe, "Hume's Reception in France," 43–45.

25. See Peter Jones, editor, *The Reception of David Hume in Europe*, vol. 1: xix. It is true that Voltaire and Madame Du Châtelet could both read English, as could Diderot, but that was rare among the *philosophes*, so it is difficult to make the case for someone's work to be canonical if it's not in either Latin (still the lingua franca of the seventeenth century) or in French.

26. Newton's *Principia* was available in Latin from the beginning, and in the case of the *Opticks*, written in English, it was available in Latin already in 1706; Locke's *Essay* was available in the famous Pierre Coste translation published in Amsterdam in 1700. Coste translated a later version of the *Opticks* into French. He also relayed to the French Enlightenment some of Newton's private views that he had shared with Locke, especially the idea—one famous to scholars from Newton's unpublished manuscript *De Gravitatione*—of how

God may have created matter, which Locke discusses in his *Essay Concerning Human Understanding*, IV.X.17. See the discussion in A. C. Fraser's edition of the *Essay*, vol. 2: 321–22 note 2, and the intriguing analysis in Koffi Maglo, "Mme Du Châtelet, *l'Encyclopédie* et la philosophie des sciences," 262.

27. According to Proust, Brucker and Diderot shared an almost violent opposition to Scholasticism—see *Diderot et l'Encyclopédie*, 251 note 94.

28. As Christia Mercer notes, seventeenth-century histories of philosophy often provided discussions of various sects—e.g., Platonism, Stoicism—and then presented thinkers like Descartes or Gassendi as falling into one of them. They did not present a canon. For related details, see Mercer's Presidential Address to the American Philosophical Association, "Empowering Philosophy." Moreover, Brucker also could have endorsed the view found in some early Enlightenment texts according to which "modern philosophy" involved neither a set of positions nor a canon, but rather a set of engagements with Cartesianism—see Massimo Mazzotti, *The World of Maria Gaetana Agnesi*, 63.

29. See Mbembe, *Critique of Black Reason*, 67–68. For an insightful discussion of Brucker's understanding of modern eclecticism, see Leo Catana, "The Concept 'System of Philosophy': The Case of Jacob Brucker's Historiography of Philosophy," 82–83. Intriguingly, Catana then connects Brucker's triumphal characterization of eclecticism's importance to his notion that modern philosophers independently developed their own "systems" of philosophy which are understood, in turn, as the projects of autonomous individuals.

30. The *locus classicus* of all contemporary discussions of canon formation in modern philosophy is Eileen O'Neill, "Disappearing Ink"; the 110 footnotes of O'Neill's paper contain a treasure trove of citations to original texts written by women throughout the early modern era (see 42–62). She argues that the German scholars of the nineteenth century who exerted such a powerful influence on the specific shape of the modern canon in the European, and indeed the Anglo-American, world sought to react to the frightening potential for an increase in women's rights and in women's access to institutional structures in the decades following the American and the French revolutions.

31. The first European institution to admit women formally was the University of Zurich in 1866—see Dalia Nassar and Kristin Gjesdal, editors, *Women Philosophers in the Long Nineteenth Century*, 5.

32. Joanna Russ provides an exquisitely detailed, historically rich, decidedly witty account of numerous modes of literary exclusion in *How to Suppress Women's Writing*. Her wit helps to inoculate the reader against the depressing attitude that might seem to be a natural accompaniment to the realization

that familiar patriarchal modes of exclusion have persisted for centuries. Although some of those modes emerged in the Renaissance, they remain perfectly familiar to readers in the twenty-first century, requiring almost no analysis. Russ is famous for her science fiction, but this work deserves more attention than it has received.

33. As we have seen, he himself had written on many of the same topics, and he could have copied directly from Wolff himself in either German or Latin, which he did in his own *La Belle Wolffienne*. See Formey, *La Belle Wolffienne*, vol. 4: 3, and following.

34. Formey never lost interest in her work or regretted having used so much of it for his *Encyclopedia* entries. In 1752, with permission, Formey published Voltaire's "éloge historique," along with a long discussion of Du Châtelet's work, in the *Bibliothèque Impartiale* (Jan–Feb, 1752, 136–46), and he also praised her work five years later in a eulogy for Wolff. See Marcu, "Formey and the Enlightenment," 113, and Reichenberger, *Emilie Du Châtelets Institutions Physiques*, 95 note 80.

35. In fact, Brucker was aware of Formey's role in the pre-history of the *Encyclopedia* as well as his importance as the secretary of the Berlin Academy— see Ursula Behler's short biography of Brucker, "Eine unbeachtete Biographie Jacob Bruckers," 40 note 99. For more details of Brucker's life, see Braun, *Histoire de l'histoire de la Philosophie*, 119–23.

36. See Du Châtelet, *Correspondance*, vol. 1: 83. Du Châtelet thanks Bernoulli for his support in this regard in a letter of June 1743: see Du Châtelet, *Correspondance*, vol. 2: 123. Brucker's *Bilder-Sal heutiges Tages lebender und durch Gelahrtheit berühmter Schriftseller* was arranged by the author without pagination. Du Châtelet appears in the 1745 volume. In the 1752 volume, he discusses Formey at length, noting his text *La belle Wolfienne*. For two very helpful and erudite discussions, see John Iverson, "A Female Member of the Republic of Letters," and Sabrina Ebbersmeyer, "From a 'Memorable Place' to 'Drops in the Ocean,'" 451–53.

37. See Brucker, *Historia Critica Philosophiae*, vol. 4.2: 643–44. He mentions Princess Elisabeth once, but only in passing: see *Historia Critica Philosophiae*, vol. 4.2: 382.

38. Kant, *Gedancken* in *Gesammelte Schriften*, vol. 1: 133; quoted from the translation in Kant, "Thoughts," (2012, 116).

39. In the modern age, Molière promotes the trope most forcefully, making fun of an academy of women. On the use of "ridicule" to exclude women from knowledge, see Estelle Cohen, "'What the Women at All Times Would Laugh

At,' " 135; and in a more contemporary context, see the fascinating discussion in Rae Langton, *Sexual Solipsism*, 272.

40. A rare exception is Londa Schiebinger, *The Mind Has no Sex?*, 271–72, who also provides an insightful discussion of the Enlightenment more generally.

41. In an intriguing twist, it turns out that Du Châtelet not only knew about Dacier's scholarly work but also mentioned it as an inspiration for her own research—see Judith Zinsser, "Entrepreneur of the 'Republic of Letters,' " 599, 606.

42. Remarkably, Ruth Hagengruber has shown in detail that in his famous dispute with Kant near the end of the eighteenth century, Eberhard quotes from the original 1742 French edition of Du Châtelet's *Institutions*—despite its availability in a German translation—and uses it as an authoritative source ("Du Châtelet and Kant: Claiming the Renewal of Philosophy," 58, 63–65).

43. There is little doubt that for a moderate Lutheran pastor like Brucker, or Formey for that matter, Scholasticism was also bound up with Catholicism's historically important intellectual dominance—see Longo, "A 'Critical' History of Philosophy and the Early Enlightenment: Johann Jacob Brucker," 494. But of course, many Catholics, like Galileo and Descartes, were also strongly anti-Scholastic in orientation, as were radical Protestants like Newton, who questioned the Trinity and other orthodoxies in a way that would have shocked Brucker or Formey.

44. Diderot, "Éclectisme," in *Histoire de la philosophie ancienne et moderne* in the *Encyclopédie*—see the version in *Oeuvres completes de Diderot*, vol. 14: 304; see also Proust, *Diderot et l'Encyclopédie*, 238–42 and Daniel Brewer, "The Encyclopédie: Innovation and Legacy," 51. In addition, the "Philosophy" article informs the reader of the "excellent" history of philosophy by Brucker in *Historia Critica*, discussing eclecticism in some depth. The article is not attributed. So Brucker's influence on the text may actually reach further than imagined, since we're not sure if this text was written by Formey or Diderot.

45. Ironically, this conception is more historically accurate than the later scholarly obsession, not with schools precisely, but with general philosophical movements. The common attempt throughout the nineteenth and twentieth centuries to describe modern philosophy by focusing on the great debate between the "rationalists" and the "empiricists" has numerous flaws. Leaving aside the common complaint that it wrongly gives pride of place to a Kantian conception of modern philosophical history—echoing the thought

that Kant's revolution would overcome the division between rationalism and empiricism—it also leads to an anachronistic separation between science and philosophy. For instance, Brucker, Diderot, and D'Alembert had no trouble expressing the importance of Newton's writings to modern philosophy, but later historians went to considerable lengths to force him artificially into the "empiricist" camp or left him out entirely. The Enlightenment without Newton is like a car without an engine. In tandem, the obsession with the empiricist reaction in the eighteenth century to the rationalism of the seventeenth has led to an overemphasis on Berkeley and Hume, and the concomitant ignorance of far more significant figures like Euler, who fits into neither camp. The Enlightenment without Euler is like a car without wheels.

46. Kästner first praises Du Châtelet's *Institutions* as a more fundamental exposition than Voltaire's *Elémens*, but insists on determining whether she is really a follower of Newton, of Leibniz, or of Wolff (*Belustigungen des Verstandes*, 1743, 301–3); see also Baasner, *Abraham Gotthelf Kästner, Aufklärer*, 533–38. As Judith Zinsser notes, one of Dortous de Mairan's complaints was that Cirey had become, in his words, "une école Leibnitienne"—see Zinsser, "Émilie Du Châtelet and the Enlightenment's *Querelle des femmes*," 139, who also intriguingly argues that Mairan turned his *vis viva* dispute with Du Châtelet into an instance of the famous *Querelle des femmes* (35–37).

47. This notion connects, in turn, to Diderot's more general views about women, the supposed failures of their imaginations, and what he regarded as their passive tendency to be molded by another's ideas—for discussion, see Joan Wallach Scott, *Only Paradoxes to Offer*, 27–35.

48. Iverson's extremely helpful article not only transcribes the original German from Faktur (Gothic) into modern roman script, but it also provides a translation of the text. The quotation above is my translation, but it deviates from Iverson's excellent version only slightly: see John Iverson, "A Woman in the Republic of Letters," 61.

49. See the excellent discussion of Princess Elisabeth's philosophical views in Lisa Shapiro's introduction to *The Correspondence between Princess Elisabeth and René Descartes*, 22–25.

50. Technically speaking, the 1738 review was anonymous, but intellectuals in this period often knew through one means or another who had authored an unattributed piece. In the case of the review, Fontenelle's biographer Troublet apparently figured out that she had written it. See Christophe Martin, "From One Marquise to Another: Émilie Du Châtelet and Fontenelle's *Conversations on the Plurality of Worlds*," 420.

51. See Hans Droysen, "Die Marquise du Châtelet, Voltaire und der Philosoph Christian Wolff," 233; cf. Frauke Böttcher, "Die Reaktion der Wolffianer in Deutschland auf die *Institutions physiques*," 274–79. Wolff himself wrote Du Châtelet a flattering letter in Latin in May of 1741 (Du Châtelet, *Correspondance*, vol. 2: 29–32), but changed his mind about her a few years later. William Barber at first reads the *Institutions* specifically as an "attempt to popularize Wolff" in his *Leibniz in France*, 135. Later in his text, however, he seems to waver a bit, concluding: "Madame du Châtelet's philosophy as here presented is thus essentially the philosophy of Wolff, with some concessions to Leibnizian terminology, offered to the public as an exposition of the views of Leibniz" (139).

52. For these aspects of Wolff's conception of philosophy, see, inter alia, §33 of his *Preliminary Discourse on Philosophy*, §31 of the *Deutsche Metaphysik* (on the deduction of the Principle of Sufficient Reason), and §361 and §383 of the latter on his conception of scientific knowledge (see Wolff, *Vernünftige Gedancken*, 1720). For a helpful discussion of Wolff's conception of space, see Hogan, "Wolff on Order and Space." On Wolff's conception of science and of knowledge, see Cassirer, *Das Erkenntnisproblem*, *Werke*, vol. 3: 438–41, and also Lanier Anderson, *The Poverty of Conceptual Truth*, 1113, 125.

53. Heinrich Ostertag, *Der philosophische Gehalt des Wolff-Manteuffelschen Briefwechsels*, 42–43. Ironically, despite this complaint, Wolff had already developed a subtle set of criticisms of Newton's physics, especially the discussion of inertia and of gravity—see Katherine Dunlop, "Mathematical method and Newtonian science in the philosophy of Christian Wolff," 465–66. More generally, Wolff was fixated on the question of whether Du Châtelet would remain loyal to him, employing the kind of religious imagery also widespread in Voltaire's discussions of her—would she be his "apostle" in France, or had Voltaire "converted" her back to Newtonian ideas, rendering her an "apostate"? See Hans-Peter Neumann, "Émilie Du Châtelet within the Correspondence between Christian Wolff and Ernst Christoph of Manteuffel," 158 and 161, respectively.

54. In some cases, both (albeit seemingly contradictory) positions can be found not just in a single interpreter over a few years but even in a single text. For instance, in his magisterial account of early modern physics, *Electricity in the 17th and 18th Centuries*, Heilbron writes of Du Châtelet that "Leibniz' was the only metaphysics that satisfied her," but also calls her a "staunch Newtonian" (see 44 and 25, respectively).

55. In a letter to Voltaire of June 1741, the former secretary of the Royal Society, James Jurin, encourages him to "convert" Du Châtelet from her defense of *vis viva* to a Newtonian point of view (*Correspondence of James Jurin*, 432–33; indeed, he repeats the term twice).

56. For instance, in addition to citing Cassirer's work frequently, Peter Gay also edited and translated a short book of Cassirer's on Jean-Jacques Rousseau, first published in 1954. As we have seen, Gay relied in turn on Paul Hazard's research, which includes citations to Cassirer's book on the Enlightenment from 1932 and also to his magnum opus from years earlier— see Hazard, *La Pensée Européenne au XVIIIème siècle*, vol. 3: 6, 25, 63. As for more recent work, Cassirer is cited in prominent texts by Pagden (*The Enlightenment*, 10) and Edelstein (*The Enlightenment*, 159 note7, 160 note1), among many others.

57. Cassirer discusses Brucker's influence on Diderot in *Die Philosophie der Aufklärung*, 301. For citations to Cassirer's various published references to Brucker over the years, see Leo Catana, "The Concept 'System of Philosophy': The Case of Jacob Brucker's Historiography of Philosophy," 86–87 note 82. As Thomas Kuhn once famously said of Edward Shils, Cassirer seemed to have read everything. In his foreword to the first English translation of Ludwig Fleck's *Genesis and Development of a Scientific Fact*, which influenced Kuhn's thought before he wrote *Structure of Scientific Revolutions*, Kuhn notes that virtually no one had read Fleck's work in those days, except for Edward Shils and a personal friend of Fleck's—see *Genesis and Development*, page vii.

58. Cassirer later worked at the Warburg Institute alongside figures like Aby Warburg and Erwin Panofsky, whose idea of art reflected Cassirer's theory of "symbolic forms." Life in the multidisciplinary Warburg Institute perfectly suited Cassirer's capacious understanding of philosophy as a discipline engaged with history, art, culture and science in equal measure. For details on Cassirer's life, see Dmitry Gawronsky, "Ernst Cassirer." Late in life, Cassirer reflected on his early years and expressed his admiration for Cohen's philosophy, mentorship, and friendship—see his "Hermann Cohen." See also Gordon, *Continental Divide*, 19–21.

59. For instance, in August 1928 he delivered an address defending the Weimar Republic as reflecting a long history of German philosophical and political ideas—see Gordon, *Continental Divide*, 23. His academic career is outlined in Michael Friedman, *A Parting of the Ways*, 1–5, 87–88.

60. The deep socio-political significance of the Davos disputation is briefly, but movingly, described by Jürgen Habermas in "The German Idealism of

the Jewish Philosophers," 32–33. The Enlightenment was also on Cassirer's mind at the end of his life: in October 1944, just months before his death, he was working at Columbia University and wrote the preface to a "little book" that serves as a "sort of introduction" to his *Philosophy of the Enlightenment*: see Cassirer, *Rousseau, Kant, Goethe*, preface.

61. See Gawronsky, "Ernst Cassirer: His Life and Work," 37.

62. Cassirer, *Die Philosophie der Aufklärung*, 289–90.

63. Cassirer, *Die Philosophie der Aufklärung*, 294. The conception of history developed by the *philosophes* is also a major theme of Becker's classic work, *The Heavenly City of the Eighteenth-Century Philosophers*, especially chapter 3.

64. See Susan Neiman, *The Unity of Reason*, chapter 5, and the extensive discussion in Peter Gay, *The Enlightenment: The Science of Freedom*, 170–81.

65. Cassirer's most prominent follower in the United States, Peter Gay, concurs with his overall analysis, but adds: "Voltaire began his great *Essai sur les moeurs* after discussions with his mistress Madame du Châtelet." See Gay, *The Enlightenment: The Rise of Modern Paganism*, 176; cf. also Ira Wade, *Voltaire and Madame du Châtelet*, 4 and 194.

66. Cassirer, *Das Erkenntnisproblem in der Philosophie und Wissenschaft der neuren Zeit*, reprinted in the Hamburg edition of Cassirer's *Gesammelte Werke*; volumes two and three are especially relevant. The text has never been fully translated into English, although Ashraf Noor helpfully translated the introduction to the first edition for *Science in Context* in 1996. For a philosophical interpretation, see Michael Friedman, *A Parting of the Ways*, 89–91.

67. That would include influential works by Edwin Burtt, Alexandre Koyré, E. J. Dijksterhuis, Émile Meyerson, Anneliese Maier, and Hélène Metzger. See Friedman, "Ernst Cassirer and Thomas Kuhn," 180. As Friedman notes, Cassirer also greatly influenced Thomas Kuhn, who explicitly cites Koyré, Meyerson, Metzger, and Maier as major influences (Kuhn, *Structure of Scientific Revolutions*, vi), all of whom were deeply influenced, in turn, by *The Problem of Knowledge*. Moreover, the dean of American history of science in the post-war period, I. B. Cohen at Harvard, was greatly influenced by Koyré and collaborated extensively with him, e.g., on their monumental critical edition of Newton's *Principia mathematica*, published in 1972. Unlike the German historians of philosophy who Cassirer would have read in his youth, such as Kuno Fischer, Cassirer discusses both science (especially Newton) and philosophy in his masterwork, emphasizing key developments in both fields in the eighteenth century. As a result, the *Problem of Knowledge* is far more historically accurate than Fischer's work, and to his great credit, Cassirer does

not assume that philosophy begins in Greece; he analyzes the originality of Greek thought in comparison with ancient Egyptian geometry and even Buddhist philosophy. This is an important theme of the introduction to the first edition: see, e.g., Cassirer, *Das Erkenntnisproblem*, vol. 1: 26 on the distinction between the work of Pythagoras and of Egyptian geometers, and the subsequent discussion of Indian and specifically Buddhist thought at 28–29.

68. See Roger Ariew and Eric Watkins, editors, *Modern Philosophy: An Anthology of Primary Sources*, v–vi, issued in a new edition in 2019. In her book *Pandora's Breeches: Women, Science and Power in the Enlightenment*, vii, Patricia Fara had already attempted to disrupt this tendency; see also the intriguing discussion in Sarah Tyson, *Where Are the Women?*, 117–18. Sarah Hutton calls this the "coat-tail syndrome" (see "Women, Philosophy and the History of Philosophy," 687), and Charlotte Witt wittily calls it "the Best Supporting Actress approach" in her "Feminist Interpretations of the Philosophical Canon," 542. For a novel approach to the canon, see Marcy Lascano and Lisa Shapiro, editors, *Early Modern Philosophy*; for the shifting fortunes of the early modern canon, see especially Christia Mercer, "The Contextualist Revolution in Early Modern Philosophy."

69. See Gideon Rosen et al., editors, *The Norton Introduction to Philosophy*, v–xviii and 1125. The first text included in the anthology by a woman is G. E. M. Anscombe's famous "Mr. Truman's Degree" from 1958 (which was published following a discussion in Oxford in 1956). She opposed the proposal to award Truman an honorary degree on the grounds that dropping the bombs on Hiroshima and Nagasaki was a war crime.

70. In the second edition of the text, Rosen et al. include a single page of text from Princess Elisabeth's correspondence with Descartes at 320. One is reminded of Charlotte Witt's remark about her philosophical education in the late 1970s: "For the most part what we learned about women in the history of philosophy was nothing" (see "Feminist Interpretations of the Philosophical Canon," 537).

Chapter 6

1. The literature on these topics is justly vast. See, inter alia, Srinivas Aravamudan, *Enlightenment Orientalism*; the discussion of cosmopolitan travel in Lloyd, *Enlightenment Shadows*, chapter 1; the groundbreaking discussions in Samia Spencer, editor, *French Women and the Age of Enlightenment*; Dorinda Outram, *The Enlightenment*, especially chapters 4–6; and, Shmuel Feiner, *The Jewish Enlightenment*.

2. Jesuit reviewers, not to mention the Pope himself, saw the *Encyclopedia* as a dangerously radical enterprise. Figures like Brucker and Formey were more moderate in their intellectual orientations: they sought to promote "modern" science and philosophy, undermining the old Scholasticism in the process, but in fact they were concerned about challenges to religious authority and other social mores. Brucker (e.g.) defended the reasonableness of Christianity and could not endorse the apparent materialism, not to say atheism, that Diderot embraced in various texts. See Rainer Jehl, "Jacob Brucker und die 'Encyclopédie,'" 254–55, for a helpful discussion, not only of *Historica Critica* but also of Brucker's earlier reflections on the history of philosophy. For Formey's conservatism, his tensions with Diderot, and his desire to avoid endorsing authors who questioned the social and religious order, see Martin Meiske, "Formey als Encyklopädist," 42–47. Israel distinguishes the "radical" and the "moderate" Enlightenment throughout his *Enlightenment Contested*, describing Diderot and D'Alembert as radicals and Voltaire, Clarke, and Newton as moderates—see 12–13, 37–39. Finally, see Isaiah Berlin's classic essay, "The Counter-Enlightenment."

3. Here I am guided by the important question raised in a recent article by Zinsser and Hayes, "what is at stake if the history of the Enlightenment includes a woman as *philosophe*?" (see Zinsser and Hayes, "The Marquise as *Philosophe*," 31).

4. Like Formey, Brucker was a Protestant pastor. See the illuminating discussion of Diderot's use of Brucker's history in Proust, *Diderot et l'Encyclopédie*, 266–67.

5. In her famous work on Du Châtelet, Elisabeth Badinter makes the strongest case in the literature for the view that Voltaire was a kind of feminist in his attitudes toward "femmes savantes" and in his promotion of Du Châtelet's work as a philosopher—see *Émilie, Émilie*, 233–35, 238–49, 257–59. I believe her case is compatible with my argument that even Voltaire, for all his promotion of her work, did not view Du Châtelet as a *modern* philosopher, a thinker who is truly independent of any school.

6. Much as Kant did forty years later in his imposing treatise, *Metaphysical Foundations of Natural Science*. On Kant's *Metaphysical Foundations*, published in 1786 between the first and second editions of the *Critique of Pure Reason*, see the extensive interpretation in Friedman, *Kant's Construction of Nature*. For discussion, see Linda Gardiner Janik, "Searching for the Metaphysics of Science: The Structure and Composition of Mme. Du Châtelet's *Institutions de physique*, 1737–1740"; Andrea Reichenberger, *Émilie Du Châtelets Institutions physiques*, 83, 92; and Geoffrey Sutton, *Science for a Polite*

Society, 261–64. More generally, the early eighteenth century saw a number of attempts to harmonize the apparently conflicting views of Newton and Leibniz—for discussion, see Cassirer, *Das Erkenntnisproblem, Werke*, vol. 3: 426–27.

7. See Du Châtelet, *Institutions*, 1742, preface, XII, 13.

8. The determined interpreter may continue to use the old lens through which to view her work, but that approach leads to odd interpretive twists and turns. For instance, Barber, who views the *Institutions* overall as an attempt to "popularize Wolff," acknowledges that "the purely scientific part of the book" is "Newtonian in its principles, except on the subject of dynamics," thereby presumably attempting to account for the *vis viva* chapter (Barber, *Leibniz in France*, 135 and 185, respectively).

9. See Du Châtelet, *Institutions*, 1742, §2. As Anne-Lise Rey argues in "La minerve vient de faire sa physique," one explanation for Du Châtelet's sometimes negative reception in the eighteenth century lies in the difficulty of labeling the *Institutions* as a Cartesian or Lockean or Newtonian work. Its unique approach hampered its scholarly uptake. See also Rey, "Agonistic and Epistemic Pluralisms: A New Interpretation of the Dispute between Emilie du Châtelet and Dortous de Mairan," 51.

10. As Julie Candler Hayes puts it, one of Du Châtelet's goals in the *Institutions* is not just to find connections between physics and metaphysics, but also to engage in "figuration" or self-presentation—see *Reading the French Enlightenment*, 94–96.

11. On this key point, it seems that Du Châtelet's approach toward autonomous thinking within philosophy coheres with the famous account developed by Michelle le Doeuff in *Hipparchia's Choice*, 59–60, who also argues that to accept disciples as a so-called "master" thinker is to deprive them of philosophy itself (153–55, 162–70). For an excellent discussion of this theme in the *Institutions*, see Tinca Prunea-Bretonnet, "Émilie, Friedrich der Große und die 'Leibniz-Wolff'sche' Metaphysik," 312–13.

12. Indeed, Newton sought for his views to be disseminated by Bentley's popular lectures, Cotes's famous preface, and Clarke's extensive correspondence. See the classic discussion in Margaret Jacob, "Newtonianism and the Origins of the Enlightenment," especially on the importance of the Boyle lectures—given by figures like Bentley, Whiston, and Clarke—in promoting Newtonianism of various kinds to a wide audience. Indeed, this version of Newtonianism was often more influential and more popular than anything gleaned directly from Newton's writings.

13. Many thanks to Lisa Shapiro for a memorable conversation about this important point.

14. In *Critique of Black Reason* (80–84), Mbembe identifies an analogous tension within classic liberal thought: the promotion of freedom (for some) and the promotion of colonialism and slavery at the very same historical moment (54–55); he notes a similar tension in the thought of major figures like Burke, Diderot, and Kant.

15. See the classic account in Genevieve Lloyd, *The Man of Reason*, especially vii–x, and more recently, Lloyd's introduction to her edited collection, *Feminism and History of Philosophy*, especially 7–14. For an intricate discussion of Lloyd's work and its connections with more recent French feminist scholarship, see Rosi Braidotti, *Patterns of Dissonance*, 185–200.

16. This striking passage is from Du Châtelet's preface to her planned translation of Mandeville's *Fable of the Bees*: see Bour and Zinsser, editors, *Selected Philosophical and Scientific Writings*, 48–49, and for the original, which I have translated here a bit differently from Bour and Zinsser, see Ira Wade, *Studies on Voltaire, with Some Unpublished Papers of Madame Du Châtelet*, 136.

BIBLIOGRAPHY

ARCHIVAL SOURCES

1. Madame Du Châtelet

Essai sur l'optique. Handschriftenband: L I a 755, fo. 230–265, Universität Basel, Switzerland.

Essai sur l'optique, Aristophil private collection, Museé de manuscrits et des lettres, Paris. [Later impounded by the French government.]

Manuscript of *Institutions de Physique* [1738–1740], ffr. 12.265. Bibliothèque Nationale de France, Paris.

Manuscripts in Voltaire Collection, National Library of Russia, St. Petersburg:

   a. *Sur "Descartes" par Mme du Châtelet*. Voltaire Collection, vol. IX: 122.

   b. *Notes sur la "physique" par la même*. Voltaire Collection, vol. IX: 123.

   c. *Essai inédit de Mme du Châtelet, chap. v: Sur la liberté*. Voltaire Collection, vol. IX: 126.

   d. *Pensées de Madame du Châtelet*. Voltaire Collection, vol. IX: 150.

   e. *Traduction de la Fable des abeilles de Mandeville*. Voltaire Collection, vol. IX: 153; and *préface de cette traduction*, Voltaire Collection, vol. IX: 217.

2. Voltaire
The Library of Voltaire, National Library of Russia, St. Petersburg, Russia. See Gorbatov (2007) in the bibliography below for details.

3. Jean-Henri Samuel Formey
Nachlass Formey, Staatsbibliothek zu Berlin, Germany.

4. Christian Wolff
"Abschrift der von Suhm für den Kronprinzen 1736 angefirtigen französischen Uebersetzung von Wolffs Metaphysik, enthaltend sie §§771–1089 (Schluss)." Folio. Handschrift. Stiftung Preußicher Schlösser und Garten, Berlin-Brandenburg, Germany.

PUBLISHED PRIMARY SOURCES

Algarotti, Franceso. 1738. *Newtonianismo per le dame.* Venice.

Algarotti, Franceso. 1791–94. *Opere del conte Algarotti.* New edition. Venice.

Bentley, Richard. 1842. *The Correspondence of Richard Bentley.* Edited by C. Wordsworth. London: John Murray.

Bentley, Richard. 1976. *Eight Boyle Lectures on Atheism, 1692.* New York: Garland.

Brucker, Johann Jacob. 1741–1755. *Bilder-Sal heutiges Tages lebender und durch Gelahrtheit berühmter Schriftseller . . .* Augsburg. Ten volumes.

Brucker, Johann Jacob. 1742–44. *Historia Critica Philosophiae.* Leipzig. Five volumes.

Du Châtelet, Émilie [anonymous]. 1738. "Lettre sur les <u>Eléments de la Philosophie de Newton</u>." *Journal des sçavans* (September): 534–41. Paris edition.

Du Châtelet, Émilie.1739. *Dissertation sur la nature et la propagation du feu.* In *Recueil des pièces qui ont remporté le prix de l'Académie royale des Sciences en 1738,* 85–168. Paris: Imprimerie royale.

Du Châtelet, Émilie [anonymous].1740. *Institutions de physique.* Paris: Prault.

Du Châtelet, Émilie.1741. *Réponse de madame * * * à la Lettre que M. de Mairan, secrétaire perpétuel de l'Académie royale des Sciences, lui a écrite le 18 février 1741 sur la question des forces vives.* Bruxelles: Foppens.

Du Châtelet, Émilie.1741. *Zwo Schriften, welche von der Frau Marquise von Chatelet, gebohrener Baronessinn von Breteuil, und dem Herrn von Mairan, beständigem Sekretär bei der französischen Akademie der Wissenschaften, das Maaß der lebendigen Kräfte betreffend, gewechselt worden.* Translated by Louise Gottsched. Leipzig: Bernh. Breitkopf.

Du Châtelet, Émilie. 1742. *Institutions physiques de madame la marquise du Chastellet adressés à M. son fils: Nouvelle édition, corrigée et augmentée considérablement par l'auteur.* Amsterdam: Aux dépens de la Compagnie.

Du Châtelet, Émilie.1743. *Der Frau Marquisinn von Chastellet Naturlehre an ihren Sohn. Erster Theilnach der zweyten Französischen Ausgabe.* Translated by Wolfgang Balthasar von Steinwehr. Halle/Leipzig: Rengerische Buchhandlung.

Du Châtelet, Émilie.1743. *Istituzioni di Fisica di Madama la Marchesa du Chastelet indiritte a suofi gliuolo. Traduzione dal linguaggio francese nel toscano, accresciuta con la Dissertazione sopra le forze motrizi di M. de Mairan.* Venice: Presso Giambatista Pascali.

Du Châtelet, Émilie.1759. "Exposition abrégée du Système du monde, et explication des principaux phénomènes astronomiques tirée des Principes de M. Newton." In *Principes mathématiques de la philosophie naturelle de Newton: Par feue madame la marquise Du Chastellet.* Paris: Desaint et Saillant.

Du Châtelet, Émilie.1961. *Discours sur le bonheur.* Introduction et notes de Robert Mauzi. Paris: Les Belles-Lettres.

Du Châtelet, Émilie. 2009. *Selected Philosophical and Scientific Writings.* Translated by Isabelle Bour and Judith P. Zinsser. Chicago: University of Chicago Press.

Du Châtelet, Émilie. 2018. *La Correspondance d'Émilie du Châtelet.* Sous la direction de Ulla Kölving et Andew Brown. Ferney-Voltaire: Centre Internationale D'Étude Du XVIIIe Siècle. Two volumes.

Clarke, Samuel. 1705/1998. *A Demonstration of the Being and Attributes of God.* Edited by Ezio Vailati. Cambridge: Cambridge University Press.

Clarke, Samuel. 1728. "A Letter from the Rev. Dr. Samuel Clarke to Mr. Benjamin Hoadly, F. R. S. Occasion'd by the Present Controversy among Mathematicians, concerning the Proportion of Velocity and Force in Bodies in Motion." *Philosophical Transactions of the Royal Society* 35: 381–88.

Clarke, Samuel, and G. W. Leibniz. 1717. *A Collection of Papers, Which Passed between the Late Learned Mr. Leibnitz and Dr. Clarke, in the Years of 1715 and 1716.* London.

Clarke, Samuel, and G. W. Leibniz. 1956. *The Leibniz-Clarke Correspondence.* Edited by H.G. Alexander. Manchester: Manchester University Press.

Clarke, Samuel, and G. W. Leibniz. 2000. *G.W. Leibniz and Samuel Clarke: Correspondence.* Edited by Roger Ariew. Indianapolis: Hackett.

Condillac, Etienne Bonnot de. 1980. *Les Monades*. Edited by Lawrence Bongie. *Studies on Voltaire and the Eighteenth Century* 187. Oxford: Voltaire Foundation.

Cousin, Victor. 1828. *Cours de Philosophie, Introduction a l'histoire de la Philosophie*. Paris.

Cousin, Victor. 1829. *Cours de l'histoire de la philosophie, Histoire de la Philosophie du dix-huitième siècle*. Paris.

Cousin, Victor. 1852. *Course of the History of Modern Philosophy*. Translated by O. W. Wight. New York.

D'Alembert, Jean Le-Rond. 1743. *Traité de Dynamique*. Paris. First edition.

D'Alembert, Jean Le-Rond. 1750/2000. *Discours Préliminaire de l'Encyclopédie*. Edited by Michel Malherbe. Paris: Vrin.

D'Alembert, Jean Le-Rond. 1759/1805. *Essai sur les éléments de philosophie*. In *Oeuvres philosophiques, historiques et littéraires de D'Alembert*. Paris: Bastien.

D'Alembert, Jean Le-Rond. 1995. *Preliminary Discourse to the Encyclopedia of Diderot*. Translated by Richard Schwab. Chicago: University of Chicago Press. Second edition.

Des Maizeaux, Pierre. 1720. *Recueil de diverses pieces, sur la philosophie, la religion naturelle, l'histoire, les mathematiques, &c.* Amsterdam: Chez H. Du Sauzet.

Desaguliers, J. T. 1745. *A Course of Experimental Philosophy*. London. Second edition.

Descartes, René. 1996. *Oeuvres de Descartes*. Edited by Charles Adam and Paul Tannery. Eleven volumes. Paris: Vrin.

Diderot, Denis. 1754. *Penseés sur l'interpretation de la Nature*. Paris.

Diderot, Denis. 1876. *Oeuvres complètes de Diderot*. Edited by J. Assézat. Paris.

Diderot, Denis. 1955. *Correspondance. Volume One: 1713–1757*. Edited by Georges Roth. Paris: Les editions de minuit.

Diderot, Denis. 1989. *Sur les femmes*. Reprinted in *Qu'est-ce qu'une femme?* Paris: P.O.L.

Diderot, Denis, and Jean Le-Rond D'Alembert, editors. 1750–65. *Encyclopédie, ou, Dictionnaire raisonné des sciences, des arts et des métiers*. Paris.

Edleston, J.E., editor. 1850. *Correspondence of Sir Isaac Newton and Professor Cotes*. London: John Parker.

Elisabeth, Princess, and René Descartes. 2007. *The Correspondence between Princess Elisabeth of Bohemia and René Descartes*. Edited and translated by Lisa Shapiro. Chicago: University of Chicago Press.

Enfield, William. 1791. *The History of Philosophy . . . Drawn Up from Brucker's Historia critica philosophiae.* London.

Euler, Leonhard. 1746. *Gedancken von der Elementen der Cörper.* Berlin. [Reprinted in *Leonhardi Euleri Opera Omnia.* Third series. Volume Two. Societatis Scientiarum Naturalium Helveticae. 1960.]

Euler, Leonhard. 1748. "Réflexions sur l'espace et le tem[p]s." *Histoire de l'Academie Royale des Sciences et belles lettres* 4: 324–33.

Euler, Leonhard. 1752. "Recherches sur l'origine des forces." *Mémoires de l'académie des Sciences de Berlin* 6: 419–47.

Euler, Leonhard. 1768. *Lettres à une Princesse D'Allemagne sur Divers sujets de physique et de philosophie.* Saint Petersbourg: Academie Impériale des Sciences. [Reprinted in *Leonhardi Euleri Opera Omnia.* Third series. Volume One. Edited by Andreas Speiser. Societatis Scientiarum Naturalium Helveticae. 1960.]

Fontenelle, Bernard le Bovier de. 1686/1991. *Entretiens sur la pluralité des mondes habités.* In *Oeuvres complètes.* Volume Two. Edited by Alain Niderst. Paris: Fayard.

Fontenelle, Bernard le Bovier de. 1990. *Conversations on the Plurality of Worlds.* Translated by H. A. Hargreaves. Introduction by Nina Rattner Gelbart. Berkeley: University of California Press.

Formey, Samuel. 1741–1753. *La Belle Wolfienne.* The Hague. Six volumes. [Reprinted in Christian Wolff, *Gesammelte Werke,* Third Abteilung, Volume 16.1–2. Zürich: Georg Olms Verlag, 1983.]

Formey, Samuel. 1750. *The Logic of Probabilities.* London.

Formey, Samuel.1760. *Abrégée de l'histoire de la philosophie.* Amsterdam.

Formey, Samuel. 1789. *Souvenirs d'un Citoyen.* Berlin. Two volumes.

Goethe, J. W. 1858. "Geschichte der Farbenlehre." In *Goethe's sämmtliche Werke in vierzig Bänden.* Band 39. Stuttgart und Augsburg.

s'Gravesande, Wilhelm. 1747. *Mathematical Elements of Natural Philosophy, or, An Introduction to Sir Isaac Newton's Philosophy.* Translated by J. T. Desaguliers. London.

Hartsoeker, Nicolas. 1730. *Cours de physique.* Paris.

Huygens, Christiaan. 1690/1944. *Discours sur la cause de la Pesanteur.* In *Oeuvres complètes.* Volume 21. The Hague: Société Hollandaise des Sciences.

Jurin, James. 1745. "An Inquiry into the Measure of the Force of Bodies in Motion: With a Proposal of an Experimentum Crucis, to Decide the Controversy about It." *Philosophical Transactions of the Royal Society,* 43: 423–40.

Jurin, James. 1996. *The Correspondence of James Jurin (168–1750), physician and secretary to the Royal Society*. Edited and translated by Andrea Rusnock. Amsterdam: Rodopi.

Kant, Immanuel. 1902—. *Gesammelte Schriften*. Berlin: Deutschen Akademie der Wissenschaften.

Kant, Immanuel. 1990. *Kritik der reinen Vernunft*. Edited by Raymund Schmidt. Hamburg: Felix Meiner Verlag.

Kant, Immanuel. 1998. *Critique of Pure Reason*. Translated by Paul Guyer and Allen Wood. Cambridge: Cambridge University Press.

Kant, Immanuel. 2012. "Thoughts on the True Estimation of Living Forces . . ." Translated by Jeffrey Edwards and Martin Schönfeld. In *The Cambridge Edition of the Works of Immanuel Kant: Natural Science*. Edited by Eric Watkins. Cambridge: Cambridge University Press.

Kästner, Abraham Gotthelf. 1743. "Brief über den leeren Raum, bey Zurucksendung der Naturlehre der Marquise von Chatelet." *Belustigungen des Verstandes und des Witzes*. Volume Four. Leipzig: Christoph Breitkopf.

Kästner, Abraham Gotthelf. 1755. *Vermischte Schriften*. Witenburg.

Leibniz, Gottfried Wilhelm. 1686. "Brevis demonstratio erroris memorabilis cartesii." Reprinted in *Leibnizens mathematische Schriften*, Volume 6: 117–19.

Leibniz, Gottfried Wilhelm. 1689. "An Essay on the Causes of Celestial Motions." Translated by Domenico Bertoloni Meli in *Equivalence and Priority*.

Leibniz, Gottfried Wilhelm. 1695. "Specimen Dynamicum." Reprinted in *Leibnizens mathematische Schriften*, Volume 6: 234–46.

Leibniz, Gottfried Wilhelm. 1849. *Leibnizens mathematische Schriften*. Edited by C. J. Gerhardt. Berlin: Asher.

Leibniz, Gottfried Wilhelm. 1931. "Streitschriften zwischen Leibniz und Clarke." In *Die philosophischen Schriften von Gottfried Wilhelm Leibniz*. Edited by C.J. Gerhardt. Volume Seven. Leipzig: Alfred Lorenz Buchandlung.

Leibniz, Gottfried Wilhelm. 1989. "Specimen Dynamicum." In *Philosophical Essays*. Translated by Roger Ariew and Daniel Garber. Indianapolis: Hackett.

Leibniz, Gottfried Wilhelm. 2000. *Leibniz and Clarke: Correspondence*. Edited by Roger Ariew. Indianapolis: Hackett.

Locke, John. 1823. *The Works of John Locke*. London: Thomas Tegg.

Locke, John. 1959. *Essay Concerning Human Understanding*. Edited by A. C. Fraser. New York: Dover. Two volumes.

Mairan, Jean-Jacques Dortous de. 1741. "Lettre de M. de Mairan, secretaire perpetuel de l'Académie Royale des Sciences, &c. à Madame ** sur la question des forces vives, en réponse aux objections qu'elle lui fait sur ce sujet dans ses *Institutions de physique*." Paris.

Maupertuis, Pierre L.M. 1732. *Discours sur les differentes figures des astres . . . avec une exposition abbrégée des systemes de M. Descartes & de M. Newton.* Paris.

La Mettrie, Julien Offray. 1747. "Lettre Critique de M. de La Mettrie sur l'Histoire Naturelle de l'Âme à Mme. La Marquise du Châtelet." Appended to *L'Histoire Naturelle de l'Âme.* Oxford [Paris].

La Mettrie, Julien Offray. 1996. *Machine Man and Other Writings.* Translated and edited by Ann Thomson. Cambridge: Cambridge University Press.

Newton, Isaac. 1731. *A Treatise of the System of the World.* London. Second edition.

Newton, Isaac. 1739–42. *Philosophiae naturalis principia mathematica.* Edited by T. Le Seur and F. Jacquier. Geneva.

Newton, Isaac. 1952. *Opticks.* Based on the fourth edition of 1730. New York: Dover Publications.

Newton, Isaac. 1972. *Philosophiae naturalis principia mathematica.* Variorum edition. Edited by I.B. Cohen and Alexandre Koyré, with the assistance of Anne Whitman. Cambridge, MA: Harvard University Press.

Newton, Isaac. 1959–77. *Correspondence of Isaac Newton.* Edited by H.W. Turnbull et al. Seven Volumes. Cambridge: Cambridge University Press.

Newton, Isaac. 1999. *Mathematical Principles of Natural Philosophy.* Edited and translated by I. B. Cohen with the assistance of Anne Whitman. Berkeley: University of California Press.

Newton, Isaac. 2014. *Philosophical Writings.* Edited by Andrew Janiak. Cambridge: Cambridge University Press. Second edition.

Nollet, Abbé. 1749. *Leçons de physique experimentale.* Paris.

Rohault, Jacques. 1671. *Traité de physique.* Paris.

Rohault, Jacques. 1729. *Rohault's System of Natural Philosophy, illustrated with Dr. Samuel Clarke's Notes, Taken Mostly Out of Sir Isaac Newton's Philosophy.* London. Second edition.

Rousseau, Jean-Jacques. 1953. *Confessions.* Translated by J. M. Cohen. New York: Penguin.

Saverien, Alexandre. 1760. *Histoire des philosophes modernes.* Paris: Brunet.

Staël, Germaine de. 1987. *Major Writings of Germaine de Staël.* Edited and translated by Vivian Folkenflik. New York: Columbia University Press.

Vallé, Gilbert-Joseph. 1747. *Lettre sur la nature de matière et de la mouvement a l'auteur des institutions de physique.* Paris.

Vallé, Gilbert-Joseph. 1754. *Réfutation du Système des Monades.* Paris.

Voltaire, F. M. A. 1752. "Éloge historique de Madame du Chastellet." *Bibliothéque Impartiale* (Jan–Feb): 136–46.

Voltaire, F. M. A. 1937. *Traité de métaphysique.* Edited by H. T. Patterson. Manchester: Manchester University Press.

Voltaire, F. M. A. 1980. *Letters on England.* Translated by Leonard Tancock. London: Penguin.

Voltaire, F. M. A. 1986. *Lettres philosophiques.* Edited by Frédéric Deloffre. Paris: Gallimard.

Voltaire, F. M. A. 1992. *Élemens de la philosophie de Newton. The Collected Works of Voltaire,* Volume 15. Edited by R.L. Walters and W.H. Barber. Oxford: The Voltaire Foundation.

Voltaire, F. M. A. 2017. *Micromégas.* In *Les Oeuvres Complètes de Voltaire,* Volume 20C. Edited by Nicholas Cronk and J. B. Shank. Oxford: Voltaire Foundation.

Winckelmann, Johann Joachim. 1755/1987. *Reflections on the Imitation of Greek Works in Painting and Sculpture.* Translated by Elfriede Heyer and Roger Norton. Bi-lingual edition. La Salle: Open Court.

Wolff, Christian. 1720. *Vernünftige Gedancken von Gott, der Welt und der Seele des Menschen, auch allen Dingen überhaupt.* Leipzig.

Wolff, Christian. 1723. *Vernunftige Gedancken von den Würkungen der Natur.* In *Gesammelte Werke, Erste Abteilung.* Volume Six.

Wolff, Christian. 1962—. *Gesammelte Werke.* Hildesheim: Georg Olms Verlag.

Wolff, Christian. 2003. *Metafisica Tedesca, con le annotazioni alla Metafisica Tedesca.* Translated, with notes, by Raffaele Ciafardone. Bilingual edition. Milano: Bompiani.

Wolff, Christian. 2007. *Rational Thoughts on God, the World and the Soul of Human Beings, also All Things in General* (1751 edition). Edited and translated by Eric Watkins in *Kant's "Critique of Pure Reason": Background Source Materials.* Cambridge: Cambridge University Press.

SECONDARY SOURCES

Ahnert. Thomas. 2019. "Newton in the German Speaking Lands." In *The Reception of Isaac Newton in Europe.* London: Bloomsbury.

Aiton, Eric. 1972. *The Vortex Theory of Planetary Motions.* New York: American Elsevier.

Anderson, Lanier. 2015. *The Poverty of Conceptual Truth: Kant's Analytic/ Synthetic Distinction and the Limits of Metaphysics.* Oxford: Oxford University Press.

Anderson, Wilda. 1984. *Between the Library and the Laboratory.* Baltimore: Johns Hopkins University Press.

Anderson, Wilda. 1990. *Diderot's Dream.* Baltimore: Johns Hopkins University Press.

Anstey, Peter. 2014. "D'Alembert, the 'Preliminary Discourse' and Experimental Philosophy." *Intellectual History Review* 24: 495–516.

Anstey, Peter. 2018. "Bacon, Experimental Philosophy and French Enlightenment Natural History." In *Natural History in Early Modern France.* Edited by Raphaële Garrod and Paul Smith. Leiden: Brill.

Applebaum, Wilbur, editor. 2005. *Encyclopedia of the Scientific Revolution.* London: Routledge.

Arato, Franco. 2005. "Minerva and Venus: Algarotti's *Newton's Philosophy for the Ladies.*" In *Men, Women and the Birthing of Modern Science.* DeKalb: Northern Illinois University Press.

Aravamudan, Srinivas. 2012. *Enlightenment Orientalism.* Chicago: University of Chicago Press.

Ariew, Roger, and Eric Watkins, editors. 2019. *Modern Philosophy: An Anthology of Primary Sources.* Indianapolis: Hackett Press. Third edition.

Baasner, Rainer. 1991. *Abraham Gotthelf Kästner, Aufklärer (1719–1800).* Tübingen: Max Niemeyer Verlag.

Badinter, Elisabeth. 1983. *Émilie, Émilie: l'ambition féminine au dix-huitième siècle.* Paris: Flammarion.

Badinter, Elisabeth, editor. 1989. *Qu'est-ce qu'une femme?* Paris: P.O.L.

Baker, Keith. 1988. "Revolution." In *The French Revolution and the Creation of Modern Political Culture.* Edited by Colin Lucas. Oxford: Oxford University Press.

Barber, William. 1955. *Leibniz in France: Arnauld to Voltaire.* Oxford: Oxford University Press.

Bassi, Romana. 2022. "Émilie Du Châtelet and Antonio Conti: The Italian Translation of the *Institutions physiques.*" In *Époque Émilienne: Philosophy and Science in the Age of Émilie Du Châtelet (1706–1749).* Cham: Springer Verlag.

Beck, Lewis White. 1969. *Early German Philosophy.* Cambridge, MA: Harvard University Press.

Becker, Carl. 1932. *Heavenly City of the Eighteenth-Century Philosophers.* New Haven: Yale University Press.

Behler, Ursula. 1998. "Eine unbeachtete Biographie Jacob Bruckers." In *Jacob Brucker: Philosophe und Historiker der europäischen Aufklärung*. Berlin: Akademie Verlag.

Berlin, Isaiah. 1982. "The Counter-Enlightenment." In *Against the Current: Essays in the History of Ideas*. New York: Penguin.

Bernal, Martin. 1987. *Black Athena, The Afroasiatic Roots of Classical Civilization*. vol. 1, *The Fabrication of Ancient Greece, 1785—1985*. New Brunswick: Rutgers University Press.

Bertoloni Meli, Domenico. 1993. *Equivalence and Priority: Leibniz vs. Newton*. Oxford: Oxford University Press.

Bertoloni Meli, Domenico. 2002. "Newton and the Leibniz-Clarke Correspondence." In *The Cambridge Companion to Newton*. Edited by I.B. Cohen and George Smith. Cambridge: Cambridge University Press.

Bertoloni Meli, Domenico. 2006. *Thinking with Objects: The Transformation of Mechanics in the Seventeenth Century*. Baltimore: Johns Hopkins University Press.

Bergès, Sandrine. 2015. "On the Outskirts of the Canon: The Myth of the Lone Female Philosopher, and What to Do about It." *Metaphilosophy* 46: 380–97.

Besterman, Theodore. 1976. *Voltaire*. Chicago: University of Chicago Press. Third edition.

Biener, Zvi. 2020. "Newton's *Regulae Philosophandi*." In *The Oxford Handbook of Isaac Newton*. Edited by Eric Schliesser and Chris Smeenk. Oxford: Oxford University Press.

Biener, Zvi, and Chris Smeenk. 2012. "Cotes's Queries: Newton's Empiricism and Conception of Matter." In *Interpreting Newton*. Cambridge: Cambridge University Press.

Blackwell, Constance. 1998. "Jacob Brucker's Theory of Knowledge and the History of Natural Philosophy." In *Jacob Brucker: Philosophe und Historiker der europäischen Aufklärung*. Berlin: Akademie Verlag.

Boas, Marie. 1952. "The Establishment of the Mechanical Philosophy." *Osiris* 10: 412–541.

Bonnefon, Paul. 1899. "Diderot prisonnier à Vincennes." *Revue d'histoire littéraire de la France* 6: 200–24.

Bos, Henk. 1980. "Mathematics and Rational Mechanics." In *The Ferment of Knowledge: Studies in the Historiography of Eighteenth-Century Science*. Edited by G.S. Rousseau and Roy Porter. Cambridge: Cambridge University Press.

Böttcher, Frauke. 2019. "Die Reaktion der Wolffianer in Deutschland auf die *Institutions physiques*." In *Emilie Du Châtelet und die deutsche Aufklärung*. Wiesbaden: Springer.

Brading, Katherine. 2019. *Émilie Du Châtelet and the Foundations of Physical Science*. London: Routledge.

Brading, Katherine, and Qiu Lin. 2023. "Du Châtelet on Absolute and Relative Motion." In *Current Debates in Philosophy of Science: In Honor of Roberto Torretti*. Edited by Cristián Soto. Cham: Springer Verlag.

Brading, Katherine, and Marius Stan. 2024. *Philosophical Mechanics in the Age of Reason*. New York: Oxford University Press.

Braidotti, Rosi. 1991. *Patterns of Dissonance*: *A Study of Women in Contemporary Philosophy*. Translated by Elizabeth Guild. London: Routledge.

Braun, Lucien. 1973. *Histoire de l'histoire de la philosophie*. Paris: Ophrys.

Brewer, Daniel. 2011. "The *Encyclopédie*: Innovation and Legacy." In *New Essays on Diderot*. Edited by James Fowler. Cambridge: Cambridge University Press.

Broman, Thomas. 2012. "Metaphysics for an Enlightened Public." *ISIS* 103: 1–23.

Calinger, Ronald. 2016. *Euler: Mathematical Genius in the Enlightenment*. Princeton: Princeton University Press.

Carus, Clara. 2022. "Du Châtelet's Contribution to the Concept of Time." In *Époque Émilienne: Philosophy and Science in the Age of Émilie Du Châtelet (1706–1749)*. Cham: Springer Verlag.

Cassirer, Ernst. 1902. *Das Erkenntnisproblem in der Philosophie und Wissenschaft der neueren Zeit*. Berlin. [Reprinted in Cassirer, *Gesammelte Werke, Hamburger Ausgabe*. Felix Meiner, 1999].

Cassirer, Ernst. 1932. *Die Philosophie der Aufklärung*. Tübingen: Verlag Mohr.

Cassirer, Ernst. 1943. "Hermann Cohen." *Social Research* 10 (May): 219–32.

Cassirer, Ernst. 1943. "Newton and Leibniz." *The Philosophical Review* 52: 366–91.

Cassirer, Ernst. 1947. *Rousseau, Kant, Goethe*. Translated by James Gutmann, Paul Oskar Kristeller, and John Hermann Randall Jr. Princeton: Princeton University Press.

Cassirer, Ernst. 1996. "From the Introduction to the First Edition of *The Problem of Knowledge in Modern Philosophy and Science*." Translated by Ashraf Noor. *Science in Context* 9: 195–215.

Catana, Leo. 2005. "The Concept 'System of Philosophy': The Case of Jacob Brucker's Historiography of Philosophy." *History and Theory* 44: 72–90.

Chaplin, Joyce. 2006. *The First Scientific American: Benjamin Franklin and the Pursuit of Genius*. New York: Basic Books.

Chomsky, Noam. 2016. *What Kind of Creatures Are We?* New York: Columbia University Press.

Cohen, Estelle. 1997. "'What the Women at All Times Would Laugh At': Redefining Equality and Difference, circa 1660–1760." *Osiris* 12: 121–42. Special issue, "Women, Gender and Science." Edited by Sally Gregory Kohlstedt and Helen Longino.

Cohen, I. Bernard. 1956. *Franklin and Newton: An Inquiry into Speculative Newtonian Experimental Science and Franklin's Work in Electricity as an Example thereof*. Philadelphia: American Philosophical Society.

Cohen, I. Bernard. 1985. *Revolution in Science*. Cambridge, MA: Harvard University Press.

Cohen, I. B., and Alexandre Koyré. 1962. "Newton and the Leibniz-Clarke Correspondence." *Archives internationale d'histoire des sciences* 15: 101–2.

Costabel, Pierre. 1983. *La question des forces vives. Cahiers d'histoire et de philosophie des sciences*. No. 8.

Cunningham, Vinson. 2021. "Review of Jefferson's Bible." *New Yorker*, January 4–11.

Curran, Andrew. 2019. *Diderot and the Art of Thinking Freely*. New York: Other Press.

Darnton, Robert. 1975. *The Business of Enlightenment: A Publishing History of the Encyclopédie, 1775–1800*. Cambridge, MA: Harvard University Press.

Darnton, Robert. 1985. *The Great Cat Massacre and Other Episodes in French Cultural History*. New York: Vintage.

Detlefsen, Karen. 2014. "Émilie du Châtelet." *Stanford Encyclopedia of Philosophy*, online resource.

Detlefsen, Karen. 2019. "Du Châtelet and Descartes on the Roles of Hypothesis and Metaphysics in Natural Philosophy." In *Feminist History of Philosophy*. Cham: Springer Verlag.

DiSalle, Robert. 2006. *Understanding Space-time*. Cambridge: Cambridge University Press.

Dobre, Mihnea. 2013. "Rohault's Cartesian Physics." In *Cartesian Empiricisms*. Edited by Mihnea Dobre and Tammy Nyden. Berlin: Springer Verlag.

Le Doeuff, Michèle. 2007. *Hipparchia's Choice: An Essay on Women, Philosophy, etc.* Translated by Trista Selous. New York: Columbia University Press.

Droysen, Hans. 1910. "Die Marquise du Châtelet, Voltaire und der Philosoph Christian Wolff." *Zeitschrift für Französische Sprache und Literatur* 35: 226–48.

Ducheyne, Steffen. 2011. "Newton on Action at a Distance and the Cause of Gravity." *Studies in History and Philosophy of Science* 42: 154–59.

Ducheyne, Steffen. 2012. *The Main Business of Natural Philosophy.* Dordrecht: Springer.

Dugas, René. 1988. *A History of Mechanics.* Translated by J. R. Maddox. New York: Dover.

Dunlop, Katherine. 2013. "Mathematical Method and Newtonian Science in the Philosophy of Christian Wolff." *Studies in History and Philosophy of Science* 44: 457–69.

Earman, John. 1989. *World Enough and Space-time.* Cambridge, MA: MIT Press.

Ebbersmeyer, Sabrina. 2019. "From a 'Memorable Place' to 'Drops in the Ocean': On the Marginalization of Women Philosophers in German Historiography of Philosophy." *British Journal of the History of Philosophy* 28: 442–62.

Edelstein, Dan. 2010. *The Enlightenment: A Genealogy.* Chicago: University of Chicago Press.

Edelstein, Dan, Robert Morrissey, and Glenn Roe. 2013. "To Quote or not to Quote: Citation Strategies in the *Encyclopédie*." *Journal of the History of Ideas* 74: 213–36.

Ehrman, Esther. 1986. *Mme du Châtelet: Scientist, Philosopher, and Feminist of the Enlightenment.* Leamington Spa: Berg.

Einstein, Albert. 1961. *Relativity: The Special and the General Theory.* Translated by Robert Lawson. New York: Crown.

Fara, Patricia. 2002. "Images of Émilie du Châtelet." *Endeavour* 26: 39–40.

Fara, Patricia. 2004. *Pandora's Breeches: Women, Science and Power in the Enlightenment.* London: Pimlico.

Feiner, Shmuel. 2004. *The Jewish Enlightenment.* Translated by Chaya Naor. Philadelphia: University of Pennsylvania Press.

Feingold, Mordechai. 2004. *The Newtonian Moment.* Oxford: Oxford University Press.

Feynman, Richard, Robert Leighton, and Matthew Sands. 1977. *The Feynman Lectures on Physics.* Reading, MA: Addison-Wesley.

Findlen, Paula. 1993. "Science as a Career in Enlightenment Italy: The Strategies of Laura Bassi." *ISIS* 84: 441–69.

Findlen, Paula. 2003. "Becoming a Scientist: Gender and Knowledge in Eighteenth-Century Italy." *Science in Context* 16: 59–87.

Findlen, Paula. 2011. "Calculations of Faith: Mathematics, Philosophy and
    Sanctity in Eighteenth-Century Italy (New Work on Maria Gaetana
    Agnesi)." *Historia mathematica* 38: 248–91.
Firode, Alain. 2001. *La dynamique de D'Alembert*. Paris: Vrin.
Fischer, Kuno. 1867. *Geschichte der neuren Philosophie*. Heidelberg:
    Bassermann.
Fleck, Ludwig. 1935/1976. *Genesis and Development of a Scientific Fact*.
    Translated by Fred Bradley and Thaddeus Trenn. Chicago: University
    of Chicago Press.
Fox-Genovese, Elisabeth. 1987. "Women and the Enlightenment." In *Becoming Visible: Women in European History*. Edited by Renate Bridenthal,
    Claudia Koonz, and Susan Stuard. Boston: Houghton Mifflin.
Friedman, Michael. 1992. *Kant and the Exact Sciences*. Cambridge, MA:
    Harvard University Press.
Friedman, Michael. 2000. *A Parting of the Ways: Carnap, Cassirer, Heidegger*.
    La Salle: Open Court Press.
Friedman, Michael. 2010. "Ernst Cassirer and Thomas Kuhn: The Neo-
    Kantian Tradition in the History and Philosophy of Science." In *Neo-Kantianism in Contemporary Philosophy*. Edited by Rudolf Makreel and
    Sebastian Luft. Bloomington: Indiana University Press.
Friedman, Michael. 2013. *Kant's Construction of Nature*. Cambridge: Cambridge University Press.
Furbank, P. N. 1992. *Diderot: A Critical Biography*. New York: Knopf.
Gandt, François de. 2001. "Qu'est ce qu'être Newtonien en 1740?" In *Cirey
    dans la vie intellectuelle: La reception de Newton en France. Studies on Voltaire and the Eighteenth Century*, 2001: 11. Oxford: Voltaire Foundation.
Gandt, François de, editor. 2001. *Cirey dans la vie intellectual: La reception de
    Newton en France. Studies on Voltaire and the Eighteenth Century*, 2001:
    11. Oxford: Voltaire Foundation.
Garber, Daniel. 1995. "Leibniz: Physics and Philosophy." In *The Cambridge
    Companion to Leibniz*. Edited by Nicholas Jolley. Cambridge: Cambridge University Press.
Garfield, Jay, and Brian van Norden. 2016. "If Philosophy Won't Diversify,
    Let's Call It What It Really Is." *New York Times*, May 16.
Gascoigne, John. 1985. *Cambridge in the Age of the Enlightenment*. Cambridge: Cambridge University Press.
Gaukroger, Stephen. 1982. "The Metaphysics of Impenetrability: Euler's
    Conception of Force." *British Journal for the History of Science* 15:
    132–54.

Gavanelli, Sonia Carboncini. 2007. "Das paradox der Aufklärung: Christian Wolff und die *Encyclopédie*." In Christian Wolff, *Gesammelte Werke*, Part III, 101, Teil 1. Hildesheim: Georg Olms.

Gawronsky, Dmitry. 1949. "Ernst Cassirer: His Life and Work." In *The Philosophy of Ernst Cassirer*. Evanston: Library of Living Philosophers.

Gay, Peter. 1966. *The Enlightenment: The Rise of Modern Paganism*. New York: Knopf.

Gay, Peter. 1969. *The Enlightenment: The Science of Freedom*. New York: Knopf.

Geissler, Rolf. 1992. "Formey critique des philosophes français." *Studies on Voltaire and the Eighteenth Century* 303: 507–10.

Gelbart, Nina Rattner. 2021. *Minerva's French Sisters: Women of Science in Enlightenment France*. New Haven: Yale University Press.

Gessell, Bryce. 2019. "'Mom petit essai': Émilie Du Châtelet's *Essai sur l'optique* and Her Early Natural Philosophy." *British Journal for the History of Philosophy* 27: 860–79.

Gillispie, Charles. 1959. "The *Encyclopédie* and the Jacobin Philosophy of Science." In *Critical Problems in the History of Science*. Edited by Marshall Clagett. Madison: University of Wisconsin Press.

Goodman, Dena. 1989. "Enlightenment Salons: The Convergence of Female and Philosophic Ambitions." *Eighteenth-Century Studies* 22: 329–50.

Goodman, Katherine. 2013. "Louise Gottsched, Freethinker." In *"Wenn sie das Wort Ich gebraucht": Festschrift für Barbara Becker-Cantarino von FreundInnen, SchülerInnen und KollegInnen*. Edited by John Putejovsky and Jacqueline Vansant. Amsterdam: Rodopi.

Gorbatov, I. 2007. "From Paris to St. Petersburg: Voltaire's Library in Russia." *Libraries & the Cultural Record* 42: 308–24.

Gordon, Peter. 2010. *Continental Divide*. Cambridge, MA: Harvard University Press.

Götze, Jannis, and Martin Meiske, editors. 2016. *Jean-Henri-Samuel Formey: Wissenschaftsmultiplikatur der berliner Aufklärung*. Hannover: Wehrhahn Verlag.

Gould, Stephen Jay. 1990. *Rocks of Ages: Science and Religion in the Fullness of Life*. New York: Ballantine.

Gray, Jeremy. 2020. "Non-Euclidean Geometry." In *Space: A History*. Oxford: Oxford University Press.

Grimsley, Ronald. 1963. *Jean D'Alembert*. Oxford: Oxford University Press.

Guerlac, Henry. 1981. *Newton on the Continent*. Ithaca: Cornell University Press.

Guicciardini, Niccolò. 1999. *Reading the* Principia: *The Debates on Newton's Mathematical Methods for Natural Philosophy from 1687 to 1736*. Cambridge: Cambridge University Press.

Guicciardini, Niccolò. 2015. "Editing Newton in Geneva and Rome: The Annotated Edition of the *Principia* by Calendrini, Le Seur and Jacquier." *Annals of Science* 72: 337–80.

Guilbaud, Alexandre. 2017. "D'Alembert's Contribution to the *Encyclopédie*." *Centaurus* 59: 320–28.

Habermas, Jürgen. 1985. "The German Idealism of the Jewish Philosophers." In *Philosophical-Political Profiles*. Translated by Frederick Lawrence. Cambridge, MA: MIT Press.

Habermas, Jürgen. 1989. *The Structural Transformation of the Public Sphere: An Inquiry into a Category of Bourgeois Society*. Translated by Thomas Burger and Frederick Lawrence. Cambridge, MA: MIT Press.

Hagengruber, Ruth, editor. 2012. *Émilie Du Châtelet Between Leibniz and Newton*. Dordrecht: Springer.

Hagengruber, Ruth, editor. 2022. *Époque Émilienne: Philosophy and Science in the Age of Émilie Du Châtelet (1706–1749)*. Cham: Springer Verlag.

Hagengruber, Ruth. 2022. "Du Châtelet and Kant: Claiming the Renewal of Philosophy." In *Époque Émilienne: Philosophy and Science in the Age of Émilie Du Châtelet (1706–1749)*. Cham: Springer Verlag.

Hagengruber, Ruth, and Hartmut Hecht, editors. 2019. *Emilie Du Châtelet und die deutsche Aufklärung*. Wiesbaden: Springer.

Hahn, Roger. 1971. *The Anatomy of a Scientific Institution: The Paris Academy of Sciences, 1666–1803*. Berkeley: University of California Press.

Hankins, Thomas. 1970. *Jean D'Alembert: Science and the Enlightenment*. Oxford: Oxford University Press.

Hankins, Thomas. 1985. *Science and the Enlightenment*. Cambridge: Cambridge University Press.

Harman, P.M. 1982. *Metaphysics and Natural Philosophy: The Problem of Substance in Classical Physics*. Sussex: Harvester Press.

Harper, William. 2011. *Isaac Newton's Scientific Method*. Oxford: Oxford University Press.

Harré, Rom. 1980. "Knowledge." In *The Ferment of Knowledge: Studies in the Historiography of Eighteenth-Century Science*. Edited by G.S. Rousseau and Roy Porter. Cambridge: Cambridge University Press.

Harth, Erica. 1992. *Cartesian Women: Versions and Subversions of Rational Discourse in the Old Regime*. Ithaca: Cornell University Press.

Hatfield, Gary. 1996. "Was the Scientific Revolution Really a Revolution in Science?" In *Tradition, Transmission, Transformation*. Edited by F. Jamil Ragep and Sally Ragep. Leiden: Brill.

Hayes, Julie Candler. 1999. *Reading the French Enlightenment: System and Subversion*. Cambridge: Cambridge University Press.

Hazard, Paul. 1946. *La Pensée Européenne au XVIIIème siècle*. Paris. Three volumes.

Heilbron, J. L. 1979. *Electricity in the Seventeenth and Eighteenth Centuries: A Study of Early Modern Physics*. Berkeley: University of California Press.

Heilbron, J. L. 1980. "Experimental Natural Philosophy." In *The Ferment of Knowledge: Studies in the Historiography of Eighteenth-Century Science*. Edited by G.S. Rousseau and Roy Porter. Cambridge: Cambridge University Press.

Henry, John. 2011. "Gravity and De Gravitatione: The Development of Newton's Ideas on Action at a Distance." *Studies in History and Philosophy of Science* 42:11–27.

Hepburn, Brian. 2020. "The Quiet Scientific Revolution: Problem Solving and the Eighteenth-Century Origins of 'Newtonian' Mechanics." In *The Oxford Handbook of Isaac Newton*. Edited by Eric Schliesser and Chris Smeenk. Oxford: Oxford University Press.

Hesse, Mary. 1961. *Forces and Fields: The Concept of Action at a Distance in the History of Physics*. London: Nelson.

Hine, Ellen McNiven. 1979. *A Critical Study of Condillac's Traité des systèmes*. The Hague: Martinus Nijhoff.

Hobson, Marian. 2006. "Diderot, the European Underground and English Radical Thought." In *Diderot and European Culture*. Edited by Frédéric Ogée and Anthony Strugnell. *Studies on Voltaire and the Eighteenth Century*. Oxford: Voltaire Foundation.

Hogan, Desmond. 2007. "Wolff on Order and Space." In *Wolff und die europäische Aufklärung: Akten des Ersten Internationalen Wolff-Kongresses, Teil 3*. Edited by Jürgen Stolzenberg and Oliver-Pierre Rudolph. Hildesheim: Georg Olms Verlag.

Hutton, Sarah. 2004. "Émilie du Châtelet's 'Institutions de physique' as a Document in the History of French Newtonianism." *Studies in History and Philosophy of Science* 35: 515–31.

Hutton, Sarah. 2012. "Between Leibniz and Newton: Emilie du Châtelet and Samuel Clarke." In *Emilie du Châtelet between Leibniz and Newton*. Cham: Springer Verlag.

Hutton, Sarah. 2019. "Women, Philosophy and the History of Philosophy." *British Journal for the History of Philosophy* 27: 684–701.

Hutton, Sarah. 2019. "Emilie du Châtelet." In *The Reception of Isaac Newton in Europe*. London: Bloomsbury.

Hutton, Sarah. 2022. "Émilie du Châtelet and Italy: The Italian Translation of Her *Institutions physiques* and the Issue of the *forces vives*." In *Époque Émilienne: Philosophy and Science in the Age of Émilie Du Châtelet (1706–1749)*. Cham: Springer Verlag.

Iltis, Carolyn. 1977. "Madame du Châtelet's Metaphysics and Mechanics." *Studies in History and Philosophy of Science* 8: 29–48.

Israel, Jonathan. 2001. *Radical Enlightenment: Philosophy and the Making of Modernity, 1650–1750*. Oxford: Oxford University Press.

Israel, Jonathan. 2006. *Enlightenment Contested*. Oxford: Oxford University Press.

Iverson, John. 2006. "A Female Member of the Republic of Letters: Du Chatelet's Portrait in the Bilder-Sal." In *Émilie du Châtelet: Rewriting Enlightenment Science and Philosophy*. Oxford: The Voltaire Foundation.

Jacob, Margaret. 1976. *The Newtonians and the English Revolution, 1689–1720*. Ithaca: Cornell University Press.

Jacob, Margaret. 1977. "Newtonianism and the Origins of the Enlightenment." *Eighteenth-Century Studies* 11: 1–25.

Janiak, Andrew. 2007. "Newton and the Reality of Force." *Journal of the History of Philosophy* 45: 127–47.

Janiak, Andrew. 2008. *Newton as Philosopher*. Cambridge: Cambridge University Press.

Janiak, Andrew. 2013. "Three Concepts of Causation in Newton." *Studies in History and Philosophy of Science* 44: 396–407.

Janiak, Andrew. 2015. *Newton*. London: Wiley-Blackwell.

Janiak, Andrew. 2018. "Émilie du Châtelet: Physics, Metaphysics and the Case of Gravity." In *Early Modern Women on Metaphysics*. Edited by Emily Thomas. Cambridge: Cambridge University Press.

Janiak, Andrew, editor. 2020. *Space: A History*. Oxford: Oxford University Press.

Janiak, Andrew. 2021. "Émilie Du Châtelet's Break from the French Newtonians." *Revue d'Histoire des Sciences* 74: 265–96.

Janik, Linda Gardiner. 1982. "Searching for the Metaphysics of Science: The Structure and Composition of Mme. Du Châtelet's *Institutions de physique*, 1737–1740." *Studies on Voltaire and the Eighteenth Century* 201: 85–113.

Jehl, Rainer. 1998. "Jacob Brucker und die 'Encyclopédie'." In *Jacob Brucker: Philosophe und Historiker der europäischen Aufklärung*. Berlin: Akademie Verlag.

Jones, Peter, editor. 2013. *The Reception of David Hume in Europe*. London: Thoemmes.

Kafker, Franz. 1996. *The Encyclopedists as a Group*. *Studies on Voltaire and the Eighteenth Century*. Oxford: Voltaire Foundation.

Kawashima, Keiko. 2022. "Anonymity and Ambition: Émilie Du Châtelet's *Dissertation de feu* (1744)." In *Époque Émilienne: Philosophy and Science in the Age of Émilie Du Châtelet (1706–1749)*. Cham: Springer Verlag.

Kelly, Joan. 1984. *Women, History and Theory*. Chicago: University of Chicago Press.

Kleinbaum, Abby. 1970. "Jean Jacques Dortous de Mairan (1678–1771): A Study of an Enlightenment Scientist." PhD dissertation, Columbia University.

Kochiras, Hylarie. 2009. "Gravity and Newton's Substance Counting Problem." *Studies in History and Philosophy of Science* 40: 267–80.

Kochiras, Hylarie. 2011. "Gravity's Cause and Substance Counting: Contextualizing the Problems." *Studies in History and Philosophy of Science* 42:167–84.

Kölving, Ulla, and Andrew Brown, editors. 2022. *Émilie Du Châtelet: son monde, ses travaux*. Ferney-Voltaire: Centre International d'Étude du xviii-eme Siècle.

Kölving, Ulla, and Olivier Courcelle, editors. 2008. *Émilie Du Châtelet: éclairages et documents nouveaux*. Ferney-Voltaire: Centre International d'Étude du xviii-eme Siècle.

Koslow, Arnold. 1965. "Changes in the Concept of Mass from Newton to Einstein." PhD dissertation, Columbia University.

Kovács, Eszter. 2022. "'La liberté est la santé de l'âme': du pouvoir soi-mouvant au culte de la liberté chez Émilie Du Châtelet." In *Émilie Du Châtelet: son monde, ses travaux*. Ferney-Voltaire: Centre Internationale D'Étude Du XVIIIe Siècle.

Koyré, Alexandre. 1968. *Newtonian Studies*. Chicago: University of Chicago Press.

Kuehn, Manfred. 2001. *Kant, a Biography*. Cambridge: Cambridge University Press.

Kuhn, Thomas. 1970. *Structure of Scientific Revolutions*. Chicago: University of Chicago Press. Second edition.

Langton, Rae. 2009. *Sexual Solipsism*. Oxford: Oxford University Press.

Larsen, Anne. 2016. *Anna Maria van Schurman, "the Star of Utrecht."* New York: Routledge.

Lascano, Marcy, and Lisa Shapiro, editors. 2021. *Early Modern Philosophy: An Anthology.* Broadview Press.

Lloyd, Genevieve. 1984. *The Man of Reason: "Male" and "Female" in Western Philosophy.* Minneapolis: University of Minnesota Press.

Lloyd, Genevieve, editor. 2002. *Feminism and History of Philosophy.* Oxford: Oxford University Press.

Lloyd, Genevieve. 2013. *Enlightenment Shadows.* Oxford: Oxford University Press.

Locqueneux, Robert. 2001. "Physique expérimentale vers 1740." In *Cirey dans la vie intellectuelle: La reception de Newton en France. Studies on Voltaire and the Eighteenth Century,* 2001: 11. Oxford: Voltaire Foundation.

Longo, Mario. 2011. "A 'Critical' History of Philosophy and the Early Enlightenment: Johann Jacob Brucker." In *Models of the History of Philosophy,* vol. 2. Edited by Gregorio Piaia and Giovanni Santinello. Heidelberg: Springer.

Lough, John. 1968. *Essays on the Encyclopédie.* Oxford: Oxford University Press.

McMullin, Ernan. 1978. *Newton on Matter and Activity.* Notre Dame: University of Notre Dame Press.

Mandelbrote, Scott, and Helmut Pulte, editors. 2019. *The Reception of Isaac Newton in Europe.* Three volumes. London: Bloomsbury.

Maglo, Koffi. 2008. "Mme Du Châtelet, *l'Encyclopédie* et la philosophie des sciences." In *Émilie Du Châtelet: éclairages et documents nouveaux.* Ferney-Voltaire: Centre Internationale D'Étude Du XVIIIe Siècle.

Malherbe, Michel. 2013. "Hume's Reception in France." In *The Reception of David Hume in Europe.* London: Bloomsbury.

Malueg, Sara Ellen Procious. 1984. "Women and the *Encyclopédie.*" In *French Women and the Age of Enlightenment.* Edited by Samia Spencer. Bloomington: Indiana University Press.

Marcu, Eva. 1952. "Formey and the Enlightenment." PhD dissertation, Columbia University.

Martin, Christophe. 2022. "From One Marquise to Another: Émilie Du Châtelet and Fontenelle's *Conversations on the Plurality of Worlds.*" In *Époque Émilienne: Philosophy and Science in the Age of Émilie Du Châtelet (1706–1749).* Cham: Springer Verlag.

Mazzotti, Massimo. 2004. "Newton for Ladies: Gentility, Gender and Radical Culture." *British Journal for the History of Science* 37: 119–46.

Mazzotti, Massimo. 2007. *The World of Maria Gaetana Agnesi, Mathematician of God*. Baltimore: Johns Hopkins University Press.

Mbembe, Achille. 2017. *Critique of Black Reason*. Translated by Laurent Dubois. Durham, NC: Duke University Press.

Meiske, Martin. 2016. "Formey als Encyklopädist." In *Jean-Henri-Samuel Formey: Wissenschaftsmultiplikatur der berliner Aufklärung*. Hannover: Wehrhahn Verlag.

Mercer, Christia. 2019. "The Contextualist Revolution in Early Modern Philosophy." *Journal of the History of Philosophy* 57: 529–48.

Mercer, Christia. 2020. "Empowering Philosophy." Presidential Address. *Proceedings and Addresses of the American Philosophical Association* 94: 68–96.

Nagel, Fritz. 2012. "'Sancti Bernoulli orate pro nobis': Emilie du Châtelet's Rediscovered *Essai sur l'optique* and Her Relation to the Mathematicians from Basel." In *Emilie Du Châtelet Between Leibniz and Newton*. Cham: Springer Verlag.

Nagel, Fritz. 2022. "'Les corps agissent sur la lumière.' Émilie Du Châtelet's Deliberations on the Nature of Light in Her *Essai sur l'optique*." In *Époque Émilienne: Philosophy and Science in the Age of Émilie Du Châtelet (1706–1749)*. Cham: Springer Verlag.

Nassar, Dalia, and Kristin Gjesdal, editors. 2021. *Women Philosophers in the Long Nineteenth Century: The German Tradition*. Oxford: Oxford University Press.

Neiman, Susan. 1994. *The Unity of Reason*. Oxford: Oxford University Press.

Neumann, Hans-Peter. 2014. "Der preusissiche Kronprinz Frederich und die französische Übersetzung der 'Deutschen Metaphysik' Christian Wolffs im Jahr 1736." *Forschungen zur brandenburgischen und preusissichen Geschichte* 24: 35–68.

Neumann, Hans-Peter. 2022. "Emilie du Châtelet within the Correspondence between Christian Wolff and Ernst Christoph of Manteuffel." In *Époque Émilienne: Philosophy and Science in the Age of Émilie Du Châtelet (1706–1749)*. Cham: Springer Verlag.

O'Neill, Eileen. 1998. "Disappearing Ink: Early Modern Women Philosophers and Their Fate in History." In *Philosophy in a Feminist Voice*. Edited by Janet Kourany. Princeton: Princeton University Press.

O'Neill, Eileen, and Marcy Lascano, editors. 2018. *Feminist History of Philosophy: The Recovery and Evaluation of Women's Philosophical Thought*. Springer Verlag.

Ostertag, Heinrich. 1910. *Der philosophische Gehalt des Wolff-Manteuffelschen Briefwechsels*. Leipzig: Olms.

Outram, Dorinda. 2005. *The Enlightenment*. Cambridge: Cambridge University Press. Second edition.

Paganini, Gianni. 2022. "Rehabilitating Hypotheses in the French Enlightenment: Émilie Du Châtelet and Condillac." In *Émilie Du Châtelet: son monde, ses travaux*. Ferney-Voltaire: Centre Internationale D'Étude Du XVIIIe Siècle.

Pagden, Anthony. 2013. *The Enlightenment and Why It Still Matters*. New York: Random House.

Pal, Carol. 2012. *Republic of Women: Rethinking the Republic of Letters in the Seventeenth Century*. Cambridge: Cambridge University Press.

Park, Peter K. J. 2013. *Africa, Asia and the History of Philosophy: Racism in the Formation of the Philosophical Canon*. Albany: SUNY Press.

Paz, Octavio. 1988. *Sor Juana, or the Traps of Faith*. Translated by Margaret Sayers Peden. Cambridge, MA: Harvard University Press.

Pfeiffer, Rudolf. 1976. *History of Classical Scholarship: From 1300 to 1850*. Oxford: Clarendon Press.

Pocock, J.G.A. 2008. "Historiography and Enlightenment: A View of Their History." *Modern Intellectual History* 5: 83–96.

Proust, Jacques. 1962. *Diderot et l'Encyclopédie*. Paris: Armand Colin.

Prunea-Bretonnet, Tinca. 2019. "Émilie, Friedrich der Große und die 'Leibniz-Wolffsche' Metaphysik." In *Emilie Du Châtelet und die deutsche Aufklärung*. Wiesbaden: Springer

Rée, Jonathan. 2002. "Women Philosophers and the Canon." *British Journal for the History of Philosophy* 10: 641–52.

Reedy, Gerard. 1985. *The Bible and Reason*. Philadelphia: University of Pennsylvania Press.

Reichenberger, Andrea. 2016. *Émilie Du Châtelets Institutions Physiques: über die Rolle von Prinzipien und Hypothesen in der Physik*. Cham: Springer Verlag.

Reichenberger, Andrea. 2018. "Émilie Du Châtelet's Interpretation of the Laws of Motion in the Light of Eighteenth-Century Mechanics." *Studies in History and Philosophy of Science* 69: 1–11.

Reichenberger, Andrea. 2019. "Die Rolle der Familie Keyserlingk und des Gottsched-Kreises für Kants Du Châtelet-Rezeption." In *Emilie Du Châtelet und die deutsche Aufklärung*. Wiesbaden: Springer

Reichenberger, Andrea. 2022. "The Reception of Émilie Du Châtelet in the German Enlightenment." In *Époque Émilienne: Philosophy and*

Science in the Age of Émilie Du Châtelet (1706–1749). Cham: Springer Verlag.

Rey, Anne-Lise. 2008. "La figure du Leibnizianisme dans les *Institutions de physique*." In *Émilie Du Châtelet: éclairages & documents nouveaux*. Ferney-Voltaire: Centre Internationale D'Étude Du XVIIIe Siècle.

Rey, Anne-Lise. 2017. "La minerve vient de faire sa physique." *Philosophiques* 44 (Autumn): 233–53.

Rey, Anne-Lise. 2017. "Agonistic and Epistemic Pluralisms: A New Interpretation of the Dispute between Emilie du Châtelet and Dortous de Mairan." *Paragraph* 40: 43–60.

Rey, Anne-Lise. 2022. "The Vis Viva Controversy." In *The Cambridge History of Philosophy of the Scientific Revolution*. Edited by David Marshall Miller and Dana Jalobeanu. Cambridge: Cambridge University Press.

Riskin, Jessica. 2002. *Science in the Age of Sensibility: the Sentimental Empiricists of the French Enlightenment*. Chicago: University of Chicago Press.

Roche, Daniel. 2006. "Encyclopedias and the Diffusion of Knowledge." In *Cambridge History of Eighteenth-Century Political Thought*. Edited by Marc Goldie and Robert Wolker. Cambridge: Cambridge University Press.

Roe, Glenn. 2018. "A Sheep in Wolff's Clothing: Émilie Du Châtelet and the *Encyclopédie*." *Eighteenth Century Studies* 51: 179–96.

Rosen, Gideon et al., editors. 2015. *The Norton Introduction to Philosophy*. New York: W.W. Norton. Second edition, 2018.

Le Ru, Véronique. 1994. *D'Alembert philosophe*. Paris: Vrin.

Le Ru, Véronique. 2019. *Émilie Du Châtelet philosophe*. Paris: Classiques Garnier.

Russ, Joanna. 1983. *How to Suppress Women's Writing*. Austin: University of Texas Press.

Schaffer, Simon. 1980. "Natural Philosophy." In *The Ferment of Knowledge: Studies in the Historiography of Eighteenth-Century Science*. Edited by G. S. Rousseau and Roy Porter. Cambridge: Cambridge University Press.

Schaffer, Simon. 1996. "Contextualizing the Canon." In *The Disunity of Science*. Edited by Peter Galison and David Stump. Stanford: Stanford University Press.

Schiebinger, Londa. 1989. *The Mind Has no Sex? Women in the Origins of Modern Science*. Cambridge: Harvard University Press.

Schilpp, Paul Arthur, editor. 1949. *The Philosophy of Ernst Cassirer*. Evanston: Library of Living Philosophers.

Schliesser, Eric. 2011. "Newton's Substance Monism, Distant Action, and the Nature of Newton's Empiricism." *Studies in History and Philosophy of Science* 42: 160–66.

Schliesser, Eric. 2017. *Adam Smith: Systematic Philosopher and Public Thinker.* Oxford: Oxford University Press.

Schliesser, Eric, and Chris Smeenk, editors. 2020. *The Oxford Handbook of Isaac Newton.* Oxford: Oxford University Press.

Schmidt-Biggemann, Wilhelm, and Theo Stammen, editors. 1998. *Jacob Brucker: Philosophe und Historiker der europäischen Aufklärung.* Berlin: Akademie Verlag.

Scott, Joan Wallach. 1996. *Only Paradoxes to Offer: French Feminists and the Rights of Man.* Cambridge, MA: Harvard University Press.

Shank. J. B. 2005. "Neither Natural Philosophy, nor Science, nor Literature—Gender, Writing, and the Pursuit of Nature in Fontenelle's *Entretiens sur la pluralité des mondes habités.*" In *Men, Women, and the Birthing of Modern Science.* DeKalb: Northern Illinois University Press.

Shank. J. B. 2008. *The Newton Wars and the Beginning of the French Enlightenment.* Chicago: University of Chicago Press.

Shank. J. B. 2018. *Before Voltaire: The French Origins of "Newtonian" Mechanics, 1680–1715.* Chicago: University of Chicago Press.

Shapiro, Lisa. 2016. "Revisiting the Early Modern Philosophical Canon." *Journal of the American Philosophical Association* 2: 365–83.

Sloan, Phillip. 2019. "Metaphysics and 'Vital' Materialism: Émilie Du Châtelet and the Origins of French Vitalism." In *Philosophy of Biology before Biology.* Edited by Cécilia Bognon-Küss and Charles Wolfe. London: Routledge.

Smeall, Cheryl. 2011. "How to Become a Renowned Writer: Francesco Algarotti and the Uses of Networking in Eighteenth-Century Europe." PhD dissertation, McGill University.

Smeltzer, Ronald. 2022. "Printing Du Châtelet's *Institutions de physique*: The Variant Texts." In *Époque Émilienne: Philosophy and Science in the Age of Émilie Du Châtelet (1706–1749).* Cham: Springer Verlag.

Smith, George E. 1999. "How Did Newton Discover Universal Gravity?" *St. John's Review* 45: 32–63.

Smith, George E. 2006. "The Vis Viva Dispute: A Controversy at the Dawn of Dynamics." *Physics Today* (October): 31–36.

Smith, George E. 2022. "Du Châtelet's Commentary on Newton's *Principia*: An Assessment." In *Époque Émilienne: Philosophy and Science in the Age of Émilie Du Châtelet (1706–1749).* Cham: Springer Verlag.

Smith, Margarete. 1993. "In Defence of an Eighteenth-Century Academician: Philosopher and Journalist Jean-Henri-Samuel Formey." *Studies on Voltaire and the Eighteenth Century* 311: 85–100.

Speranskaya, Natalia. 2022. "Émilie Du Châtelet's Manuscripts Preserved at the National Library of Russia." In *Époque Émilienne: Philosophy and Science in the Age of Émilie Du Châtelet (1706–1749)*. Cham: Springer Verlag.

Stan, Marius. 2018. "Emilie Du Châtelet's Metaphysics of Substance." *Journal of the History of Philosophy* 56: 477–96.

Stein, Howard. 1990. "On Locke, 'The Great Huygenius, and the Incomparable Mr. Newton.'" In *Philosophical Perspectives on Newtonian Science*. Edited by Phillip Bricker and R. I. G. Hughes. Cambridge, MA: MIT Press.

Stein, Howard. 2002. "Newton's Metaphysics." *The Cambridge Companion to Newton*. Edited by I. B. Cohen and George Smith. Cambridge: Cambridge University Press.

Steinbrügge, Lieselotte. 1995. *The Moral Sex: Woman's Nature in the French Enlightenment*. Translated by Pamela Selwyn. Oxford: Oxford University Press.

Sutcliffe, Anthony. 1993. *Paris: An Architectural History*. New Haven: Yale University Press.

Sutton, Geoffrey. 1986. *Science for a Polite Society: Gender, Culture and the Demonstration of the Enlightenment*. Boulder: Westview Press.

Terrall, Mary. 1995. "Émilie du Châtelet and the Gendering of Science." *History of Science* 33: 283–310.

Terrall, Mary. 1995. "Gendered Spaces, Gendered Audiences: Inside and Outside the Paris Academy." *Configurations* 3: 210.

Terrall, Mary. 1999. "Mathematics, Metaphysics and the Gendering of Science in France." In *The Sciences in Enlightened Europe*. Edited by William Clark, Jan Golinski, and Simon Schaffer. Chicago: University of Chicago Press.

Terrall, Mary. 2002. *The Man Who Flattened the Earth*. Chicago: University of Chicago Press.

Terrall, Mary. 2004. "Vis viva Revisited." *History of Science* 42: 189–209.

Thomson, Ann. 2022. "Émilie Du Châtelet and La Mettrie." In *Époque Émilienne: Philosophy and Science in the Age of Émilie Du Châtelet (1706–1749)*. Cham: Springer Verlag.

Toulmonde, Michel. 2022. "Émilie Du Châtelet and Newton's *Principia*." In *Époque Émilienne: Philosophy and Science in the Age of Émilie Du Châtelet (1706–1749)*. Cham: Springer Verlag.

Truesdell, Clifford. 1968. *Essays in the History of Mechanics*. Berlin: Springer Verlag.

Tyson, Sarah. 2018. *Where Are the Women? Why Expanding the Archive Makes Philosophy Better*. New York: Columbia University Press.

Vanzo, Alberto. 2016. "Empiricism and Rationalism in Nineteenth-Century Histories of Philosophy." *Journal of the History of Ideas* 77: 253–82.

Verbeek, Theo. 1988. *Le Traité de l'Ame de la Mettrie: edition critique du texte avec une introduction et un commentaire historique*. Utrecht: Grafisch Bedrijf. Two volumes.

Vermij, Rienk. 2019. "Newton and Huygens." In *The Reception of Isaac Newton in Europe*. London: Bloomsbury.

Wade, Ira O. 1941. *Voltaire and Madame du Châtelet: An Essay on the Intellectual Activity at Cirey*. Princeton: Princeton University Press.

Wade, Ira O.1947. *Studies on Voltaire with Some Unpublished Papers of Madame du Châtelet*. Princeton: Princeton University Press.

Waithe, Mary Ellen. 2015. "From Cannon Fodder to Canon Formation: How Do We Get There from Here?" *The Monist* 98: 21–33.

Wandall, Anne-Sophie Sørup. 2024. "Contested Identities: Challenging Discourses on Female Intellectuality." PhD dissertation, University of Copenhagen.

Wellman, Kathleen. 1992. *La Mettrie: Medicine, Philosophy, and Enlightenment*. Durham, NC: Duke University Press.

Wilson, Curtis. 1992. "Euler on Action at a Distance and Fundamental Equations in Continuum Mechanics." In *The Investigation of Difficult Things: Essays on Newton and the History of the Exact Sciences in Honor of D. T. Whiteside*. Edited by P. M. Harman and Alan Shapiro. Cambridge: Cambridge University Press.

Winter, Ursula. 2012. "From Translation to Philosophical Discourse—Emilie du Châtelet's Commentaries on Newton and Leibniz." In *Emilie du Châtelet between Leibniz and Newton*. Cham: Springer Verlag.

Witt, Charlotte. 2006. "Feminist Interpretations of the Philosophical Canon." *Signs* 31: 537–52.

Yeo, Richard. 2003. "Classifying the Sciences." In *The Cambridge History of Science, Volume Four: Eighteenth-Century Science*. Cambridge: Cambridge University Press.

Zinsser, Judith P. 2001. "Translating Newton's *Principia*: The Marquise du Châtelet's Revision and Additions for a French Audience." *Notes and Records of the Royal Society* 55: 227–45.

Zinsser, Judith P. 2002. "Entrepreneur of the 'Republic of Letters': Emilie de Breteuil, Marquise du Châtelet, and Bernard Mandeville's *Fable of the Bees*." *French Historical Studies* 25: 595–624.

Zinsser, Judith P, editor. 2005. *Men, Women, and the Birthing of Modern Science*. DeKalb: Northern Illinois University Press.

Zinsser, Judith P. 2006. *La Dame d'Esprit: A Biography of the Marquise du Châtelet*. New York: Viking.

Zinsser, Judith P. 2014. "Émilie Du Châtelet and the Enlightenment's *Querelle des femmes*." In *Challenging Orthodoxies: The Social and Cultural Worlds of Early Modern Women; Essays Presented to Hilda Smith*. Edited by Sigrun Haude and Melinda Zock. Surrey, UK: Routledge.

Zinsser, Judith P. and Julie Candler Hayes. 2006. "The Marquise as Philosophe." In *Émilie du Châtelet: Rewriting Enlightenment Science and Philosophy*. Oxford: The Voltaire Foundation.

Zinsser, Judith P., and Julie Candler Hayes, editors. 2006. *Émilie du Châtelet: Rewriting Enlightenment Philosophy and Science. Studies on Voltaire and the Eighteenth Century*. Oxford: The Voltaire Foundation.

INDEX

For the benefit of digital users, indexed terms that span two pages (e.g., 52–53) may, on occasion, appear on only one of those pages.

Académie Française, 4, 204n.6
    exclusion of women, 117
Acta Eruditorum, 32–33, 124–25,
    127–28
Agnesi, Maria Gaetana, 117, 118–19
    Instituzione analitiche, 118, 122
Algarotti, Francesco, 5, 28, 172–74,
    176–77, 190
    Newtonianism for the ladies,
    119–20, 141, 174
Anderson, Wilda, 228n.65, 229n.73,
    230n.77
Anscombe, G.E.M., 244n.69
Aravamudan, Srinivas, 221n.9,
    233n.11, 244n.1
Aristotle, 40, 70–72, 75–76,
    112–13, 157, 158–59, 165,
    190–91, 194–95
Astronomy
    Copernican, 84–85
    Ptolemaic, 84–85
Atheism, 110–11

Atomism, 98–101
Axioms
    Leibniz's view of, 63, 64–65, 70–
    71
    Newton's view of, 62–63,
    64–65, 70–71

Bacon, Francis, 140–41, 161–62,
    163–64, 175, 192–93, 194–95
Basel, 109, 186–87
Bassi, Laura, 22, 117, 167–68, 170
Badinter, Elisabeth, 245n.5
Beauvoir, Simone de, 1
Bentley, Richard, 38, 46, 76
    Boyle lectures, 46–47
    correspondence with
    Newton, 46–47
Berlin Academy of Sciences, 51–52,
    94–96, 115–16, 124, 168–69
    founding, 135–36
    prize competition on monads,
    95–96

Berlin, Isaiah, 245n.2
Bernal, Martin, 233n.11, 233n.12
Bernoulli, Johann II, 5, 109, 170, 171
Bertoloni Meli, Domenico,
    205n.16, 207n.30, 208n.33,
    223n.28
Bible, 110–11, 116–17
Bologna Academy of Sciences,
    115–16, 117, 167–68, 170
Bos, Henk, 209–10n.43
Boyle, Robert, 32, 41
    air pump, 108
    Boyle lectures, endowment of, 46
Brading, Katherine, 209n.41,
    209n.42, 211n.53, 212n.7,
    213n.16, 215n.28, 218n.50,
    219n.55, 219–20n.56
Brucker, Johann Jacob
    Critical History of Philosophy
        (Historia Critica Philosophiae),
        16–17, 158–60, 170, 180–81,
        183–84, 187–88
    eclecticism, view of, 175
    exclusion of women from canon,
        17–18, 170
    "father" of modern history of
        philosophy, 158
    history of philosophy, view of,
        16–17, 158–59, 161–62, 164
    influence on Enlightenment history
        of philosophy, 16–17, 158
    Portrait Gallery, 170, 177–78,
        198n.6
    Scholasticism, rejection of, 112–
        13, 158–59, 165–66, 174–75
    Wolff, relation to, 17–18

Café Gradot, 1–3
Calculus, 49–50, 117, 209–10n.43

Canon, 17–18, 168, 188–89
    Enlightenment, conception of, 17
    philosophes, conception of, 17
Caroline, Princess of Wales, 27, 43–44
Cartesianism, 34, 105–6, 149–50,
    151–52, 165–66, 177, 190
Carus, Clara, 215n.27
Cassirer, Ernst, 180–84
    Das Erkenntnisproblem, 183–84,
        211n.56, 241n.52, 245–46n.6
    Philosophy of the Enlightenment,
        181–84, 212n.8, 232–33n.7
Cavendish, Margaret, 22, 118, 166,
    184–85
    visit to Royal Society of London, 117
Chambers, Ephraim, 137, 140–41
Chomsky, Noam, 208n.37
Christina, Queen of Sweden, 116,
    130–31, 177, 178
Clairaut, Alexis, 179, 200–1n.20
Clarke, Samuel, 34–36, 42–43
    correspondence with Leibniz,
        43–45, 63–64, 87, 130, 144
    edition of Rohault's Treatise, 141,
        217n.44
    Newton's theory of gravity,
        interpretation of, 44–45
    vis viva, discussion of, 130–31
Cohen, I.B., 200n.19, 200–1n.20,
    205n.11, 206n.21, 243–44n.67
Condillac, 96, 163–64, 184,
    214n.20
Condorcet, 140–41
Copernicus, 11, 24–25, 58–59
Cotes, Roger, 38, 40–43, 71–72
    essence of matter, conception of,
        208–9n.39
    gravity, conception of, 40–42,
        73–74

Cousin, Victor, 160, 161, 166
Curie, Marie, 117, 197n.3

Dacier, Anne, 172–73, 239n.41
D'Alembert, Jean-le-Rond
  Du Châtelet, relation to, 14–15,
    143–53,
  "Elements of Science," 144–
    48, 151
  Encyclopédie, contributions to,
    55, 137
  force, conception of, 55
  force of inertia, view of, 55
  history of philosophy, view of,
    158, 162–63, 170–71
  mechanics, view of, 55, 148
  metaphysics, conception
    of, 144–48
  Newton, relation to, 55–56, 75
  "Newtonianism," 149–52
  physics, view of, 145–46
  *Preliminary Discourse to the
    Encyclopedia*, 14–15, 75–76,
    151, 162, 175
  Treatise on Dynamics, 55, 152–53
Darnton, Robert, 227n.60, 227n.61,
    228n.65
Democritus, 94
Desaguliers, J.T., 25–27
Descartes, René, 25–26, 32, 41,
    70–71, 165, 185
  debate with Anna Maria van
    Schurman, 116–17
  "father" of modern philosophy,
    158, 161
  laws of motion, 49
  mathematics, use of, 12
  matter, view of, 40, 49
  Meditations, 71–72

motion, view of, 125, 129–30
physics, 71
Principia philosophiae (*Principles
  of Philosophy*), 49, 70–71,
  105–6, 125
vortex theory, 82, 172–73
Detlefsen, Karen, 213–14n.17
Diderot, Denis
  arrest, 153–54, 187
  Du Châtelet, view of, 8, 154, 180
  eclecticism, embrace of, 166,
    175–76, 180, 192
  Encyclopédie, conception of, 145
  Encyclopédie, contributions to,
    137, 139–41, 180–81
  "Epicureanism," 154
  history of philosophy, view of,
    158, 159–60
  imprisonment in Vincennes,
    154, 187
  Letter on the blind, 153–54
  metaphysics, conception of,
    142–43, 148
  Philosophical thoughts, 153–54
  "Prospectus to the
    Encyclopedia," 140–41
  women, views on, 139–40,
    240n.47
Doeuff, Michele Le, 197n.3,
    246n.11
Du Châtelet, Émilie
  absolute motion, discussion
    of, 91–92
  absolute space, discussion of,
    61–62, 87–88, 91–92, 93
  aristocratic standing of, 1–2,
    3–4, 6, 154–55
  Bologna Academy of Sciences,
    membership, 117

Du Châtelet, Émilie (*cont.*)
    chateau in Cirey, 4–5, 6–7
    construal as "Newtonian,"
        108–9, 151, 176–77, 189–90
    construal as "Wolffian," 177–78
    D'Alembert, relation to,
        14–15, 143–53
    death after childbirth, 155
    debate with Paris Academy
        Secretary Mairan, 123–24
    debate with Royal Society
        Secretary Jurin, 124, 176–
        77, 179–80
    Descartes, relation to, 83–84,
        103–4, 132–33
    Diderot, relation to, 154
    *Dissertation on the nature and
        propagation of fire*, 123
    Essay on optics, 109–10, 120–21
    essences, view of, 71–75
    Euler, relation to, 51–52
    exclusion from philosophy
        canon, 17–18, 168, 188–89
    *Exposition abregée du Système du
        Monde*, 84–85, 198–99n.10
    fame, 8–9
    father's salon, 3
    force, view of, 133
    German translation of
        Institutions, 8, 15–16, 121–22
    God, view of, 110–11
    gravity, conception of, 48, 72–75
    hypotheses, conception of, 1–2,
        13–14, 81–86
    influence on the Enlightenment,
        10–11, 14–15
    'institutions', meaning of, 71, 146
    *Institutions of Physics
        (Institutions physiques)*, 7–8,

        45, 48, 61–62, 63, 65–66,
        68–69, 70–71, 81, 83–84,
        91–92, 96–97, 101–4, 106–7,
        110, 113–14, 120–22, 123–24,
        133, 137, 138, 139–40, 143,
        146, 147, 151–52, 178–79,
        189–92, 194
    Italian translation of *Institutions*,
        8, 121–22
    Kant, relation to, 15–16
    Locke, relation to, 77–79, 192
    mechanical philosophy, view
        of, 106–8
    metaphor, use of, 12–14, 55–56
    metaphysics, 71–72, 96–97, 100,
        101–8, 111–12, 189–90
    Newton, view of, 48–49,
        83–84, 132–34
    Paris Academy of Sciences,
        relation to, 123, 124
    rejection of discipleship and
        partisanship, 28–29, 35–36,
        61–62, 85–86, 101–2, 113–
        14, 190–92
    philosophy, conception of, 14,
        190–92, 193–94, 195
    physics, conception of, 12–13,
        55–56, 101–8, 111–12
    prejudice, views of, 4, 195
    "revolutions in the sciences,"
        10–11, 195
    Saint-Lambert, relationship with,
        154–55, 231n.93
    simple beings, view of, 96–101
    space, conception of, 86–92,
        143–46
    translation of Mandeville's
        Fable of the Bees, 4, 118–19,
        247n.16

translation of Newton's *Principia*, 72, 84–85, 118–19, 122, 153–54, 155, 178–79, 198–99n.10

vis viva, view of, 120, 133–34, 189–90

Voltaire's philosophy, view of, 7–8, 27–28, 61–62

Voltaire, relationship with, 5–6, 21, 154–55

Du Châtelet, Florent-Claude (husband), 3–4, 6

Ducheyne, Steffen, 207n.26, 208n.37

Ebbersmeyer, Sabrina, 220n.2, 236n.22, 238n.36

Eberhard, Johann, 173, 239n.42

Egypt, 157–58, 159–60, 243–44n.67

Einstein, Albert, 47–48
general theory of relativity, 47–48, 87
Newton's view of space, conception of, 56, 61
special theory of relativity, 85–86

Elisabeth, Princess of Bohemia, 22, 166, 177, 178, 184–85

Encyclopedia Britannica, 18–19

Encyclopédie (Diderot & D'Alembert, editors), 22–23, 137–53, 158, 170–71, 175
controversial status, 245n.2
Du Châtelet's ideas in, 137–40
origins of, 137
scope of, 139
women in, 139–40

Enlightenment
differing conceptions of, 136, 139, 153, 180, 186–88, 195
French, 75–77, 118–19

history of philosophy in, 158, 159–60, 161–62, 164

Newton's role in, 29–30, 68

science, 86–87, 105, 112, 115–17, 119–20, 122, 130, 145, 190–91, 195

salons, 117–18

theology, 110–11, 139

Epicurus, 47

Ether, 73–74, 85–86, 98

Euler, Leonhard
absolute space, defense of, 66–67, 87–88
academic positions, 33–34
calculus, 49, 209–10n.43
Du Châtelet's philosophy, view of, 8–9, 51–52
"f = ma", 49–50
force, conception of, 51–52
law of inertia, 66–67, 87–88, 96
Mechanics, 52
monads, view of, 96
Newton, criticisms of, 51–53, 55–56
"Research on the origin of forces," 51–52
vis inertiae, rejection of, 51–53, 55–56
wide range of scientific and mathematical work, 33–34

Feynman, Richard, 98–99

Findlen, Paula, 220n.5, 221n.9

Fischer, Kuno, 160, 161–62, 166

Folkes, Martin, 28

Fontenelle, Bernard, 4, 119–20, 123, 173–74
Conversations on the Plurality of Worlds, 119–20

Fontenelle, Bernard (*cont.*)
  Secretary of Paris Academy of
    Sciences, 119–20
Formey, Samuel, 96, 135–39, 142
  Diderot, criticisms of, 136, 187–
    88
  Du Châtelet, copying from,
    137–42, 148–49
  Encyclopédie, contributions
    to, 136–40
  La belle Wolfienne, 119–20, 135–
    36
  metaphysics, view of, 144
  Rousseau, criticisms of, 136, 187
  Secretary of Berlin Academy of
    Sciences, 121–22, 168–69
  Short History of Philosophy, 159–60,
    168–69, 202n.25
  Wolff, support of, 137
Franklin, Benjamin, 29–30, 203n.32
Frederick the Great (Frederick II of
    Prussia), 90–91, 135, 225n.46
  Du Châtelet, view of, 8–9
  Voltaire, relation to, 5–6
Friedman, Michael, 215n.31,
    243n.66, 243–44n.67,
    245–46n.6

Galileo, 11, 12, 24–25, 32, 41, 94,
    125–26, 194–95, 200n.18
Garber, Daniel, 222n.24, 223n.25
Gauss, Christian, 47–48
Gay, Peter, 20–21, 180–81, 204n.6
Geometry
  Euclidean, 60, 61, 93, 194–95
  Non-Euclidean, 47–48
  relations with other
    disciplines, 145–46
Gessell, Bryce, 218–19n.51

God, 63, 71, 73, 76–77, 78–79,
    80–81, 103, 110–11, 227n.56
Goethe, 110, 233–34n.13
Gould, Stephen Jay, 104
Guicciardini, Niccolò, 201n.22,
    209–10n.43, 228n.68

Habermas, Jürgen, 220n.8,
    242–43n.60
Hagengruber, Ruth, 239n.42
Halley, Edmond, 25, 29–30
Hartsoeker, Nicholas, 105–6, 112
Haslanger, Sally, 212n.5
Hatfield, Gary, 202n.25, 202n.26,
    217n.43
Hayes, Julie Candler, 200n.16,
    203–4n.34, 245n.3, 246n.10
Hazard, Paul, 20–21, 180–81
Heidegger, Martin, 181–82
Heilbron, John, 211n.1, 217–18n.45,
    228n.68, 241n.54
Hegel, 161, 164, 193
Henry, John, 208n.37
Hesse, Mary, 208n.37
Hume, David, 65–66, 163–64, 184
  Enlightenment, role in, 163
  Treatise of Human Nature,
    65–66, 163
Hutton, Sarah, 200n.17, 222n.22,
    223n.27, 224n.40
Huygens, Christian, 24–26, 31
  Newton, criticisms of, 31–33
  pendulum, experiments with, 31

Infinity, 93
Israel, Jonathan, 20–21, 223n.30

Jacob, Margaret, 208n.35, 208n.36,
    213n.11, 246n.12

Jacquier, François, 141, 149–50, 200–1n.20, 222n.22
Jaucourt, Marquise de, 139–40
Jefferson, Thomas, 25
Jurin, James, 242n.55
    Secretary of Royal Society of London, 124, 176–77, 179–80

Kant, Immanuel, 94–95, 161, 162–64, 171–74, 176
    Bacon, view of, 15–16, 192–93, 194–95
    Brucker, relation to, 232–33n.7
    Critique of Pure Reason, 15–16, 65–66, 94–95, 161–62, 192–93, 194–95
    Du Châtelet, relation to, 15–16, 184–85
    fame, 94–95
    life in Königsberg, 15–16, 94–95, 115–16
    Observations on the Beautiful and the Sublime, 172–74
    "Physical Monadology," 95–97
    prize competitions, participation in, 116
    revolutionary philosophy of, 15–16
    "Thoughts on the True Estimation of Living Forces," 162–63, 171
Kästner, Abraham, 176–77, 199–200n.13, 200n.17, 215n.32
Kelly, Joan, 203n.31
Kepler, 12–13
    "laws", 82–83
Kochiras, Hylarie, 208n.37
König, Samuel, 96
Koyré, Alexandre, 206n.21, 206n.23, 243–44n.67

Kovács, Eszter, 227n.56
Kuhn, Thomas, 67–68, 242n.57, 243–44n.67

La Mettrie, Julien, 199–200n.13, 225–26n.47, 226n.53
Langton, Rae, 238–39n.39
Lascano, Marcy, 244n.68
Leibniz, Gottfried Wilhelm, 30–31, 177
    archives in Hannover, 30–31
    "Brief Demonstration," 125–26
    calculus, 30–31, 127
    Cartesians, criticisms of, 82, 124–26
    correspondence with Clarke, 43–45, 63–64, 87, 144
    "Essay on the causes of celestial motions," 32–33
    hypotheses, use of, 82–83
    Newton, criticisms of, 12, 31–33, 43, 63–64, 82
    Princess Caroline of Wales, relation to, 43
    space, conception of, 86–87, 89
    "Specimen dynamicum," 127–29, 130
    Theodicy, 43
    vis viva, 124–32
    vortex theory, 82
Lin, Qiu, 215n.28
Lloyd, Genevieve, 201n.23, 244n.1, 247n.15
Locke, John, 25–26, 34–36, 41, 75, 163–64, 165–66, 186–87, 192
    correspondence with Stillingfleet, 76–78, 79, 192
    Essay Concerning Human Understanding, 76, 192

Locke, John (*cont.*)
   Newton's theory of gravity,
     conception of, 76–77
   role in French Enlightenment, 75
   presence in *Encyclopédie*, 141
   superaddition, theory of, 76–78
London, 57

MacLaurin, Colin, 149–50, 211n.56
Maglo, Koffi, 229–30n.75, 236–
   37n.26
Maimonides, 158–59, 165
Mairan, Jean-Jacques Dortous de,
   121–22, 171, 172
   debate with Du Châtelet, 123–24,
     199n.12
   Secretary of Paris Academy
     of Sciences, 121–22, 123,
     135, 176–77
   view of women, 123–24
Mandeville, Bernard, 4, 118–19
Mass, 49, 50–51, 52, 127–28, 129
Maupertuis, Pierre-Louis, 1–2,
   179, 184
   President of Berlin Academy of
     Sciences, 124, 215n.32
Mbembe, Achille, 166, 237n.29,
   247n.14
Mechanical philosophy, 32, 41, 53,
   76–77, 106, 112–13
Mercer, Christia, 234–35n.17,
   237n.28, 244n.68
Molières, Joseph Privat de, 105–6, 112
Monads, 95–96, 116, 172–73
Montesquieu, 141–42, 168–69, 182
Moses, 160, 169

Nagel, Fritz, 109, 219n.53
Neiman, Susan, 243n.64

Newton, Isaac
   absolute motion, 59
   absolute space, 55–62
   action at a distance, 46–47, 208n.37
   ancient Greek knowledge, view of,
     10, 12, 49–50
   apple story, 2–3, 24–25
   bucket example, 60–61
   calculus, 12
   childhood, 32, 60–61
   Descartes, relation to, 49, 126
   Enlightenment, role in, 161–62
   essence of matter, view of, 39–40
   "f = ma," 49–50
   force, conception of, 41–42, 50–51
   funeral at Westminster Abbey, 27
   General Scholium, 82–83
   "Geneva edition" of *Principia*
     (Le Seur & Jacquier, editors),
     141, 149–50
   God, conception of, 53–54
   gravity, conception of, 31–32,
     36–40, 73–74, 79–80
   hero of Scientific Revolution,
     24–25
   hypotheses non fingo, 82–83,
     85–86, 112–13, 194
   laws of motion, 49–50, 53–
     54, 62–63
   Lucasian Professor of
     Mathematics, 9–10
   mass, conception of, 49,
     50–51, 127–28
   mathematics, use of, 25–26, 192
   Opticks, 42–43, 52–54, 73–74, 94,
     98, 112–13, 130, 191
   popularizations of his work,
     26–27, 79–80
   President of Royal Society, 43–44

Principia (*Mathematical Principles of Natural Philosophy*), 9–10, 25–26, 29–30, 36–37, 38, 43, 53, 62–63, 73–74, 82–83, 119–20, 126, 129, 192
Regulae philosophandi, 38–40
"stood on the shoulders of giants," 10–11, 24–25
Treatise of the System of the World, 79–81
vis inertiae (force of inertia), 50–51, 53–54
visit from Edmond Halley, 9–10, 29–30, 126–27
vis viva, reaction to, 128–29
vortex theory, rejection of, 82–83, 177
Nollet, Abbé, 152–53

O'Neill, Eileen, 204n.35, 237n.30

Pagden, Anthony, 19–20
Pal, Carol, 204n.35, 220n.4
Paradigm, 67–68
Paris
   Academy of Sciences, 4, 68–69, 115–16, 117, 134
   Bastille, 6, 154
   Notre Dame Cathedral, 3–4
   Place Royale (Place des Vosges), 3
Paz, Octavio, 157–58
Pemberton, Henry, 149–50
Philosophes, 111–12, 136–37, 139, 141–42, 163–64, 178–79, 186–87
Physics
   contemporary, 87
   eighteenth-century, 105–6
Plagiarism, 140–41

Plato, 157, 158–59, 165, 177, 185
Pope, Alexander, 25
Pre-Socratics, 157
Principle of Sufficient Reason, 63, 65, 70–71, 87–88, 89–90, 92, 138, 142–43, 172–73, 179, 189, 193–94

Reichenberger, Andrea, 200n.17, 224n.41, 226n.53, 245–46n.6
Republic of Letters, 94–95, 118–19, 120–21, 135, 141–43, 153
Rey, Anne-Lise, 222n.23, 224n.39, 224n.40, 225n.42, 246n.9
Rohault, Jacques, 105–6, 112, 141, 198–99n.10
Rousseau, 141–42, 154, 168–69, 187
   Confessions, 154
Royal Academy of Sciences, Paris, *see* Paris, Academy of Sciences
Royal Society, London, 9–10, 28, 30, 43–44, 115–16, 117, 124, 149–50
   Philosophical Transactions of the Royal Society, 31, 115–16, 130–31
Ru, Véronique Le, 200–1n.20, 213n.14, 214n.21, 221n.14, 229–30n.75, 230n.84
Russ, Joanna, 237–38n.32

S'Gravesande, Wilhelm, 105–6, 131–32, 149–50
St. Petersburg Academy of Sciences, 115–16
Sartre, Jean-Paul, 1
Saint-Lambert, Jean-François, 154–55, 231n.93
Salons, 3, 117–18

Schaffer, Simon, 210n.48,
  214n.22
Schliesser, Eric, 205n.11, 208n.37
Scholasticism, 12–13, 112–13,
  165–66, 180, 190–91
Schurman, Anna Maria van, 22,
  116–17, 118–19, 166
  debate with Descartes, 116–17
  knowledge of Hebrew, 116–17,
    118
  university attendance, 116–17,
    167–68
Scientific Revolution, 72, 127
  conceptions of, 10, 67–68
  methods, 12
Scott, Joan Wallach, 240n.47
Shapiro, Lisa, 204n.35, 240n.49,
  244n.68, 247n.13
Smith, Adam, 29–30, 186–87
Smith, George, 209n.41, 222n.23,
  223n.26, 228n.68
Socrates, 157–58
Stan, Marius, 209n.42, 211n.53,
  214–15n.26, 219–20n.56
Stillingfleet, Edward, 76, 79, 192

Terrall, Mary, 221n.9, 222n.18,
  222n.21
Theology, 139
Trinity College, Cambridge, 46,
  115–16, 165

Universities
  exclusion of women, 116
  inclusion of women, 116–17
  science in, 115–16

Vincennes prison, 154
Vis viva, 120–34, 171

anachronistic discussions
    of, 129–31
Voltaire
  and story of Newton's
    apple, 14, 29
  disciple of Isaac Newton, 13–14,
    27, 28, 34–35, 190
  Du Châtelet, relationship with,
    5–6, 183
  Elements of the Philosophy of
    Newton, 7–8, 27, 34–35, 110,
    120, 121–22, 131, 148, 178–79
  Essay on Manners, 182–83
  Frederick the Great, relation
    to, 5–6
  history of modern philosophy,
    view of, 161–62
  legal troubles, 6, 27
  literary fame, 5–6
  Philosophical Letters (Lettres
    philosophiques), 6, 25, 27,
    34–35, 75, 141–42, 161–62
  visit to England, 6
  vis viva, discussion of, 131
Vortex theory, 82–83, 172–73

Winckelmann, Johann, 160
Witt, Charlotte, 204n.36, 244n.68,
  244n.70
Wolff, Christian, 61–62, 112,
  135–36, 151–52, 192–93
  corpus, 137–38
  Du Châtelet, relation to, 90–91,
    177–78, 179–80
  fame, 16–17, 105–6, 236n.21
  Formey, relation to, 135–36, 137–
    38
  German Metaphysics (Vernünftige
    Gedancken), 90–91

Leibniz, relation to, 91
physics, 105–6
space, conception of, 90–91
Wollstonecraft, Mary, 186–87

Zinsser, Judith, 21, 200n.17,
203n.31, 222n.19, 228n.67,
231n.93, 239n.41,
240n.46, 245n.3